KINGDOM WELLNESS COUNSELING & MENTORING

Taquetta Baker, M.Ed

DIVERSITY AND INCLUSION COMMITMENT

Kingdom Shifters Wellness Counseling and Mentoring Center is dedicated to serving with a commitment to diversity and inclusivity for our clients.

Dr. Taquetta Baker

Kingdom Wellness Counseling and Mentoring Center

Faith Based Counseling

Manual I

The Faith Community & Mental Health

Taquetta's Kingdom Wellness Theory (TKWT)

Kingdom Wellness Counseling and Mentoring Center

Faith Based Counseling

Manual I

TAQUETTA BAKER, M.Ed

With an Introductory Essay & Scholarly Contributions by Dr. Kathy Williams

Amazon Publications
Muncie, IN

Manual I

This manual is based in over 20 years' experience in professional counseling.

kingdomwellnesscenter@gmail.com

kingdomshifters.com

Connect with Taquetta via Facebook or YouTube

TABLE OF CONTENTS

Contents

DIVERSITY AND INCLUSION COMMITMENT i

TABLE OF CONTENTS v

FOREWORD 1

FOREWORD 2

FOREWORD 4

INTRODUCTORY ESSAY 8

TAQUETTA BAKER, FOUNDER 13

VISION STATEMENT 15

DR. KATHY WILLIAMS, FOUNDER'S TRIBUTE 16

THE FAITH COMMUNITY AND MENTAL HEALTH 18

TAQUETTA'S KINGDOM WELLNESS THEORY (TKWT) 25

TAQUETTA'S WELLNESS PARADIGM 28

EXEGETICAL PREMISE FOR HUMANITY 28

EXEGETICAL PREMISE FOR ORDAINED PURPOSE 30

EXPLORING KINGDOM WELLNESS 32

DEFINING FAITH-BASED COUNSELING 39

WHAT COUNSELING IS NOT 54

WHAT A COUNSELOR IS NOT 55

THE SPIRIT OF COUNSEL 56

UNDERSTANDING UNGODLY COUNSEL AND ERROR 67

ESSENTIAL QUALITIES OF A FAITH BASED COUNSELOR 73

THE COUNSELOR-CLIENT RELATIONSHIP 75

THE DISCERNING COUNSELOR 86

DELIVERANCE MINISTRY 101

DELIVERANCE – THE CHILDREN'S BREAD 114

MAINTAINING DELIVERANCE AND WELLNESS 118

THE PROCESS TO WHOLENESS 140

THE GRACE OF THE PROCESS 151

HEALTHY IDENTITY VERSUS UNHEALTHY IDENTITY 159

MAINTAINING A HEALTHY IDENTITY 186

MAINTAINING BIBLICAL STANDARDS 193

TEACHING CLIENTS ABOUT SELF-WORTH 201

OVERCOMING INFERIORITY 205

DESTINY AS A LIFESTYLE 211

CONNECTING CLIENTS TO GOD 226

COUNSELING SESSION ETIQUETTE 248

BALANCE: RESPITE FOR LEADERS 258

COUNSELING CENTER CHARGE 265

KSM BOOKSHELF 267

REFERENCES 269

FOREWORD

This manual written by Dr. Taquetta Baker is a breath of fresh air for the mental health community. The Kingdom Wellness manual educates, empowers, and elevates the reader. It also gives us insight of what it looks like to combine spirituality with the effective new theory that have been developed by the author. This manual operates in uniquely profound levels of concepts that collide the spiritual and psychosocial aspects along with new theories that need to be embodied in Christian Counseling and the healing experience. If you are a new counselor, this manual is for you. If you are an experienced counselor, this refreshing manual is for you. If you are a Christian counselor or a pastoral counselor and looking for in-depth broken-down material that is effective, this manual is for you. Lastly, if you are in ministry and looking for new & improved ways to impact people, this is your manual.

Dr. Baker helps us to break the barriers and strongholds that exists between the secular arena and what effective biblical counseling represents. God desires for us to be healed, whole, restored, and free mentally, physically, and emotionally. Utilization of this manual assists individuals holistically so they can effectively work on the total person. It is through God's deliverance that we can operate in his perfect will and purpose for our lives. When we are mentally, physically, and emotionally free, we able to fulfill our destiny here on earth. The *Kingdom Wellness Manual* sharpens your skills in discernment, demonic manifestations, deliverance, and inner healing. This kingdom educational manual that shows counselors how to competently operate through the Spirit of God, and develop the client in the process of healing.

Rhoshanda Camille Howell RN, BSN
Board Certified Psychiatric Mental Health Registered Nurse
Liberty University Clinical Mental Health Counseling Dept.
Mental Health Therapist Intern
Associate Pastor Eastern North Carolina- ENC-Hub

FOREWORD

It is with great pleasure that I write a forward for Taquetta Baker's newest book, *Kingdom Wellness Counseling And Mentoring Manual Volume I.* I am a licensed professional counselor, entrepreneur, pastor, wife, and mother. Since 2003, I have provided mental health services in hospitals, colleges/universities, K-12 schools, community mental health and private agencies. Currently, I own a private practice that specializes in the diagnosis and treatment of people with mental illness across the lifespan. Personally, I treat Major Depression, Anxiety, Bipolar, Post-traumatic Stress Disorder, Obsessive Compulsive Disorder, Borderline Personality Disorder and many more. I enjoy treating teens, college students young adults, couples, professionals, healthcare providers, and spiritual leaders.

I was blessed to meet Taquetta Spring 2019 in Myrtle Beach, SC at a leadership gathering for the Tribe Network. The first day of the retreat, a group of about 50 leaders in marketplace and ministry gathered from across the globe. I introduced myself to her during a short break in between session. I quickly learned about her background in professional counseling, and immediately set a lunch date to better a quaint myself with her. I am very passionate about the integration of psychology and theology, so I could not wait to discuss current issues and topics with someone from both worlds, so to speak.

Taquetta is an instrument of God who is being used to help bridge the gap between the church and wellness. There is a major gap in this area and that gap is costing God's people more than I believe we should be paying. The gap is costing us our peace, joy, contentment, stability, motivation, and so much more. *Kingdom Wellness Counseling And Mentoring Manual Volume I,* is a powerful tool because it uses both psychological and biblical frameworks to examine the concept of wholeness and provide solutions for treating God's people, mind, body, and soul.

If you are an aspiring counselor, professional counselor, life coach, pastor, or deliverance minister, this manual is for you! Taquetta provides real strategy for positively impacting the lives of people with a biblically-based, holistic approach.

I am so glad that you have chosen this book. I pray that it will bless your life, ministry, business, and community, in new and refreshing ways. I declare that God is empowering you to be his hands and feet in the Earth, spreading his healing and deliverance power wherever you go.

Rosa Jones, LPC
Licensed Professional Counselor
Christiansburg, Virginia

FOREWORD

Bishop Dr. Jackie L. Green, D. Min.

"It is hard to fight an enemy that is undiagnosed and undetected.

Mental illness and mental instability in the church has been like a stealth bomber, operating undetected and destroying lives right under our nose.

Undiagnosed mental illness and unchecked mental instability in the church affects every area of church life and every area of a person's life, hindering growth and maturity."

The church has been engaging in spiritual warfare against Satan concerning healing and deliverance with "one hand" instead of two. We have **NOT** been prepared effectively process people to wholeness, or to diagnose and detect mental illness in our congregations and bring them to Kingdom wellness. Satan has been winning this battle until now. Dr. Taquetta Baker unveils the hidden strategy of the enemy thus producing a theory that will liberate the body of Christ to wholeness. A strong key point that Dr. Baker shares is that *"The rise of suicide is our inability to detect or discern that threat, yet the person is dying on the inside."* **For that revelation alone, the body of Christ must become Kingdom minded and prepare ourselves, especially Pastoral leaders and Christian counselors for the warfare that is arising through mental illness and mental instability.**

I am so honored as well as enlightened with Dr. Baker's skill to articulate a very needed conversation on Kingdom Wellness in the Body of Christ. It is a sound spiritual, clinical, psychological treatise, that will **SHIFT** the body of Christ and the world at large into complete wellness. This book challenges the church as a whole. Moreover, it provokes ministry leaders, Christian practitioners, community counselors, social workers, mentors, and coaches, to take a hard look at how we do church and ministry, how we do deliverance and healing, how those who have not been effectively helped, and have not been sufficiently diagnosed as it relates to various levels of mental illness.

As a Pastoral Counselor that served for years on staff in a rising mega church as well as a Pastor of Prayer, my eyes were opened to an unprepared area of ministry in counseling, deliverance, and mental wellness, that remained the *"Cinderella"* ministry of the local church. Many of the principles that Dr. Baker addresses, hold the answer to the root problems we have regarding effective counseling practices, church leadership services, and among member care. It is clear to me that we have assumed that difficult members were just being problematic or divisive, when in fact many have Manic Depression, onsets of Dementia and Alzheimer's Disease, chemical imbalance, Personality Disorders, are Bi-Polar, Schizophrenic tendencies and behaviors that are undiagnosed by anyone. **These seem to be the most common in our churches today. If we could have become adept and skilled in dealing with these seven mental areas of warfare, we could save a lot of lives if we had Dr. Baker's Kingdom Wellness manual. Most of the time church leaders cannot even discern when a person is on medication and living with mental struggles.** We need trained counselors and team members to get the job done.

Most profound is Dr. Baker's TKWT theory. It is infused with wisdom nuggets that SHIFT the way we counsel and conduct deliverance in our churches and communities. Dr. Baker makes it clear that Kingdom Wellness is for Believers and Non-Believers, because *"both saved and unsaved need to know they have a specific life purpose through relationship with the Creator."* A non-believer will surely come to Christ once they have received kingdom wellness through Dr. Baker's TKWT theory if they open their hearts to God and the guidance of the counselor. TKWT enables the counselor to offer Christ through biblical counseling, while processing the non-believer into salvation and relationship with the Savior. Anointed counseling such as this, is a true key to evangelism that we have not tapped within our churches or communities.

Dr. Baker speaks clearly to those that are mental wellness counselors and ministers, where she provides instruction on the importance of maintaining self-care, while serving others. This chapter alone is a complete training course for clergy and counselors. Indeed, she stresses the need for clergy and counselors to have personal and professional balance and boundaries.

This Kingdom Wellness manual is a "**Counselor's Dream Course.**" It is balanced with biblical principles, spiritual insight, physical, psychiatric, deliverance and practical wisdom for churches, pastors, Christian Counselors, and non-Christian counselors to help clients become free and whole.

As I close this review, our greatest hindrance to putting Kingdom Wellness in place is the fact that most **ministries do not have the discernment, time, or trained staff to really invest in the mentally wellness within our congregations**. The body of Christ wants a quick fix just like most of society, or we are overloaded dealing with other issues. My experience suggests that many of our church fellowship issues are due to our lack of pastoral and leadership discernment regarding mentally wellness. Depending on the issue, it could take years to walk a person THROUGH to mental wellness. The Kingdom approach takes discipline and investing time in the lives of broken people. *It also takes a team working as a team and not just players wearing the same jersey.*

The Pastor cannot do it all. In my experience with counseling our first schizophrenic member, we had a ministry team of four leaders, skilled in discipleship, discernment, deliverance, and medical education. It took eight years of counseling, casting out demons, progressive spiritual regiments, accountability, prayer and intercession, and holding the person accountable to see breakthrough. Because of that process, the person was able to accept her call to preach the Gospel, was licensed as an evangelist, and as an elder in the church. Every area of her life was brought to Kingdom wellness. That individual is now able to minister to others. Dr. Baker's Kingdom Wellness Manual will equip ministry teams and give them the tools they need to walk people through to Kingdom wholeness. This manual is a gift to the Body of Christ. It will open our spiritual eyes to those undiagnosed and to undetected warfare in the Body of Christ that has kept us from being effective.

I am grateful for this manual, a fresh *piece of armored revelation* that will help us process people all the way through to mental wholeness. We can begin by seeking Jesus Christ, the Wonderful Counsellor and then as Dr. Baker says, "We do not value counseling, mental health agencies and social services organizations." *Let us begin today to value those that daily minister to the mentally and socially broken in our communities and especially in the Kingdom of God!*

Encouraged and Excited!

Bishop Dr. Jackie L. Green,
JGM Enternational PrayerLife Institute, Redlands, CA

INTRODUCTORY ESSAY

By Dr. Kathy Williams

Any construction effort begins with a foundation. Let's look at the foundation that has been laid throughout church history that brings us to the 21st century faith-based counselor. Many believe that there were only 12 apostles plus one replacement for Judas; however, the scripture testifies to the contrary. It is quite intriguing that the modern church has such difficulty with both the title and function of apostle, when, in fact, apostles were the primary leaders of the early church. Any institution that is guided by humans is subject to the ebb and flow of history. By the end of the first century, much of the early church had transitioned from apostles as the principal leaders to pastors as shepherds. In the Medieval Period, the spectrum broadened further to consider bishops and priests as the more important vocations. The presence of Gregory the Great (540-604) as the first pope embedded an oxymoron of politics, corruption, and a manual *Book of Pastoral Rule* that became a standard for the monastic church. "During the thousand-year period from Nicea to Wycliffe, ministry took place in spite of the church more than because of the official church."[1]

Between the Medieval Period and the Modern Period (1649 – now) resides the Reform Period. Perhaps we have circled around to Stitzinger's thought that ministry is taking place in spite of the church more than because of the church. No more than we can dismiss pioneers as only those who traveled in covered wagons across this country can we dismiss the biblical validation of apostles as only existing in the aftermath of Jesus' ascension. For purposes of this writing, we are not pursuing the concept of apostle for title but for empowerment and assignment. Understanding history gives permission for us to embrace our present and make preparations for our future. It is critical that we identify those who are positioned to facilitate that journey.

---

[1] James F. Stitzinger. (1995, Fall). Pastoral ministry in history. Retrieved from *The Master's Seminary* website at https://www.tms.edu/m/tmsj6f.pdf

It is attested by this writer that the late 20th- century restoration of fivefold ministry and spiritual gifts has been generally misconstrued. *Ephesians 4:11 And He Himself gave some to be apostles, some prophets, some evangelists, and some pastors and teachers.* For reasons that are not quite clear, the institution of the church has selected only portions of that scripture for validation in ministry. Particularly with society's current state-of-affairs, there is a need for total ministry, and not a select portion of the available roles. Our world is in a downward spiral of ongoing catastrophes, including a global food crisis, more than 40 war zones, terrorist attacks, human trafficking, child soldiers, political corruption, environmental emergencies, medical shortages, threats of nuclear war, an opioid epidemic, mental illness, racial injustices, domestic and child abuse, suicide, and much more. For any one person to believe that they have been positioned as leadership of a church or ministry is simply an inadequate and delusional statement. We live in a world that demands teamwork through empowerment. We also live in a world where the need for true church leadership resides on us SHIFTING out of the four walls of the church and effectively delivering, healing, saving, and transforming lives and communities. Jesus started his ministry by empowering his team. *Matthew 10:1 And when He had called His disciples to Him, He gave them power over unclean spirits, to cast them out, and to heal all kinds of sickness and all kinds of diseases.* The first action guaranteed after Jesus ascension was an impartation of power, *Acts 1:8 But you shall receive power after the Holy Spirit has come upon you . . ..* Paul's ministry was noted for many signs and wonders due to *the power of the Holy Spirit **Romans 15:19.***

The physician Luke writes in his gospel of a time when Jesus sent 70 specially appointed harbingers by 35 teams of two. His instructions carry a mandate critically important to our current state of affairs. *Luke 10:2 Then He said to them, "The harvest truly is great, but the laborers are few; pray the Lord of the harvest to send laborers into His harvest."* With perpetual gratitude to the elderly African-American "church mothers" who built a foundation of "doing" in me, I share the same teachings. *Ecclesiastes 9:10 Whatever your hands find to do, do it with your might . . .."* Evangelism had nothing to do with a title but, *2 Timothy 4:5 But you be watchful in all things, endure afflictions, do the work of an evangelist, fulfill your ministry.* Taquetta Baker brings the heart of "doing" to her commitment toward building faith based counseling as a viable tool for our broken society.

It is intriguing that the concept of wellness initially coincides with the historical period of the Modern Period (1640's). While Hippocrates is often credited with being the first physician to work toward preventing disease rather than simply treating it, the notion did not take root until the mid-17th century.

> *"The use of the word "wellness" in the English language – meaning the opposite of "illness" or the "state of being well or in good health" – dates to the 1650s, according to the Oxford English Dictionary. The earliest published reference is from the 1654 diary entry of Sir Archibald Johnston: "I ... blessed God ... for my daughter's wellness." The first citation with modern spelling is from a 1655 letter from Dorothy Osborne to her husband, Sir William Temple: "You ... never send me any of the new phrases of the town... Pray what is meant by wellness and unwellness?"*[2]

The modern concept of wellness took root in the 1950's. In a 1979 broadcast, Dan Rather is quotes as saying, *"Wellness,* there's a word you don't hear everyday." But "more than three decades later," the New York Times notes, *"wellness* is, in fact, a word that Americans might hear every day..."[3] It does not take much to do the math and project the increase for the few years between the chart below and the present day.

---

[2] History of wellness. (n.d.) Retrieved from the *Global Wellness Institute* website at https://globalwellnessinstitute.org/industry-research/history-of-wellness/
[3] Ibid, n.d.

Figure 0.0 Global Wellness Economy

GLOBAL WELLNESS ECONOMY:
$3.7 trillion in 2015

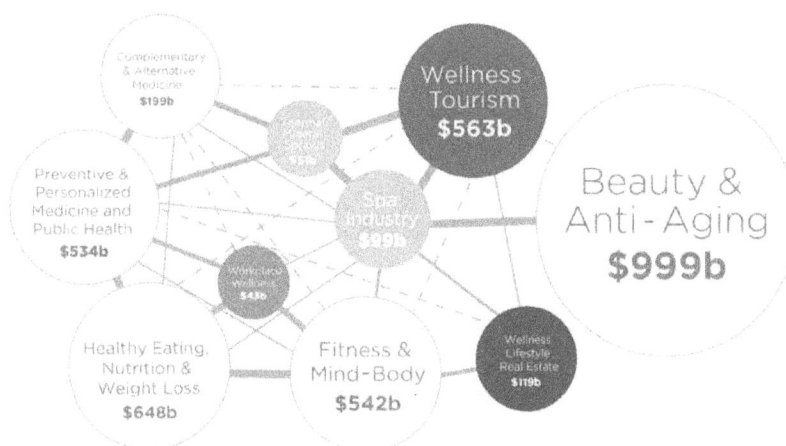

Complementary
& Alternative
Medicine
$199b

Wellness
Tourism
$563b

Preventive &
Personalized
Medicine and
Public Health
$534b

Spa
Industry
$99b

Beauty &
Anti-Aging
$999b

Workplace
Wellness
$43b

Wellness
Lifestyle
Real Estate
$119b

Healthy Eating,
Nutrition &
Weight Loss
$648b

Fitness &
Mind-Body
$542b

Note: Numbers may not add due to overlap in segments. The thickness of the lines in the chart
indicates the strength of the relationships and synergies between sectors.
Source: Global Wellness Institute, Global Wellness Economy Monitor, January 2017.

GLOBAL WELLNESS
INSTITUTE

Source: Global Wellness Institute, 2018

The diagram begs the simplest question, "What happened to us?" When did we stop believing and applying the principles of the Word? My questions are an inquiry and not an accusation. Did the body of believers we call "the church" let their assignment of wellness slip through their fingers and land in the lap of the secular experts? My examination is in hopes of prompting a reset of our thinking. Briefly try to estimate the number of churches in your local community. Have we become entangled in a religious franchise war with location competition by building across the street from one another, while not providing adequate spiritual wellness that the world can depend on? Perhaps the answer is in the "doing" mentality mentioned earlier. Perhaps it begins with an experience of kenosis. Kenosis is the doctrine that Christ relinquished his divine attributes as to experience human suffering.

"For us to participate in the *kenosis* of God, which is our calling, as God's image, means that we must give up all that we conceal from ourselves and others: it means *to be willing to be emptied.*"[4] Over and over in this manual, the message reverts to the infallible truth of God's

---

[4] Maggie Ross. (1987). *The Fountain & the Furnace: The Way of Tears and Fire.* New York, NY: Paulist Press

word and the necessity of his presence in our lives. What we are experiencing through this manuscript is a revolutionary change in our world view. The telescope that was given as a Christmas present to a fifth grader is inadequate to the intrinsic demands of exploring galaxies. There is a new relativism on the horizon. Taquetta Baker is pioneering this relativism with counseling theory that is as desperately needed as water in the desert. A revolution changes the domain, changes even the very language in which we speak about some aspect of nature."[5] You are invited to be a partaker in a culture of empowerment that will bring a permanent SHIFT in how we perceive faith-based counseling, healing, and deliverance. It is time to reconsider wellness through the lens of God's intentional design.

*To everything there is a season, and a time for every purpose under heaven. **Ephesians 3:11***

---

[5] Thomas S. Kuhn. (2012). *The Structure of Scientific Revolutions.* Chicago, IL: The University of Chicago Press

TAQUETTA BAKER, FOUNDER

As an adopted child, Taquetta knows the lifelong journey of appreciating both spiritual and natural relationships and encounters. She understands being strengthened by the pain that life can bring while embracing the joy of unexpected connections. Taquetta has transformed her experiences to establish a legacy of pioneering and fearlessly leading others.

Taquetta Baker is the founder of Kingdom Shifters Ministries (KSM), Kingdom Shifters Empowerment Church, and Kingdom Wellness Counseling and Mentoring Center. She has authored over 38 books and two prayer CD's. Taquetta has a Doctorate in Ministry, a Master's Degree in Community Counseling with an emphasis on Marriage, Children and Family Counseling, a Bachelor's Degree in Psychology and Associate Degree in Business Administration. Taquetta is a Certified Life Coach, Certified Professional Coach, and Certified Executive Leadership Coach, through Breakthrough Coaching & Leadership Academy. Taquetta has a Therapon Belief Therapist Certification from the Therapon Institute, which provides faith-based counseling and ministry training.

Taquetta serves in the mental health field as a Behavioral Consultant. She enjoys working with individuals and families who experience a broad range of psychological, emotional, social, relational, and spiritual challenges. Her outreach demonstrates cultural agility across a spectrum of ages, ethnicities, and socio-economic backgrounds. She is committed to empowering others with launching ministries, businesses, and books. She provides mentoring, counseling and vision launching through her Kingdom Wellness Counseling and Mentoring Center. With over 22 years of faith-based and professional counseling experience, her reputation is one who transforms lives and families through balancing biblical principles with applicable tools and strategies.

Taquetta serves on the Board of Directors for New Day Community Ministries, Inc. and is a graduate of the Eagles Dance Institute under Dr. Pamela Hardy with a license in liturgical dance. Before pioneering her own ministry, Taquetta was a dedicated member of Christ

Temple Global Ministries for 14 years. She served and pioneered Shekinah Expressions dance ministry and served in the role of prophet, teacher, presbytery board member, and overseer of the Altar Workers Ministry. Taquetta receives mentoring and ministry covering from Bishop Jackie Green, Founder of JGM-National Prayer Life Institute (Phoenix, AZ), and was ordained as an Apostle on June 7, 2014.

The Bible is full of stories that are centered around digging or receiving from wells which represent stability and deep places of renewal. Taquetta flows through the spiritual wells of warfare, worship, counseling and deliverance. Taquetta's mantle is an apostolic directive of judging and establishing God's kingdom in people, ministries, communities, and regions. Taquetta travels in foreign missions and throughout the United States. She has mentored and established dance teams, altar workers, counseling programs, and deliverance and prophetic ministries. Taquetta ministers in the areas of fine arts, systems of prayer, fivefold ministry, deliverance, healing, miracles, atmospheric worship, and counseling. Her mission is to empower and train others to identify and embrace their destiny.

The difficult beginnings of life have blossomed into a mature and committed advocate for wellness. That vision now encompasses multiple generations. The concept of Kingdom Shifters comes from prompting others to move from a place of stagnation to a place of renewed purpose. This manual and others encompasses revolutionary works that will set a fresh momentum in the field of counseling. They are birthed from Taquetta's journey, knowledge, experience, and above all, her passionate quest to be a blessing to others.

VISION STATEMENT

Kingdom Wellness offers a revolutionary theory of bridging mental and physical health with biblical truths, faith-based counseling, deliverance and healing principles. This is a holistic ideology of the total person – body, soul (mind, will, emotions), and spirit becoming one.

Kingdom Wellness

Mental & Physical Health

Spiritual Well-Being

"Psychological theories are valuable for guiding practice in education, mental health, business, and other domains. They provide answers to intrinsically interesting questions concerning many kinds of thinking including perception, emotion, learning, and problem-solving."[6]

---

[6] Paul Thagard, Ph.D. (2017). What is a psychological theory? Retrieved from *Psychology Today* website at www.psychologytoday.com

DR. KATHY WILLIAMS, FOUNDER'S TRIBUTE

As founder of Kingdom Wellness Counseling Center and Taquetta's Kingdom Wellness Theory, I would like to make a special tribute to Dr. Kathy E. Williams for her contribution as editor and scholarly writer of this manual. Dr. Williams is a Doctor of Strategic Leadership from Regent University, and holds a Master's Degree in Strategic Management from Indiana Wesleyan University. Dr. Williams is the founder of New Day Ministries of Muncie, IN. Her passion is to mentor, mother, and restore incarcerated men and women, while proving that their destiny can be recaptured through patience, godly guidance, and empowerment to face and overcome life obstacles. She is a social media guru who brings love, laughter, encouragement, salvation, hope, and transformation to those who frequent her platforms and partake of her jokes, stories, and ministerial revelation that SHIFTS people from darkness to light. Dr. Williams has authored eight books of her own (and counting) that can be purchased on Amazon.com or Kingdomshiftingbooks.com. My nickname for Dr. Williams is "GENIUS" as she is indeed that in every sense of the word. She has a special gift of adding a unique perspective, divine tactility, and educational ingenuity to everything and everyone she touches. She is definitely in my hall of fame and added contributions to this manual that will impart God's true spirit of counsel into every reader. Thank you, Dr. Williams, for who you are to the world and to my life. Thank you for the countless hours you worked on this manual, prayed over me and the writings as you edited this book, and for helping to capture God's theory and heart of a New Testament Counselor for such a time as this. May your name forever be scribed from generation to generation as the legacy of who you are radiates from the "GENIUS" that you are to me and to the world.

With Heartfelt Blessings,
Taquetta Baker, Founder
Kingdom Wellness Counseling & Mentoring Center

Kingdom Wellness Counseling and Mentoring Center

Faith Based Counseling

Manual I

Part 1: (Chapters 1 – 4)

Learning Objectives:

- To develop a baseline concept of the relationship between the faith community and the influence of faith-based counseling in the field of mental health.
- To explore self-actualization through a reciprocal relationship between God and individuals, families, communities, and organizations.
- To understand the paradigm of Taquetta's wellness model.
- To understand kingdom wellness through biblical principles and concepts.

Chapter 1

THE FAITH COMMUNITY AND MENTAL HEALTH

The World Health Organization defines mental health in the following terms:

> "... a state of well-being in which the individual realizes his or her own abilities, can cope with the normal stresses of life, can work productively and fruitfully, and is able to make a contribution to his or her community." The WHO stresses that mental health "is not just the absence of mental disorder."[7]

Mental health is *"a person's condition with regard to their psychological and emotional well-being."*[8] The world of psychology would contend that mental health encompasses the balanced, appropriate, or satisfactory psychological (mental) level or condition of a person's emotional or behavioral ability to take care of themselves and to live safely among others.

Often when we consider mental health, we focus on the extreme mentally ill. Though there are broad spectrums of mental illness where people can be diagnosed with a psychological disorder, every person can be challenged with mental illness or mental instability at some point in their lives. ***James 1:8*** contends, *"A double-minded man is unstable in all his ways."*

Double-minded is _dipsychos_ (Greek):
1. two-spirited, i.e. vacillating (in opinion or purpose)
2. wavering, uncertain, doubting, divided in interest

---

[7] Christian Nordqvist. (2017). What is mental health? Retrieved from *Medical News Today* website at https://www.medicalnewstoday.com/articles/154543.php
[8] Retrieved from dictionary.com

Figure 1.0. Alternative Expressions for Unstable

Inconsistent	Not fixed or firm	Uncertain	Sensitive	Unsteady
Insecure	Unsteadfast	Unsettled	Fickle	Wavering
Restlessness	Unreliable	Borderline	Irrational	Volatile
Erratic	Untrustworthy	Unstable	Unpredictable	Suspect

Source: Baker, 2018

Every person will experience double-mindedness from time to time, which means we are operating in two spirits:

- One that is our true identity and reality.
- The other which is our false identity and false reality.
- Without healing, we become at risk for living double-minded which can lead to experiencing and operating through other splits in our personality.

As we consider this concept, there is a vast population of people with mental illness who are undiagnosed and who would be appalled if you suggested they are mentally challenged. There is also a vast population of people who live a lifestyle of demonstrated mental instability but are able to care for themselves and live within society without being a severe safety hazard to themselves or others.

"Without being severe" is an essential descriptor as anytime there is mental instability, the person is a challenge to themselves and others and carries the potential to become a safety hazard without warning. It is my position that this is the basis for the rise of suicide and our inability to detect or discern that threat. God's measure set in *James 1:8* is true, and mental illness has reached epic proportions to become a contemporary plague.

- We accept doublemindedness as commonplace behavior.
- We tend to be reactive rather than proactive regarding mental illness.
- We live in extremes, so the adverse double-minded individual goes undetected and without treatment, deliverance, and healing to restore their mental health.

- We tend to hide mental illness through personality facades, learned survival tactics/endurances, and lifestyle successes that present as mental stability, yet the person is dying on the inside.
- We do not value counseling, mental health agencies, and social services organizations, so people are ashamed about having to receive services. They refuse services or hide the fact that they are receiving them.

Society is shocked when a (perceived) stable or successful person takes their life. The shock increases with examining conversations, comments, and behaviors, and realization that the person was double-minded, unstable in many and perhaps all of their ways. Their conflicted public persona and private self-reflected a tearing in their soul.

When considering, mental health and faith, the topic and complexities are challenging. The faith community has endeavored to provide deliverance and healing to the mentally challenged, however, the methods have been more contextual to the literal writings within the scriptures rather than really seeking God for effective strategies that provide sufficient wellness and breakthrough to the mental health community.

Often the faith community is focused specifically on demonology when it comes to mental health. Speedy altar prayers or abbreviated deliverance session are frequently utilized with minimal to no follow-up as part of the plan. Counseling and social service programs are rarely available or considered to further provide the person with inner healing and skills building to process and sustain in mental wellness. Quick fixes with prayer and clichés *"just stand and believe,"* *"praise your way through,"* *"put on the garment of praise for heaviness,"* and other rhetoric, are also utilized as cures for complex struggles that require a journey of being processed to wellness.

After people stand, believe, and praise, they are often without sufficient applicable tools and inner healing. If there is a chemical imbalance connected to their mental instability, there is a need for medication to assist toward breaking through to psychological health and being single-minded in thoughts and emotions.

Though addressing the presence of demonic infiltration and strongholds is essential, balanced deliverance and healing is vital if the faith community is going to really manifest the wellness of God in the area of mental health as it relates to their members and with assisting communities. I believe one of the main reasons God wanted churches and ministries to be planted in communities is to be an edifice for deliverance and healing for the people, the land, and the region.

God wanted this to be an operable orderly system which is the purpose for *Ephesians 4:11-13*:

And he gave some, apostles; and some, prophets; and some, evangelists; and some, pastors and teachers; For the perfecting of the saints, for the work of the ministry, for the edifying of the body of Christ: Till we all come in the unity of the faith, and of the knowledge of the Son of God, unto a perfect man, unto the measure of the stature of the fulness of Christ.

Part of the work of apostles, prophets, evangelists, pastors, and teachers is to be strategic leaders that seek God in developing events, programs, and services through churches and ministries. The goals and objectives include perfecting the wellness and well-being of saints (believers) by training, equipping, and releasing them into their ordained destiny. The outcome is that they can effectively minister the heart, mind, will, and purpose of God to the community and to the world.

According to the ancient philosopher Aristotle, "Nature abhors a vacuum." It is applicable to the church leaving a vacuum of providing services to people. The secular world steps in and fills the void, leaving the church on the outside looking in rather than in its intended role. Churches and ministries have become many other things that are far from deliverance and healing centers, while hospitals, counseling centers, and social service organizations have become governmental institutions with new age and non-faith based biblical kingdom values and practices.

- Many church members are not equipped in their destiny.

- Many who operate as counselors, mental health agents, and social service professionals, are educated and trained by world systems and utilize their degrees in worldly organizations where they are not able to consistently or effectively implement biblical principles and standards.

- Many pastors and leaders shun counseling and organizational services and view these entities as ungodly or possessing a lack of faith.

- Many pastors and leaders shun members receiving counseling and organizational assistance outside of the ministry. Many pastors and leaders shun members from receiving counseling from other persons, even if it is other ministers within their ministry or the body of Christ. Many deem this as betrayal or usurping their authority.

- Many churches and ministries do not have in-house counseling and social service programs, and if they do, some of the programs are operated by uneducated professionals who consider their role to be mentors or outreach ministers.

- Pastors and leaders tend to provide counseling and mental health services, and often they are not equipped with the educational training, skills, applicable tools, financial or community resources. Most do not have the time to adequately process people to wellness.

- Many seminaries do not teach about demonization or deliverance as part of their counseling and social service curriculum; therefore, this component is overlooked by those who may have faith-based counseling education but no deliverance training or awareness. With certainty, we know demonization and deliverance ministry are not taught in the world's systems.

If *Ephesians 4* was implemented into churches and ministries, the result is that professional health care workers (counselors, case managers, social workers, psychologists, and psychiatrists), could be utilized to establish a faith-based biblical counseling and social service center. That is the paradigm necessary for an effective 21st-century church. This center could provide balanced deliverance, counseling, psychological and psychiatric treatment, case management and social services to people within the church and from the community.

Thomas Kuhn posits that there are a series of paradigm shifts required by the sciences, including normal science, puzzle-solving, paradigm, anomaly, crisis, and revolution. The concept of mental health and the faith community falls under the title of *incommensurability*. "That is the idea that, in the course of a revolution and paradigm shift, the new ideas and assertions cannot be strictly compared to the old ones."[9] The result is not the development of a new theory that merely substitutes fresh insights but a demonstrative change in world view. That is the radical objective of this manual.

The component of spirituality that needs to be in the forefront of mental health would be present, along with applicable tools, skills, and resources needed to produce well-balanced people and communities. Spirituality is essential. We are created by a God who is a complete spiritual being. We are made in his likeness. We therefore cannot live a balanced life of wellness apart from relationship and guidance from him.

Figure 1.1. Trichotomy of Humanity

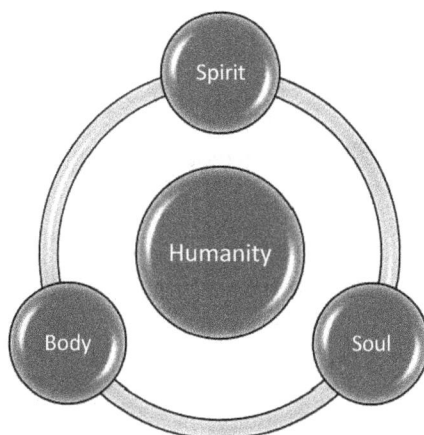

Source: Williams, 2018

The trichotomy of man (humanity) is consistently inclusive of the spirit, yet our culture has made self-care about every other dimension of our being except the spirit. Society is saturated with messages concerning the body and soul, while woefully neglecting spiritual care in a model that is inclusive of our Creator.

Shift! My ambition is that the faith community SHIFTS back into its rightful place as a center for wellness. Someone said once (while holding up the Bible), "What if we really believed this book?" We

---

[9] Thomas S. Kuhn. (2012). *The Structure of Scientific Revolutions.* Chicago, IL: The University of Chicago Press

can equip, train, and produce faith-based professionals. Those individuals will operate in biblical counseling, mental health, and social service agencies in addition to serving as a holistic resource. The outcome will be a revolutionary SHIFT for healing and stabilizing individuals, families, and communities. Join me in steadfastly believing that this revelation will burn in the spirits of leaders, saints, and ministries in the name of Jesus.

Decreeing A Kingdom Wellness SHIFT into the earth!

Chapter 2

TAQUETTA'S KINGDOM WELLNESS THEORY (TKWT)

The concept of kingdom wellness holds the premise that in order to maintain healing in the mind, heart, body, and soul, a person has to live and cultivate wellness through their spirit. There are nearly 500 mentions of the word *through* in the scripture. One that most are familiar with is **Philippians 4:13,** *I can do all things through Christ which strengthens me.* We have spent too much time trying to invert that concept and do Christ through all things. Wellness through the spirit has a relational order that cannot be modified or placed in secular terms.

Humans are primarily spirit even though we are made of flesh and encompass thoughts, emotions, and a will. In order to cultivate spiritual wellness, a person has to be connected to God as true wellness cannot be attained without him. He is the creator, a spiritual being, and the source of all wellness.

Genesis 1:27 *So God created man in his own image, in the image of God created he him; male and female created he them.*

Proverbs 20:27 *The spirit of man is the lamp of the LORD, Searching all the innermost parts of his being.*

Ecclesiastes 2:7 *Then the dust will return to the earth as it was, and the spirit will return to God who gave it.*

John 3:24 *God is a Spirit: and they that worship him must worship him in spirit and in truth.*

John 32:8 *But it is a spirit in man, And the breath of the Almighty gives them understanding.*

1 Corinthians 2:11 *For what man knoweth the things of a man, save the spirit of man which is in him? even so the things of God knoweth no man, but the Spirit of God.*

God teaches through his word and through relationship with him, how to live through our spirit, so that every other facet of our lives is empowered through a pure well that renews life, while flushing out instability, illness, impurities, and death. "Wells represent life, prosperity and abundance. No wonder numerous biblical characters from Abraham to Isaac, Jacob and Moses - even our Lord Jesus Christ had a story to tell regarding or while by a well."[10]

Since God created mankind, he is the source of our existence and identity. It is essential to have relationship with him, so that we can acquire and maintain mental stability and overall wellness.

Wellness is a continually evolving journey. Once we obtain wellness, it is essential to keep on receiving guidance from God for sustained wholeness.

Taquetta's Kingdom Wellness Theory (TKWT) holds the belief that when God is the head and center of a person's life, he or she can sufficiently self-actualize to wellness. It is a spiritually reciprocal relationship. *Galatians 6:9b* assures us, *. . . he who sows to the Spirit will of the Spirit reap life everlasting.* That concept not only refers to the afterlife, but of perpetual development that encompasses past, present, and future.

God has ordained a specific purpose for every individual that can only be fulfilled when we partner in relationship with him. TKWT believes that as a person SHIFTS into revelation of who he or she is in God and who God is in them, true healthiness, wellness, and sustaining success in and throughout life can occur. That revelation avails by:

- Learning one's divine purpose in life.
- Receiving deliverance and healing from experiences, thoughts, feelings, behaviors, and demonic strongholds, that hinder and thwart one's purpose.
- Creating life standards based on biblical principles where the person can exercise their divine purpose as a daily lifestyle.

---

[10] Bode Ayodele. (2007). The significance of spiritual wells. Retrieved from *Sermon Central website at* https://www.sermoncentral.com/sermons/the-significance-of-spiritual-wells-bode-ayodele-sermon-on-holy-spirit-in-believers-111359

- Partnering in relationship with God to maintain that standard, while journeying in a life of wellness with him.

TKWT believes that the greatest need of a person is to know that they have a specific life purpose and the only way to know that purpose is through relationship with the Creator. Through one's purpose, a person is self-actualized. Self-actualized means to become real or actual. When you are authentic you are not a copy of someone else and you are not a facade of yourself. It is an issue of semantics for a person to believe that self-actualization is contradictory to discipleship. The Bible is not void of theories of self-worth. In fact, quite the opposite is true. The scripture is filled with God calling individuals by speaking to them about their destiny and greatness. **Jeremiah 29:11,** *For I know the plans I have for you, declares the Lord, plans to prosper you and not to harm you, plans to give you hope and a future.*

Self-actualization is about the person and the Creator envisioning the same plan. It is where a person is operating in his or her unique original self, while reaching his or her greatest potential. As a person comprehends their purpose, he or she becomes self-actualized, the result is activating a fulfilled life in God. When a person strives to live life outside a relationship with God, it constructs a reality that provides temporary fulfillment. With God, true fulfillment and contentment occurs as a person learns who they were designed to be and masters living in that truth. **Romans 8:37,** *Yet in all these things we are more than conquerors through Him who loved us.*

Be a Healthy You!

Chapter 3

TAQUETTA'S WELLNESS PARADIGM

Figure 3.0. Wellness Paradigm

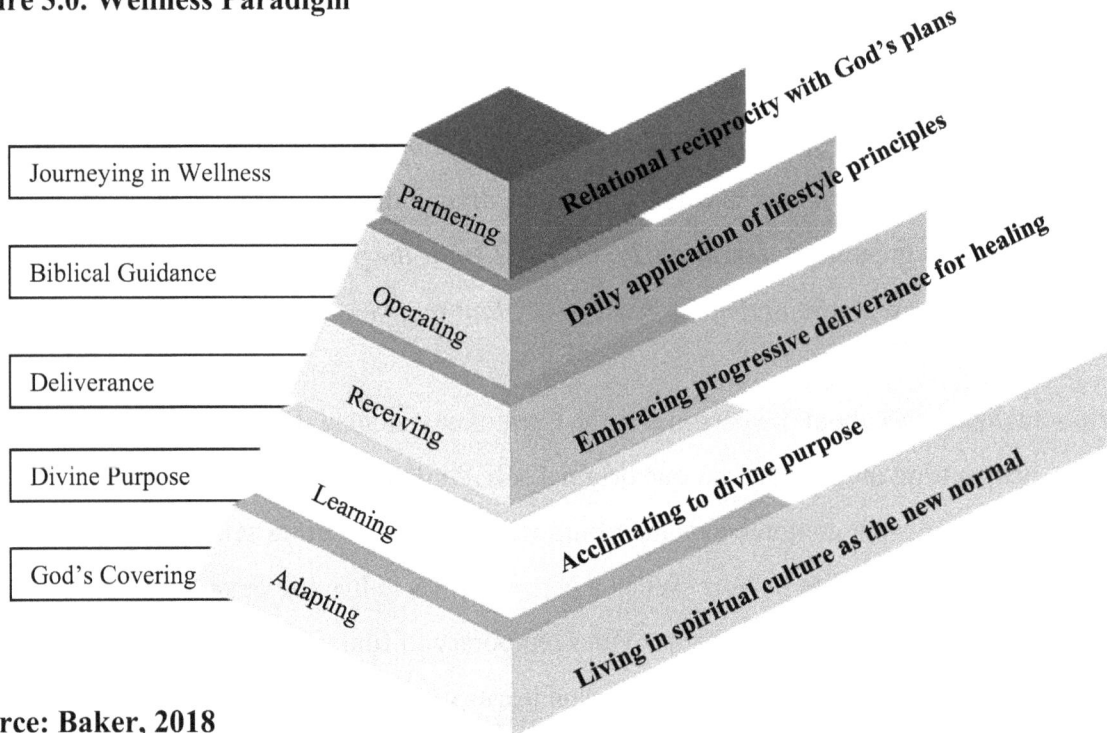

Journeying in Wellness	Partnering	Relational reciprocity with God's plans
Biblical Guidance	Operating	Daily application of lifestyle principles
Deliverance	Receiving	Embracing progressive deliverance for healing
Divine Purpose	Learning	Acclimating to divine purpose
God's Covering	Adapting	Living in spiritual culture as the new normal

Source: Baker, 2018

So love the Lord your God with all your heart, with all your soul, with all your mind, and with all your strength.' The second most important commandment is this: 'Love your neighbor as you love yourself.' No other commandment is greater than these." Mark 12:30-31 (GW)

EXEGETICAL PREMISE FOR HUMANITY

Genesis 1:26-27 *And God said, Let us make man in our image, after our likeness: and let them have dominion over the fish of the sea, and over the fowl of the air, and over the cattle, and over all the earth, and over every creeping thing that creepeth upon the earth. So God created man in his own image, in the image of God created he him; male and female created he them.*

Psalm 8:3-6 When I consider thy heavens, the work of thy fingers, the moon and the stars, which thou hast ordained; What is man, that thou art mindful of him? and the son of man, that thou visitest him? For thou hast made him a little lower than the angels, and hast crowned him with glory and honour. Thou madest him to have dominion over the works of thy hands; thou hast put all things under his feet:

Psalm 100:3 Know ye that the LORD he is God: it is he that hath made us, and not we ourselves; we are his people, and the sheep of his pasture.

Psalm 119:73 Thy hands have made me and fashioned me: give me understanding, that I may learn thy commandments.

Psalm 138:8 The LORD will perfect that which concerneth me: thy mercy, O LORD, endureth for ever: forsake not the works of thine own hands.

Psalm 139:14 I will praise thee; for I am fearfully and wonderfully made: marvellous are thy works; and that my soul knoweth right well.

Job 4:17 Can mortal man be just before God, or be more right than He is? Can a man be pure before his Maker, or be more cleansed than He is? (AMP)

Isaiah 43:7 Even every one that is called by my name: for I have created him for my glory, I have formed him; yea, I have made him.

Isaiah 45:12 I have made the earth, and created man upon it: I, even my hands, have stretched out the heavens, and all their host have I commanded.

EXEGETICAL PREMISE FOR ORDAINED PURPOSE

Exodus 9:16 *And in very deed for this cause have I raised thee up, for to shew in thee my power; and that my name may be declared throughout all the earth.*

Job 42:2 *I know that You can do all things, and that no thought or purpose of Yours can be restrained or thwarted. (AMP)*

Proverbs 19:21 *Many are the plans in a person's heart, but it is the Lord's purpose that prevails.*

Proverbs 20:5 *The purposes of a person's heart are deep waters, but one who has insight draws them out.*

Jeremiah 29:11 *For I know the thoughts that I think toward you, saith the LORD, thoughts of peace, and not of evil, to give you an expected end.*

Isaiah 14:24 *The LORD of hosts hath sworn, saying, Surely as I have thought, so shall it come to pass; and as I have purposed, [so] shall it stand.*

Isaiah 14:27 *For the LORD of hosts hath purposed, and who shall disannul [it]? and his hand [is] stretched out, and who shall turn it back?*

Acts 26:16 *But rise, and stand upon thy feet: for I have appeared unto thee for this purpose, to make thee a minister and a witness both of these things which thou hast seen, and of those things in the which I will appear unto thee.*

John 15:16 *Ye have not chosen me, but I have chosen you, and ordained you, that ye should go and bring forth fruit, and [that] your fruit should remain: that whatsoever ye shall ask of the Father in my name, he may give it you.*

Matthew 28:19 *Go ye therefore, and teach all nations, baptizing them in the name of the Father, and of the Son, and of the Holy Ghost:*

Ephesians 1:11 *In whom also we have obtained an inheritance, being predestinated according to the purpose of him who worketh all things after the counsel of his own will.*

Philippians 2:12-13 *Therefore, my dear friends, as you have always obeyed—not only in my presence, but now much more in my absence—continue to work out your salvation with fear and trembling, for it is God who works in you to will and to act in order to fulfill his good purpose.*

Romans 8:28 *And we know that in all things God works for the good of those who love him, who have been called according to his purpose.*

2 Timothy 1:9 *[For it is He] Who delivered and saved us and called us with a calling in itself holy and leading to holiness [to a life of consecration, a vocation of holiness]; [He did it] not because of anything of merit that we have done, but because of and to further His own purpose and grace (unmerited favor) which was given us in Christ Jesus before the world began [eternal ages ago]. (AMP)*

The etymology of the word purpose stirs little change from its use in ancient times to present, spiritual application. Its Greek origin refers to putting something on display or putting it in plain view.[11] Amazingly, it historically refers to the shewbread in the temple. God wants to put you on display!

God wants wellness on display!

[11] Lexicon: Strong's G4286. (n.d.) Retrieved from *The Blue Letter Bible* website at
https://www.blueletterbible.org/lang/lexicon/lexicon.cfm?Strongs=G4286&t=KJV

Chapter 4

_____

EXPLORING KINGDOM WELLNESS

God's original design for humanity did not include mental or physical illness. Before the fall in the Garden of Eden, mankind existed by the breath of God – fully spirit - and completely whole.

Genesis 2:6 *Then the LORD God formed a man from the dust of the ground and breathed into his nostrils the breath of life, and the man became a living being. (NIV)*

The fall of man produced sin and suffering in the earth. The disobedience of eating from the tree of the knowledge of good and evil brought consequences that are still applicable today (Study ***Genesis 3***). "God revealed fundamental truths in the Bible that medical science has taken thousands of years to confirm. Regrettably, many theologians do not understand the value of the health principles recorded in Scripture—and as a result they have failed to perform an important God-given function!"[12]

The Bible is a narrative of God's efforts to bring restoration to his creation. His primary investment is in the man and woman who were made in his image. God performed miracles, deliverance, and healings with a consistent agenda of restoring the mental and physical well-being of humanity. It is unfortunate that in our 21st-century society, there is such a need to convince those who profess a lifestyle in God to accept biblical principles for healing. We revert back to a question posed earlier, "Do we really believe this book?" No wonder that the prophet Isaiah was compelled to ask, *Who has believed our report? And to whom is the arm of the Lord revealed (**Isaiah 53:1**)*

_____

[12] Douglas S. Winnail. (2009, May-June). Biblical principles of health. Retrieved from *Tomorrow's World* website at https://www.tomorrowsworld.org/magazines/2009/may-june/bible-principles-of-health

Kingdom Wellness offers bilateral persuasion for both believers and non-believers to access ancient principles of wellness. A living portrait of empirical data can be gathered from the legacy of scriptural documentation concerning healing. The spectrum of people represents a pluralism comparable to today's global community.

A Hebrew name of God is "Jehovah Raphah," meaning the God who heals

Raphah also means:
1. to mend (by stitching), heal individual hurts
2. (figuratively) to cure, to (cause to) heal
3. to be healed by or likened unto a physician
4. to repair, thoroughly, make whole, make healthful
5. heal national defects and distresses or hurts, restore national favor

Exodus 15:26 *And said, If thou wilt diligently hearken to the voice of the Lord thy God, and wilt do that which is right in his sight, and wilt give ear to his commandments, and keep all his statutes, I will put none of these diseases upon thee, which I have brought upon the Egyptians: for I am the Lord that healeth thee.*

Deuteronomy 32:39 *See now that I, even I, am he, and there is no god with me: I kill, and I make alive; I wound, and I heal: neither is there any that can deliver out of my hand.*

2 Chronicles 7:14 *If my people, which are called by my name, shall humble themselves, and pray, and seek my face, and turn from their wicked ways; then will I hear from heaven, and will forgive their sin, and will heal their land.*

Psalm 41:3 *The LORD will sustain him upon his sickbed; In his illness, You restore him to health.*

Psalm 103:5 *Praise the Lord, my soul; all my inmost being, praise his holy name. Praise the Lord, my soul, and forget not all his benefits—who forgives all your sins and heals all your diseases, who redeems your life from the pit and crowns you with love and compassion, who satisfies your desires with good thing, so that your youth is renewed like the eagle's.*

Psalm 107:20 *He sent out His word and healed them, and delivered them from their destruction.*

Isaiah 53:5 But He was pierced for our transgressions, He was crushed for our iniquities; the punishment that brought us peace was on Him, and by His wounds we are healed.

A New Testament Greek word for Healing is Therapeuo

Therapeuo means:
1. to wait upon menially
2. (figuratively) to adore (God), or (specially) to relieve (of disease)
3. to cure, heal, worship
4. to serve, do service, restore to health

Matthew 4:23 And he went throughout all Galilee, teaching in their synagogues and proclaiming the gospel of the kingdom and healing every disease and every affliction among the people.

Matthew 10:1 And He called to Him His twelve disciples and gave them authority over unclean spirits, to cast them out, and to heal every disease and every affliction.

Matthew 10:8 Heal the sick, raise the dead, cleanse those who have leprosy, drive out demons. Freely you have received; freely give.

Acts 10:38 How God anointed Jesus of Nazareth with the Holy Spirit and with power. He went about doing good and healing all who were oppressed by the devil, for God was with him.

James 5:14-15 Is anyone among you sick? Let him call for the elders of the church, and let them pray over him, anointing him with oil in the name of the Lord. And the prayer of faith will save the one who is sick, and the Lord will raise him up.

1 Peter 2:24 He personally bore our sins in His [own] body on the tree [as on an altar and offered Himself on it], that we might die (cease to exist) to sin and live to righteousness. By His wounds you have been healed.

3 John 1:2 Dear friend, I pray that you may enjoy good health and that all may go well with you, even as your soul is getting along well.

When Jesus died on the cross and ascended to the right hand of God, he restored salvation. His sacrifice completed the highest level of healing that restored mankind unto eternal life. His love gives us access to the same healing.

John 3:16 For God so loved the world, that he gave his only begotten Son, that whosoever believeth in him should not perish, but have everlasting life.

<u>Salvation or Save in Greek is *sozo* and means:</u>
1. to save, i.e. deliver or protect (literally or figuratively)
2. heal, preserve, save (self), do well, be (make) whole
3. to keep safe and sound, to rescue from danger or destruction
4. to deliver one (from injury or peril), heal, restore to health
5. to save a suffering one (from perishing), i.e. one suffering from disease, to make well
6. to preserve one who is in danger of destruction, to save or rescue

God prearranged our healing with his love.

Matthew 6:10 Your kingdom come Your will be done, On earth as it is in heaven.

Matthew 9:35 Jesus was going through all the cities and villages, teaching in their synagogues and proclaiming the gospel of the kingdom, and healing every kind of disease and every kind of sickness.

Luke 9:2 And He sent them out to proclaim the kingdom of God and to perform healing.

Luke 10:9 And heal those in it who are sick, and say to them, 'The kingdom of God has come near to you.'

Luke 11:2 And He said to them, "When you pray, say: 'Father, hallowed be Your name. Your kingdom come. Thy will be done, as in heaven, so in earth.

Luke 11:20 But if I cast out demons by the finger of God, then the kingdom of God has come upon you.

Matthew 6:10 Your kingdom come. Your will be done on earth as it is in heaven.

Jesus taught his disciples to pray with an expectation that what happens in heaven will happen in the earth. There is no mental or physical illness in heaven. We are able to have heaven on earth through the work of the cross. As New Testament believers, we are living through the redemption of salvation, and operating in the giftings that allow heaven and earth to align.

Mental health is God's eternal will for us.

Deuteronomy 28:28 *The LORD will smite you with madness and with blindness and with bewilderment of heart.*

1 Samuel 16:23 *So it came about whenever the evil spirit from God came to Saul, David would take the harp and play it with his hand; and Saul would be refreshed and be well, and the evil spirit would depart from him.*

Matthew 17:14-20 *When they came to the crowd, a man came up to Jesus, falling on his knees before Him and saying, "Lord, have mercy on my son, for he is a lunatic and is very ill; for he often falls into the fire and often into the water. "I brought him to Your disciples, and they could not cure him."*

Romans 8:22-23 *For we know that the whole creation has been groaning together in the pains of childbirth until now. And not only the creation, but we ourselves, who have the firstfruits of the Spirit, groan inwardly as we wait eagerly for adoption as sons, the redemption of our bodies.*

Philippians 4:6-7 *Be anxious for nothing, but in everything by prayer and supplication with thanksgiving let your requests be made known to God. And the peace of God, which surpasses all comprehension, will guard your hearts and your minds in Christ Jesus.*

I Peter 5:7 *Casting all your cares on him, because he cares for you.*

2 Timothy 1:7 *For God has not given us a spirit of fear, but of power, and of love, and of a sound mind.*

The Bible is filled not only with stories of healing but with a continuum of how healing manifests. In some cases, the healing was complete and instantaneous. In others, there were processes required or responsibility put on the person desiring the healing. People who are not healed instantaneously of a physical disorder can access therapeutic treatment. People who are not healed instantly of mental illness deserve access to a godly counselor, psychologist, or psychiatrist for holistic treatment. All of these avenues can be God's pathways - processing - to kingdom wellness. Kingdom-committed healers are indispensable to manifesting God's healing, whether instantaneously or through a process.

Proverbs 19:21 *There are many devices in a man's heart; nevertheless the counsel of the LORD, that shall stand.*

Proverbs 19:21 *Many are the plans in a person's heart, but it is the LORD's purpose that prevails. (NIV)*

Healing is woven throughout the scriptures. David wrote in *Psalm 73:26* *My flesh and my heart fail; But God is the strength of my heart and my portion forever.*

Diagram 4.0 Old Testament Healing

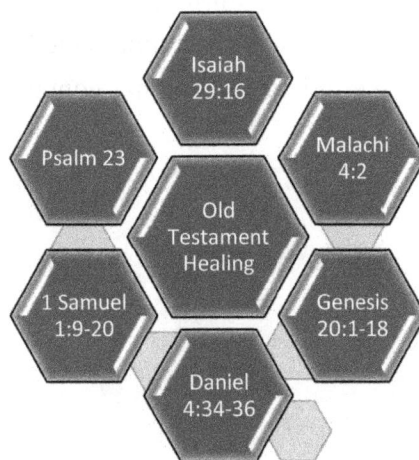

Source: Williams, 2018

Kingdom Wellness Counseling and Mentoring Center

Faith Based Counseling

Manual I

Part 2: Chapters (5 – 9)

Learning Objectives:

- To provide a definitive overview of faith-based counseling versus other mental health services, mentorships, and programs.
- To provide truths and misunderstandings regarding the pure objective of faith-based counseling.
- To provide a biblical perspective of the spirit and gift of counseling versus counseling through one's humanity or experience with traumatizing life experiences.
- To examine how ungodly and erred counseling has contaminated the effectiveness of faith-based counseling.

Chapter 5

DEFINING FAITH-BASED COUNSELING

Contemporary terminology might suggest that someone is receiving counseling; when, in fact, that may not be the case. Particularly considering the increased marketing of mentoring, life coaching, and consulting, it is essential to properly differentiate. All of these professions are beneficial and necessary to people, communities, ministries and businesses, but are not necessarily counseling. Each plays a role in helping to equip people, ministries, and the world in being healthy and focused as they journey in destiny, but their service is different from the counseling profession.

Faith Based Biblical Counseling (Therapy)

In addition to the Spirit of Counseling to which is examined in the next chapter, counselors are usually educated paid professionals that require a degree, licensing (depending on state ordinances), and ongoing training to keep them accountable and equipped to service their clients. Counseling is an in-depth exploration of past and present unresolved experiences, and of personal and generational issues. Counseling addresses personal issues, generational strongholds, sin issues, character flaws, and unresolved painful experiences. Counseling involves a course of sessions where the person is enlightened, delivered, and healed, through examination of circumstances, individuals, and choices. Deliverance and healing is woven into that course of sessions through a watchful change process (activation) and points of accountability.

Diagram 5.0 Change Process

| Activation | → | Accountability | → | Empowerment | → | Maintenance |

Source: Williams, 2018

Once an individual has engaged in resolution and healing, a skillful counselor will provide tools, skills, and guidance to move their client toward empowerment. Empowerment is the key to developing a maintenance plan. Many times, well-intended individuals will provide exploration, wisdom, and direction to a person, and assert that is counseling. Authentic counseling, however, is a strategic set of committed sessions that are ongoing until goals have been achieved. Jesus had the spirit of counsel (*Isaiah 11:2*) and, by the words of the prophet, was counselor (*Isaiah 9:6*). To say that we are a disciple of Christ includes counsel. Counseling is not the same as offering advice. It is a dedicated processing to wholeness. The counselor is not responsible for the healing but is responsible for guiding their client through the healing process.

In faith-based counseling a series of sessions based in biblical truth process the client toward healthiness and wholeness. This standard is applicable, whether the client is an individual, couple, or family. It is an authentic tool for the corporate world, government entities, or any other organized group. The Bible supports seeking counsel as wisdom and not as a sign of weakness or a measure of capability. The majority of scriptural references to counsel comes from David's psalms and Solomon's proverbs. Solomon, with the reputation of one of the wisest men to ever live, was a chief advocate for counseling.

Proverbs 11:14 Where there is no counsel, the people fall; but in the multitude of counselors there is safety.

Proverbs 19:20 *Listen to counsel and receive instruction, that you may be wise in your latter days.*

The counseling process may include:
- Completing an intake form,
- Attending a10-20 minute phone consultation to discuss the purpose of counseling,
- A succession of personal, couples, family, or group therapy,
- Deliverance ministry,
- Inner healing techniques,
- Homework assignments,
- Feedback, constructive criticism,
- Tools and skills to help reshape behavior and transform lives.

Though there are many professional counseling styles and techniques that can be used, each case is unique.

It is essential to rely on the Holy Spirit with:
- How the counseling process should unfold,
- How many therapy sessions should take place,
- What homework assignments are given,
- Whether deliverance ministry is necessary,
- What inner healing techniques should be utilized.

Legally, most people who are seeking counseling are obligated to 6-9 sessions. Anyone who professes healing in less than three sessions probably just needed advice or guidance to get beyond a specific barrier that has blocked healing or deliverance. Never discount the possibility of a miracle; however, even miracles impose a change of circumstances that will benefit from guidance.

It has been my professional experience that it takes at least three sessions to establish a comfortable relationship. Clients need to feel safe to move toward disclosure. A person may initially expose deep painful issues because they are elated to have someone to discuss them with.

That initial elation transitions to withdrawal for various reasons:

- Shame, guilt, condemnation,
- Fear of not being believed,
- Fear of their information being shared with others.

This is the reason it generally takes three sessions to establish a stable atmosphere. By the sixth session, a person is likely exposing deeper issues. In that phase, at least 3-6 additional sessions are needed to effectively explore root causes, soul wounds, issues of forgiveness, and resolution. Woven throughout the entire process is the empowerment of moving the individual to a place of sustained maintenance with each step of healing.

It is my professional position that anyone who contends they are a counselor, should be professionally educated with ongoing training. That includes those who have an identified spirit of counsel. As a sidenote, ministries who utilize spiritual gifts assessments have a responsibility to not simply issue conclusions to their members without guiding them to appropriate training for their gifts. We have to stop whipping people with scriptures as if correcting and chastising are the primary tools for the body of Christ. For those who advocate using a rod of correction, please note that the rod spoken of was a staff used by shepherds to tap a sheep from side to side for the purposes of guidance and not beating.

Our mission is to provide our clients with tools for appropriate application of biblical principles. Faith-based counselors must be aware of the numerous factors that can impact someone's life, e.g. psychological, mental, financial, economic, educational, chemical, physical, social, spiritual. Professional education and ongoing training will provide a balanced perspective of realism to the counseling ministry. With an ever-increasing scope of issues, there is a plethora of factors involved in helping our clients.

Pastoral Counseling

According to the American Association of Pastor Counseling (AAPC), Pastoral Counseling is:

Pastoral counseling is a mode of clinical health care that integrates the knowledge of psychology and the behavioral sciences with the wisdom of spirituality, religion, and theology. Pastoral counseling serves individuals, couples, families, and community systems in an effort to foster healing, renewal, reconciliation, and transformation..[13]

Because of our traditional model of church leadership where the weight of ministry centers around the pastor, numerous (if not most) pastors have provided these services with the best of intention, but no training. These men and women rely on their wisdom, faithfulness, and commitment to help people. *Proverbs 4:7* tells us, *"Wisdom is the principal thing; therefore get wisdom: and with all thy getting get understanding."* There must be clarity in the reason for the wisdom and how to apply the wisdom to produce sustaining deliverance and healing. Most pastors wear many hats. There are three primary reasons why pastors who take on the role of counseling can become problematic:

Diagram 5.1 Change Process

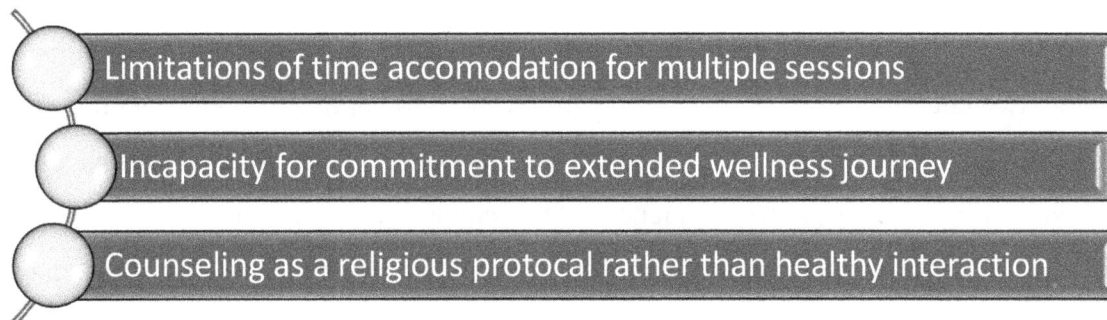

- Limitations of time accomodation for multiple sessions
- Incapacity for commitment to extended wellness journey
- Counseling as a religious protocal rather than healthy interaction

Source: Baker, 2018

To examine those three areas in more detail, we find that pastors are stretched thin and do not have the valuable resources of time and energy to meet with people for multiple sessions. Some people have expressed that their pastors do not pursue pastoral counseling because of a preconceived notion that pastors do not have time to help. In some cases, members have begun

---

[13]Jill L. Snodgrass. (n.d.) Why pastoral counseling. Retrieved from *American Association of Pastoral Counselors* website at https://www.aapc.org/page/WhyPastoral

pastoral counseling but found that it had to be stopped because of scheduling conflicts. Others have experienced hurt when receiving pastoral counseling from feeling that the pastor,

1) Did not really listen,
2) Did not take their heart into consideration,
3) Provided religious solutions but process pathway and applicable tools to sustain in their healing,
4) Lacked follow-through.

Providing quick solutions, using prayer as the primary device, and utilizing religious jargon can easily take precedence over the effective counseling need for transformation. It is important that we validate those in the pastoral role for the good that they bring to the body of Christ and remove the unrealistic burden that they have to be everything for everyone. For those pastors who choose to counsel, it is logistically impossible to counsel at every request. Establishing a counseling center, while partnering with gifted and educated counselors, would allow those who are qualified to facilitate this arm of ministry.

Secular Counseling

Like faith-based counseling, secular counseling has the ambition of helping people with their problems and improving their overall well-being. Secular counselors provide insights on human behavior based in research and practices. Most counseling theories are from respected experts who utilized research to prove a particular counseling perspective. Secular counseling believes that humanity in their finite self is good; therefore, the goal is to correct thoughts and behaviors to achieve a self-actualized life. Secular counseling tends to see the person as a catalyst for their own change, while faith-based counseling sees God and a relationship with God as the springboard for change. Secular counseling tends to focus on what the person desires. The process of counseling is designed to assist in achieving their stated goals. If the client desires a relationship with God, that is incorporated into the counseling process but is not considered an essential component. Secular counseling utilizes certain principles and practices that are not grounded in biblical truths or perspectives. These principles and practices can open doors to further binding clients to demonic strongholds, or swaying clients onto a path that is outside of God's design. Many who have experienced secular counseling have found it to help in measure or for a season of their life but not in fullness. Without the biblical grounding, wholeness is not actualized through a relationship with God as our Creator.

New Age Counseling

New age counseling claim to have faith-based values but its premise is focused on empowering people in whatever '*god*' they believe in, rather than the Almighty God. It respects a person's beliefs and incorporate principles and concepts into the counseling process from that person's spiritual belief system. Many will pursue new age counselors thinking they are faith-based; however, this paradigm lacks connection with the true Creator of life and destiny. New age counselors may claim to be respecting the client's spiritual beliefs, but the reality is that the client is impacted by the counselor's god(s), or ideologies of a god or creation. New age counselors typically utilize practices rooted in witchcraft or idolatry. These practices can incur further bondage as demons and witchcraft practices are used to assist clients with overcoming struggles and improving their well-being. The problem with this is the demonic spirits are now a part of the person's life journey, and they have to continue the witchcraft practices so the demonic spirits can continue helping to impact their life.

Romans 1:21-25 Because when they knew and recognized Him as God, they did not honor and glorify Him as God or give Him thanks. But instead they became futile and godless in their thinking [with vain imaginings, foolish reasoning, and stupid speculations] and their senseless minds were darkened. Claiming to be wise, they became fools [professing to be smart, they made simpletons of themselves]. And by them the glory and majesty and excellence of the immortal God were exchanged for and represented by images, resembling mortal man and birds and beasts and reptiles. Therefore God gave them up in the lusts of their [own] hearts to sexual impurity, to the dishonoring of their bodies among themselves [abandoning them to the degrading power of sin], Because they exchanged the truth of God for a lie and worshiped and served the creature rather than the Creator, Who is blessed forever! Amen (so be it). (Amp)

Few new age therapists have any accredited education to support their practices. In most cases, the training involved is a few week-end retreats with other likeminded individuals. Much of the new age therapy techniques are based in the concept of karma. "And when they use the karma idea in that way, it is no longer a spiritual help, it is a collective displacement of the focus backwards in time and therewith out of reality and into the unreality of the collective time."[14] Here is a sample projection by a New Age guru on the counseling process:

1) Compassionate intentionality is the illumination of the cosmic soul.

2) The transfiguration of cosmic consciousness is the astral oneness.

3) Harmonic convergence is the quantum energy of biofeedback singularity.[15]

It is a reasonable critique that most new age therapy practices are based in charismatic presentations that bring no long-lasting difference to its clients. It is eclectic with the fluidity of metaphysics that is human based.

Mentoring

Mentors may be educated in different areas, but there is not a professional degree specifically for mentoring. Many who function as mentors believe they possess a level of expertise that can better someone else's life. There are no professional guidelines to mentoring as this is usually an individually designed position. This means that even though people should be led by God in any position of positive influence, people decide if they want to be a mentor or not.

Mentoring can be for a season or a lifetime. A mentor might walk with a person in certain seasons and be absent in other seasons. A mentee might have mentors based on the needs, desires, skills, and development he or she needs for a particular season of life. Mentors generally provide wisdom, guidance, and instruction to someone that may be less experienced,

---

[14] Morton Tolloll. (n.d.) The devastating New Age turn within psychotherapy. Retrieved from Morton Tollboll's website at https://mortentolboll.weebly.com/the-devastating-new-age-turn-within-psychotherapy.html
[15] Gad Saad, Ph.D. (2014, October 31). New age gurus: Dispensers of nonsense. Retrieved from *Psychology Today* website at https://www.psychologytoday.com/us/blog/homo-consumericus/201410/new-age-gurus-dispensers-nonsense

or that need a safe relationship for self-examination, confirmation, support, empowerment, instruction, and accountability. The mentor is usually older with personal experience or knowledge in the areas to which they are imparting. That level of experience can be influential as keys are shared and implemented from one person to another. Similarly, the wisdom may help someone else avoid needless hardships. Moreover, shared commonality becomes a motivator from one to the other for development. Mentors also help cover and pray for people, while they are working on goals and life issues.

Though there may not be a professional field called mentoring, that is not to suggest it is not biblical. Mentoring is about one generation encouraging another through teaching and role modeling. Here are some scriptures that reflect mentoring:

1 Kings 20:11 The king of Israel answered, "Tell him: 'One who puts on his armor should not boast like one who takes it off.' (NIV)

Titus 2:4 In this way they will teach young women to show love to their husbands and children, (MSG)

It is worth considering whether the Holy Spirit is a reflection of mentorship for believers.

John 14:26 But the Comforter, which is the Holy Ghost, whom the Father will send in my name, he shall teach you all things, and bring all things to your remembrance, whatsoever I have said unto you.

The Greek word for Comforter is *paraklētos* which means one who is called alongside. A person who steps into the role of mentoring must have spiritual maturity, discernment, and an absolute assurance that the one they are mentoring is a divine assignment.

Though a person may share painful experiences and explore unresolved challenges with a mentor, and even receive some processing of issues, mentoring is not counseling. Mentors are usually focused on how they can SHIFT a person to the present and guide them into the future. They do not regard the past, but the present and future is there focus. Also, some mentors may not be equipped to help a person explore past issues and present unresolved issues in-depth.

This is where mentoring tends to cross boundaries that may not be beneficial to mentees. Mentors may inadvertently open wounds. Because they are not equipped to bring deliverance and healing via a process of professionally faith-based counseling, the mentee is left exposed and vulnerable. A mentor can unintentionally cause the mentee to become unstable due to not being able to handle what has been unveiled and exposed. A mature mentor will understand the scope of their influence and will readily recommend counseling to their mentee. It does not have to be an "either or" decision.

When people come into my life, I examine if it is for a season or a lifetime, but I also observe if there is a need for mentoring or a deeper need for counseling. Generally, those that can receive mentoring have maintained a level of stability. While they may have some unresolved issues, the issues are not a detriment to their present and future life. Deliverance and healing are enacted through a few guided suggestions that can usually be independently implemented. My presence becomes a point of accountability, a place of support, and a source of further direction. Those that are a counseling assignment need in-depth exploration of past and present issues, and will require committed, consistent, one-on-one attention until they fulfill a process of wellness. Mentors must be able to discern the needs of those who come to them for guidance. If they require counseling, then they should be encouraged to pursue a professional faith-based counselor. The mentor can still journey with them by providing support, encouragement, and accountability. As the person is healed, the mentor continues to journey with the person, while providing additional guidance that confirms and sustains the counseling process.

Coaching

A coach focuses on unlocking a person's potential as it relates to their talents, gifts, and goals. Some forms of coaching require no personal interaction as this field can be built and taught via books, media, and seminars. Life coaches work to help people form goals and a vision plan for getting an idea for a business, ministry, organization, or product successfully implemented. They also work with the person to improve their personal and business performance. They provide support, identity empowerment, critical thinking, constructive criticism, feedback, guidance, and accountability, as the person explores goals, ambitions, and desired achievements. Most coaches are not issue focused, and do not counsel. They will, at times, assist with exploring a specific challenge that is hindering a person's development and progress. The focus is solely on a particular block in progress with no contextual processing. They do not perform in-depth counseling. If there is an exploration of past (or a pattern) of challenges, it is often related to responsibility, accountability, and consistency in implementing and working on a desired vision plan. Coaches are future focused and seek to strengthen their clients in the areas of wisdom, confidence, and perseverance, so they can operate in their full potential. If a person has more in-depth issues, a coach will refer them to a counselor who can address those issues, while they remain focused in working with the person on their coaching vision plan. In *Exodus 18*, we find Jethro operating in the gift of coaching and administration.

There are executive coaches in the corporate world. In a *Harvard Business Review* article, the authors discuss that experts in the field have no agreement on how to quantify this field or its certification, "Commentators and coaches alike felt that the bar needs to be raised in various areas for the industry to mature, but there was no consensus on how that could be done."[16] The results of a survey issued to recipients of executive coaching show satisfaction in the services; however, those same survey result in this consensus, "The survey results also suggest that the industry is fraught with conflicts of interest, blurry lines between what is the province of coaches and what should be left to mental health professionals, and sketchy mechanisms for monitoring the effectiveness of a coaching engagement."[17] Much of the coaching field is about assisting individuals with removing distractions from a predetermined set of goals. Coaches help to create a game plan and strategies, while cheering the person on in their execution and success of completing their goals.

Consulting

A consultant provides expertise, advice, strategies, solutions, and vision plans to assist individuals or organizations with improving or succeeding in particular endeavors. My secular career is that of a Behavioral Consultant. While my overall responsibilities include a measure

---

[16]Diane Coutu and Carol Kauffman. (2009, January). What can coaches do for you? Retrieved from *The Harvard Business Review* website at https://hbr.org/2009/01/what-can-coaches-do-for-you
[17] Ibid, 2009.

of counseling and mentoring, the primary duties focus on building skills, and providing proactive treatment tools and interventions, that assist clients in overcoming limitations that thwart leading a full life. My skills extend to organizational consulting. Specifically, the goal is to function successfully despite the challenges and limitations of the client. The first step is creating a vision plan for individuals, families, or companies followed by training on how to implement that plan. Continued monitoring and offering feedback is part of the extended plan which may involve adjusting the vision plan. The objective is to stabilize a client's life with recognizable improvement. My role does not include processing personal issues with clients or organizations. The focus is more on providing the best course for achieving goals than working toward deliverance, healing, or breakthrough. The people, families, and organizations survive, not because they are delivered, but because they work the plan. When we think of this spiritually, someone can go through their entire life with a measure of success yet lack wholeness. The main purpose and foundation of salvation is for a person to be delivered, healed, and set free. *John 8:36 Therefore if the Son makes you free, you will be free indeed.* Without a spiritual element, the tactics provided by the consultant will enable but not empower for wholeness to the inner man or the inner workings of a client's life and destiny.

Social Work

Social work is facilitated by those with a bachelor's or master's degree, where professionals advocate and facilitate the welfare of individuals, families, groups, organizations, and communities. Social workers tend to work with populations that are less fortunate, impoverished, mentally challenged, or those that need assistance advocating for human rights and resources relative to their overall well-being. Social work is focused on helping people develop skills to use their own resources and those of the community to resolve and overcome life obstacles. Social workers promote social change, individual and social development, cohesion, and empowerment. Their foundation is rooted in theories of social sciences. They operate through principles of social justice, human rights, responsibility and accountability, and respect for diversity. Social workers seek to enhance peoples' lives. Some social workers take counseling positions because they are required to take a certain number of counseling classes as a college requisite. However, social work is frequently about administrating and facilitating services. Social workers also tend to be the voice for their clients. Encouraging and empowering the client to be their own voice can be secondary, and even sometimes unnecessary, as a social worker is required to uphold the rights and laws of the individual, family, group, organization, and community they represent, regardless to whether they can or will speak for themselves. Though social workers collect and know the history of their clients, this information is used to explore the needs and resources of a client, more than to help them deal with unresolved issues that affect their well-being. Social workers tend to refer clients to counseling as opposed to providing personal counseling. Many social workers have too many clients to engage in personal detail counseling services. Moreover, unless a social worker is in an established position of a counselor, it is a conflict of interest and crosses ethical boundaries, to provide counseling services, rather than referring the client for services. Social work is a respected part of the community's network of services, but is a partner of counseling, rather than a source of counseling.

Managing & Administrating

Managers and administrators achieve organizational tasks that help ministries, businesses, and organizations run successfully. Managers and administrators are focused on works. They believe issues will get resolved as duties are completed. They are focused on ensuring everyone and everything cooperates and works together despite differences and challenges. They may address small fires of conflict but are not focused on past unresolved issues, or personal quirks and issues. Managers and administrators will complete evaluations to see how they can better improve the success of an operation in the future, but their focus is implementing works, measures, and precautions to ensure a stated outcome. If that means a particular person or strategy is not a part of arriving at the stated outcome, then that person or strategy is eliminated. A manager or administrator's role is to operate in change management, implement the vision plan, and "get the job done." It is rare that there is any counseling or mentoring implemented with the plan. Their role is to be solution oriented. Their motivation is to be success driven with data that satisfies organizational vision. They will eliminate and replace in order to achieve the desired outcome. This role is essential to organizational success as it is based in the professional ability to be personnel focused rather than personal focus.

1 Corinthians 12: 27-28 *Now you [collectively] are Christ's body and [individually] you are members of it, each part severally and distinct [each with his own place and function]. So God has appointed some in the church [for His own use]:first apostles (special messengers); second prophets (inspired preachers and expounders); third teachers; then wonder- workers; then those with ability to heal the sick; helpers; administrators; [speakers in] different (unknown) tongues. (AMP)*

1 Corinthians 14:40 *But all things should be done with regard to decency and propriety and in an orderly fashion. (AMP)*

Examples of the Gift of Administration in the Bible:

- Jesus organized his ministry by choosing his inner circle of three disciples (*Mark 9:2*), appointing the twelve (*Mark 3:13-14*), and sending out the seventy two by two (*Luke 10:1*)
- Joseph was positioned over the land to govern in a time of famine (*Genesis 41:41-57; 47:13-26*)
- Titus was positioned to govern the ministries in the region (*Titus 1:5*)

A Good Administrator Possesses The Following Characteristics:

- Excited about the vision and about fulfilling tasks and duties,
- Can hear God for strategies and consistent witty ideas that advance the ministry,
- Able to use strategies and witty ideas to obtain favor, blessings, and save money,
- A people person with the capacity for cultural agility,
- Have great communication skills and can effectively communicate and give direction and guidance with clarity,
- Brings maturity and balanced perspectives,
- Able to empower others to fulfill tasks and carry the vision,
- An organizer of people, projects, tasks, money, goals within the vision,
- Capacity to proficiently administrate several projects at one time,
- Are able to solve problems and diffuse challenging conflicts and situations,
- See the future of the vision and can implement ideas, strategies, tools, etc., to progress the vision forward,
- Understands the importance of not just using people to complete tasks and fulfill roles, but are great motivators and personal esteemers of team members and workers,
- Humble, respectful, honoring, and careful not to bully, belittle and control and manipulate people,
- Willing to be hands-on when necessary to complete tasks,
- Can recognize the need to rest and refresh,
- Balanced in spiritual development while accomplishing administrative duties,

- Good decision maker, and able to step in and run and assist with the vision and overseeing parts of the vision when necessary,
- Operates in a spirit of excellence, and is willing to make personal improvements and improvements to the vision and team such that it produces excellent results,
- Possesses professional skills of an administrator or business to effectively assist with events, meetings, vision tasks.

Many people have great management and administrative skills, but these skills should not be mistaken for counseling. People may come into compliance for a while, but compliance is not introspective wholeness. People management includes the ability to recommend counseling.

All mentors are necessary but are not counseling.

In conclusion to this chapter, it is important to note that a person overcoming a challenging experience or painful situation does not mean he or she should become a counselor, social worker, life coach, or mentor. **Providing these services because of past issues without proper education results in minimal resolution. It results in a person with a career driven out of emotionalism.** Such familiarity and issues will keep that relationship in a place of rehashing negative experiences. What is thought to be healing is merely the camaraderie of connecting through familiarity. The service provider is operating out of a need to rescue others from something that really is about them rescuing themselves. Those who operate in this manner need to stop hurting people by keeping them in cycles that really feed his or her own ego for a sense of identity. Send people to someone that can really help process them to wholeness.

WHAT COUNSELING IS NOT

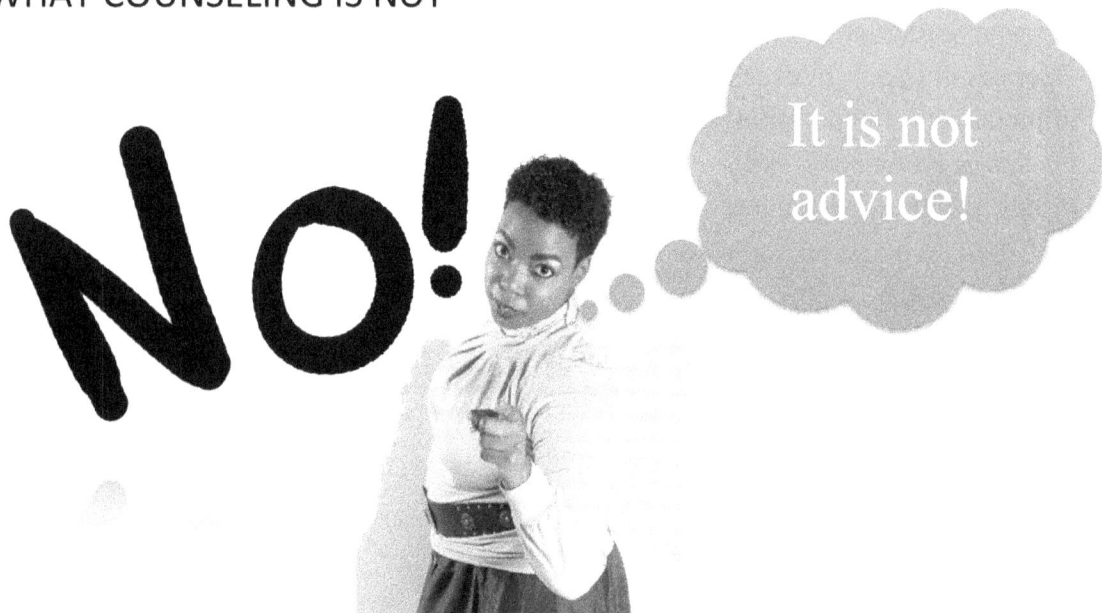

It is not advice!

- **Not mentoring.** Mentoring is a relationship rooted in acquaintance which can sometimes interfere with the counseling process. The nuance of mentoring is reciprocal where both parties benefit. Counseling is for the client ONLY!

- **Not coaching.** Coaching is for mature people who have resolved their underlying issues. Most coaches dread counseling and are **not** trying to counsel which is why they choose the profession as "COACH!" For those who do not have positive outcomes from a coaching process, it is often the result of needing counseling and not motivation-based techniques.

- **Not pastoring.** Many pastors have a wisdom, godly advice, and may have the gift of counseling, but without the educational expertise, many pastors fail to teach others how to engage in and complete the counseling process.

- **Not issue focused** but deliverance and healing focused. **SHIFT RIGHT NOW!**

- **Not a garbage can** or garbage disposal. It is a place to relieve burdens through taking on the yoke of the Lord.

- **Not an ambulance** or emergency room service. A person may attend counseling during a crisis; however, follow up and processing is often necessary as usually these 9-1-1 incidences are the product of a deeper issue.

- **Not a perfect** or fixed process. The process is tailor-made to the individual. There is not 1-2-3 process for healing or wholeness. God outlines the process.

- **Not going** to work if you do not complete the process to healing and wholeness.

- **Not a waste** of time. Wasted time is unnecessarily living with torment and pain.

- **Not optional.** It is a part of our wellness as people. Counseling may be the most undervalued form of health care in our society.

WHAT A COUNSELOR IS NOT

- **Not responsible** for the healing but is responsible as a liaison between the plan of God and the client's healing process.

  - **Not a self-exalted** expert because they may have overcome a situation. Counseling is a spiritual gift and must be God-directed.
  - **Not self-rewarding** as the counselor gets personal needs met for love, belonging, or a sense of identity.
  - **Not a place** to fulfill a COUNSELOR'S need to be needed. A needy, rescuing, fixer, type counselor will soon overstep boundaries that will present unhealthy interactions between the counselor and counselee.
  - **Not your** friend, lover, family member, mentor, pastor. These types of dual relationships can compromise the counseling process. If the person receiving counseling is not able to maintain an understanding that they are in a counseling process and not a personal relationship, it is the counselor's responsibility to cut ties and not psychologically victimize the client. People will demand the counselor steps aside and that the other relationship dynamic comes forth during times when they do not want to be accountable to or are challenged within the counseling process. Most often these types of counseling interconnections are aborted because people do not fully disclose the depth needed. Clear boundaries are essential to a healthy counseling rapport.

- **Not well liked** by people who do not want their issues exposed. Many people are challenged by counselors as counseling is perceived as a threat. There is a thought that counselors are analyzing them and can "read" and "see" their issues. Please know this is true. Most counselors can discern issues but are not at liberty by God to challenge or address everything that is revealed to them. An authentic counselor is only interested in helping people who want to help themselves or who God is leading them to counsel.

- **NOT FREE** ministry. Authentic counselors understand the importance of education and generally have a four-year degree or higher. The majority of counselors have a master's degree with updated licenses, certifications, and continuing education units, that demonstrates their accountability to consistently perfecting their profession.

Chapter 6

THE SPIRIT OF COUNSEL

Counseling has a biblical foundation verifying the interchange of God empowering us with the Spirit of Counsel so that we may empower others. The Bible contains nearly 150 verses regarding counsel. The first mention of counsel is from Moses' father-in-law Jethro (*Exodus 18*). Jethro sees Moses trying to be everything to all of the people. In his wisdom, Jethro says, "You are going to destroy yourself and be no good to the people (paraphrase)." Jethro tells Moses that he will counsel him and by listening to counsel, God will be with Moses. The first guidance Jethro offers to Moses is a perfect support for our previous chapter that advises against pastors determined to be counselors. Jethro encourages Moses to appoint leaders throughout groups of people that can relieve the burden of Moses' ambition to be everything to everyone.

One of the biggest blunders made by the faith-based community is purporting to cast the devil out and imposing areas of healing on a person when, in fact, the result is a stripping of the person's walls of protection. Many times, all of that is imposed without sufficiently providing tools and strategies to help sustain deliverance and healing. Numerous well-intended efforts are no more than throwing Bible verses, principles, and cliches out with the expectation that the recipient will know how to implement them. Typically, this approach lacks any skills development that will support improvement or stabilize a deliverance experience. The follow-up is often to rebuke the person for being carnal, worldly, lost, confused, lukewarm, backslidden, and otherwise indifferent to deliverance. This mentality has created exponential harm to the extent that many are resistant toward attending church, lack faith that church can help them, or, in the worst-case scenario no longer believe in God and his saving power. Because of such folly, restoration of the Spirit of Counsel is needed in the body of Christ like never before.

Leaders have a responsibility to properly guide those in their ministry. Every church is not going to have its own counseling center; however, there should be a camaraderie among leaders that can offer referrals to resources within the city or region. With the same confidence that we might refer someone to other professional services, there must be a network of communication to provide awareness of the nearest faith-based counseling center. There are nearly 400,000 churches in the United States. The majority attend a church with membership of 350 or more. There are approximately 600,000 clergy serving those congregations and their members. All but five states include megachurches in their demographic profile.[18] The American Association of Christian Counselors and the National Christian Counselors Association are two excellent resources for local leaders to use in locating service providers in their area. "Counselors who have been licensed by the state are held to strict ethical standards that mandate an individual's right to be free from religious influence."[19] Counseling through the Spirit of Counsel is an essential component toward assisting believers who need help. Most believers who will become clients are coming through a connection to a local church, their pastor, or other ministry leaders. Other clients will come from secular referrals when there has been a specific request for spiritually directed counsel. The unprecedented level of mental health challenges facing our current society compels those who profess a call to faith-based counseling to operate through the *Isaiah 11:1-2* standard of distinction.

Jesus asked nothing of us that he did not first do by example. Every impartation that is for us came through him. Isaiah prophesied of Jesus possessing the Spirit of counsel and power.

Isaiah 11:1-2 A shoot will come up from the stump of Jesse; from his root a branch will bear fruit. The spirit of the Lord will rest on him-the Spirit of wisdom and of understanding, the Spirit of counsel and of power, the Spirit of knowledge and of the fear of the Lord.

The word "*counsel*" in Hebrew is *etsah*, which means "*to counsel, advice, purpose.*" The root word *ya`ats* means, "*to advise, consult, give counsel, counsel, purpose, devise, plan.*"

The word "*spirit*" in Hebrew is *ruwach*, which means, "*wind, breath, mind, spirit.*"

---

[18]Fast facts about American religion. (n.d.) Retrieved from the *Hartford Institute for Religion Research* website at http://hirr.hartsem.edu/research/fastfacts/fast_facts.html

[19] State-secular vs. Christian counseling. (n.d.) Retrieved from the *Pastoral Counseling Center* website at http://www.pastoral-counseling-center.org/Christian-Counseling-vs-Secular-Counseling.htm

The "*ruwach*" aka spirit of God is the vigor, breath, life, power of counseling. The counsel is the wisdom, consultation, deliberation of God's spirit. Therefore, the intent of the spirit of counseling is to breathe life into a person and help progress them into their destined purpose in God.

Jesus is the Wonderful Counselor.

Isaiah 9:6 *For to us a child is born, to us a son is given, and the government will be on his shoulders. And he will be called Wonderful Counselor, Mighty God, Everlasting Father, Prince of Peace.*

Counseling is a mantle that serves as a governmental rule and voice for people and nations.

Jesus had the tongue of the learned.

Isaiah 50:4-5 *The Lord God hath given me the tongue of the learned, that I should know how to speak a word in season to him that is weary: he wakeneth morning by morning, he wakeneth mine ear to hear as the learned. The Lord God hath opened mine ear, and I was not rebellious, neither turned away back.*

A person that is learned has been instructed, taught, discipled. Therefore, a counselor is one who has been under the training and discipleship of the Lord, so he or she can acquire revelation for those in need of refreshing, empowerment, and transformation. A counselor receives daily word from the Lord and is obedient to what he or she hears. This scripture also lets us know that it is beneficial for a counselor to have some educational experience as a counselor. A person that has a Bachelors, Masters, or PhD in counseling or social work can be more effective in leading a client through healing and wholeness. A believer that recognizes their call to operate in the Spirit of Counsel must have a lifelong learning commitment for continued excellence.

Recommended further reading: The Book of Daniel provides an excellent role model through Daniel who is initially described as having gifts in all wisdom, possessing knowledge, and quick to understand (***Daniel 1:4***). Throughout his journey, Daniel is called to counsel those in high authority, interpret dreams, and provide guidance.

Counseling the Brokenhearted

Isaiah 61:1-3 & Luke 4:18-19 *The Spirit of the Lord is upon me, because he hath anointed me to preach the gospel to the poor; he hath sent me to heal the brokenhearted, to preach deliverance to the captives, and recovering of sight to the blind, to set at liberty them that are bruised, To preach the acceptable year of the Lord.*

Brokenhearted in Greek is *syntribo* and means:
1. to shatter, to crush completely, to break into pieces
2. break into shivers, bruise
3. to tread down, put Satan under foot, as a conqueror trample Satan

When the spirit of the Lord is upon us, we are anointed with authority and power to shatter demonic strongholds and SHIFT people into a place of towering over every challenge. Our ability to deliver the captives and set liberty to the bruised, enables us to release people from bondages and imprisonments, while producing the freedom, pardon, forgiveness, deliverance, and remission of the Lord. As we minister, we can recover the sight of the mentally and physically blind. Recovery is a counseling term.

- ✓ Counselors help people regain Godly clarity, perspective, understanding, vision, and foresight.
- ✓ Counselors help people regain their strength, composure, balance, stability, wellness, and peace.

Lack Of Counsel Breeds Death

Proverbs 11:14 *Where no counsel is, the people fall: but in the multitude of counsellors there is safety.*

Safety in Hebrew is *tshuah* and means:
1. rescue, deliverance, help, victory
2. deliverance (usually by God through human agency)
3. salvation (spiritual in sense)

Counseling Actuates the Following Projections

Figure 6.0 Counseling Activations

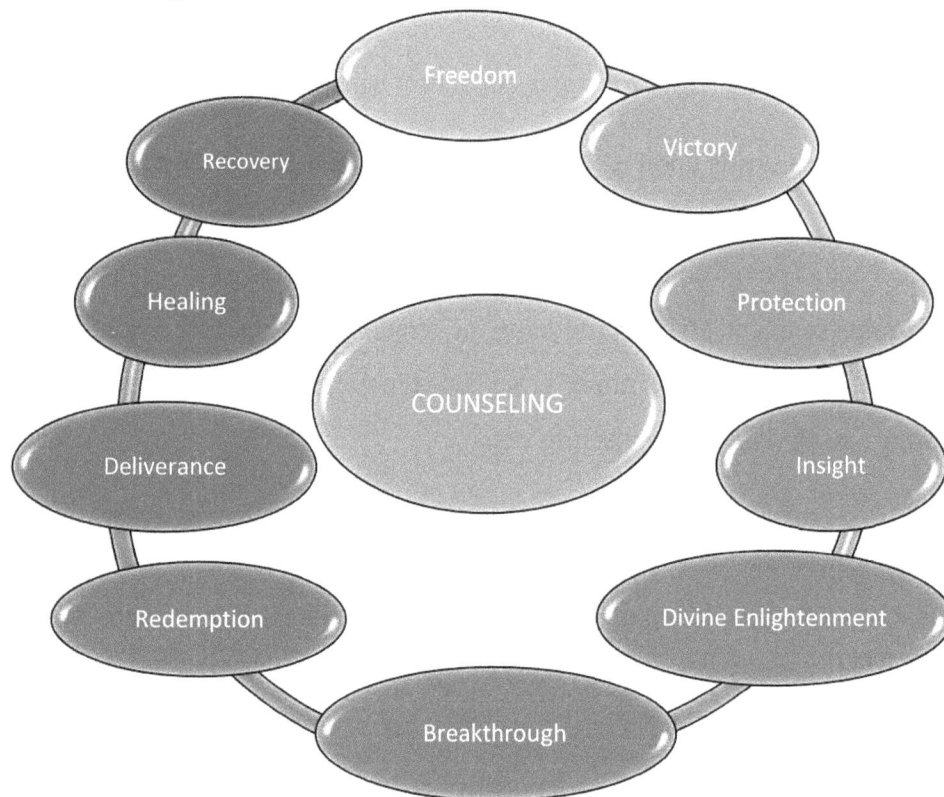

Source: Baker, 2018

Proverbs 11:4 (NIV) *For lack of guidance a nation falls, but many advisers make victory sure.*

There will be people who will perish if they fail to receive counsel. Where there is no existence of counsel, there is sure to be death. People, regions, nations, generations will die.

Nations Without Counsel

Deuteronomy 32:28 *For they are a nation void of counsel, neither is there any understanding in them.*

This scripture reveals that the plans and purposes of God can derive from counseling. Culture and society can error without sufficient counsel. The *'etsah* of this word counsel means, "*to devise and implement a plan.*" It is an advisory role for purposes of executing a plan. This entire chapter is Moses singing about Israel's journey with God. He sings about God keeping Israel as the apple of his eye and how he flutters over the nation like an eagle watching over her young. The song includes the rebellious attitude of God's chosen people and the punishments that came. Its ebb and flow rhythmically vocalize the ups and downs of humanity. In referencing the foolishness of those who choose to be enemies of God, Moses sings that they are a nation without counsel. ***The Message Version*** paraphrases it much more colorfully, *They are a nation of ninnies, they don't know enough to come in out of the rain.* Clearly, there is wisdom in functioning as a nation that leans to biblically based counsel.

Counseling Ministry

In ***Exodus 18:15-26,*** the people come to Moses for counseling. ***Numbers 1:46*** records 603,550 men over the age of 20 in the exodus. That total does not include women and children, but we can fairly surmise that the total was exponentially more than one individual could counsel. The counsel of Jethro to Moses was to select mature believers for counseling, judging, and leading the people.

> *And Moses said unto his father in law, Because the people come unto me to enquire of God: When they have a matter, they come unto me; and I judge between one and another, and I do make them know the statutes of God, and his laws. And Moses' father in law said unto him, The thing that thou doest is not good. Thou wilt surely wear away, both thou, and this people that is with thee: for this thing is too heavy for thee; thou art not able to perform it thyself alone. Hearken now unto my voice, I will give thee counsel, and God shall be with thee: Be thou for the people to God-ward, And it came to pass on the morrow, that Moses sat to judge the people: and the people stood by Moses from the morning unto the evening.*

And when Moses' father in law saw all that he did to the people, he said, What is this thing that thou doest to the people? why sittest thou thyself alone, and all the people stand by thee from morning unto even? And Moses said unto his father in law, Because the people come unto me to enquire of God: When they have a matter, they come unto me; and I judge between one and another, and I do make them know the statutes of God, and his laws. And Moses' father in law said unto him, The thing that thou doest is not good. Thou wilt surely wear away, both thou, and this people that is with thee: for this thing is too heavy for thee; thou art not able to perform it thyself alone. Hearken now unto my voice, I will give thee counsel, and God shall be with thee: Be thou for the people to God-ward, that thou mayest bring the causes unto God: And thou shalt teach them ordinances and laws, and shalt shew them the way wherein they must walk, and the work that they must do. Moreover thou shalt provide out of all the people able men, such as fear God, men of truth, hating covetousness; and place such over them, to be rulers of thousands, and rulers of hundreds, rulers of fifties, and rulers of tens: And let them judge the people at all seasons: and it shall be, that every great matter they shall bring unto thee, but every small matter they shall judge: so shall it be easier for thyself, and they shall bear the burden with thee. If thou shalt do this thing, and God command thee so, then thou shalt be able to endure, and all this people shall also go to their place in peace. So Moses hearkened to the voice of his father in law, and did all that he had said. And Moses chose able men out of all Israel, and made them heads over the people, rulers of thousands, rulers of hundreds, rulers of fifties, and rulers of tens. And they judged the people at all seasons: the hard causes they brought unto Moses, but every small matter they judged themselves.

Exodus 18:13 tells us that Moses sat from morning to evening trying to assist the people. Jethro's efforts to help his son-in-law obviously did not involve counseling in our Western culture model of repeat sessions, filling out forms, and so on. *Ya'ats* (counsel) means to assist in devising a plan and to exchange ideas. Effective contemporary counseling must include the dynamics of exchange, planning, guidance, and instilling purpose. With that as our foundation, 21st-century faith-based counselors can be grateful to Jethro for setting the precedent of the need to counsel.

To some degree, we can suggest that in ***Judges 4:4-5***, the Prophetess Deborah set up a counseling center under a tree. Her work was not the *ya'ats* of our previous story with Jethro and Moses but was a *mishpat* which refers to offering advice about how to align with ordinances. Her words provided guidance for lawful decisions and outcomes that realigned the conduct of the people to the will of God. There are multiple scenarios where a counselor needs general knowledge of law without presenting their advice as legal counsel. Faith based counseling is required to contain elements of a *mishpat*, particularly if the client is reporting intent to harm others or self-harm. There is no counseling protection for sexual crimes.

Judges 4:4-5 *And Deborah, a prophetess, the wife of Lapidoth, she judged Israel at that time. And she dwelt under the palm tree of Deborah between Ramah and Bethel in mount Ephraim: and the children of Israel came up to her for judgment.*

Faith-based counselors ultimately have the responsibility of correctly interpreting scripture for application of biblical principles. Duvall and Hays use a concept called principlizing bridge to illustrate studying the Bible in its original context and then accurately walking its meaning over to our Western culture context.

Figure 6.1 Interpretive Journey

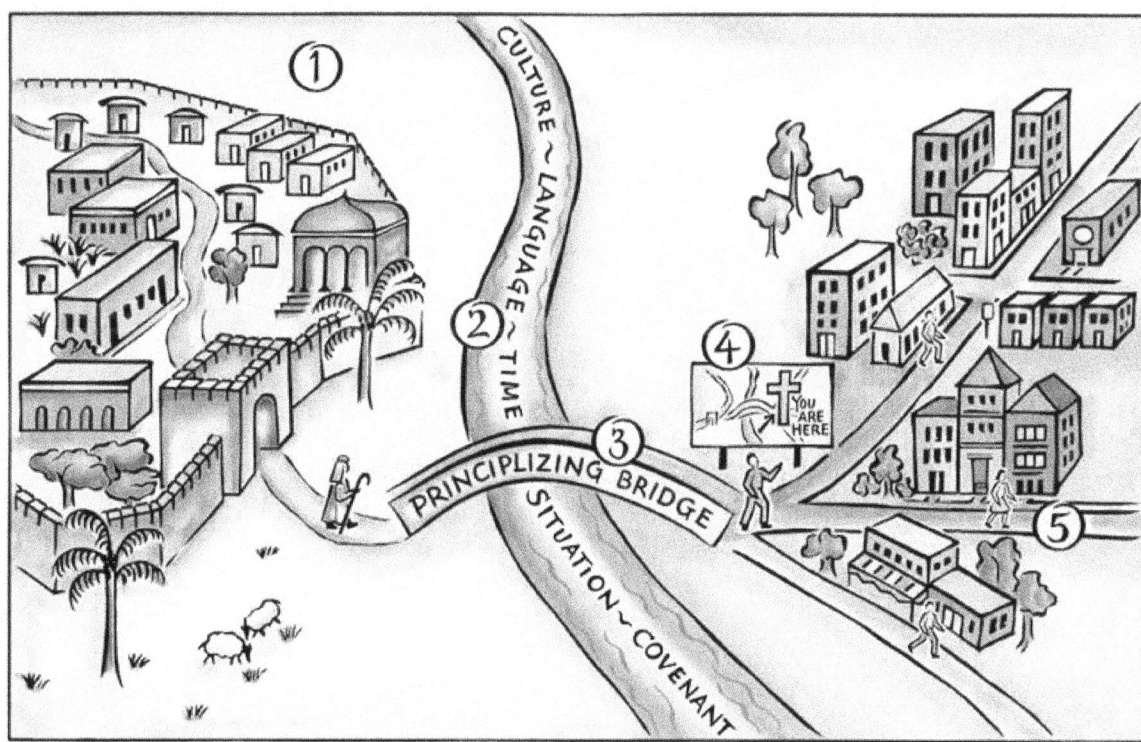

Source: Duvall and Hays, 2012[20]

---

[20] J. Scott Duvall and J. Daniel Hays. (2012). *Grasping God's Word,* 3rd ed. Grand Rapids, MI: Zondervan

Counseling and Fivefold Ministry

The Apostle Paul implemented the model of fivefold ministry, beginning with the church in Ephesus. The expectation was three-fold, including perfecting, equipping, and ministering. The collective outcome was the building up of the church.

Ephesians 4:11-12 And His gifts were [varied; He Himself appointed and gave men to us] some to be apostles (special messengers), some prophets (inspired preachers and expounders), some evangelists (preachers of the Gospel, traveling missionaries), some pastors (shepherds of His flock) and teachers. His intention was the perfecting and the full equipping of the saints (His consecrated people), [that they should do] the work of ministering toward building up Christ's body (the church). (AMP)

This assignment of fivefold ministry is not to be confused with spiritual gifts or the fruit of the Spirit. Paul taught that the fruit of the Spirit includes love, joy, peace, longsuffering, gentleness, goodness, faith, meekness, and temperance. The fruit (*karpos*) is the evidence that the Spirit of God is present in an individual's life. That standard is applicable to every believer. The gifts of the Spirit; however, will differ from person to person.

> *There is quantitative and qualitative growth when believers discover and actively use their spiritual gifts. Each part of the body depends on the rest for its well-being, and there are no useless organs. This is why edification through teaching and fellowship is so necessary in the local church. The biblical concept of koinonia or fellowship communicates the fact that isolation leads to atrophy. Just as no organ can function independently of the others, so no Christian can enjoy spiritual vitality in a relational vacuum. The Spirit has sovereignly distributed spiritual gifts to every member of the body, and no single member possesses all the gifts. Thus, growth does not take place apart from mutual ministry and dependence.[21]*

While individual counseling is not specifically named in the gifts or the offices of the New Testament church, its presence is interwoven throughout each. If we did not believe that to be true, then it is impossible to say that we believe the Bible as the word of truth. Jesus said that

---

[21]Kenneth Boa (n.d.) The gifts of the Spirit. Retrieved from *The Bible* website at https://bible.org/article/gifts-spirit

he did not come to do away with what had been established prior to his appearance, but he came as a fulfillment of all that had taken place (*Matthew 5:17*). "***Romans 15:4*** *For whatever was written in earlier times was written for our instruction, so that through perseverance and the encouragement of the Scriptures we might have hope (NET).*" The result of learning what is written in the Old Testament is that we might have hope. And we all need hope! About one in ten Americans suffers from depression and depressed people need hope.[22] The various modes of counsel we see throughout the Old Testament is relevant to the New Testament church, including our contemporary world.

It is an oxymoron that our society promotes self-actualization while suffering from an epidemic of mental health challenges. With one in six Americans taking a psychotropic medication and one in ten reporting a need for medication for ". . . problems with emotions, nerves, or mental health,"[23] there is an obvious need for solutions that heal rather than relieve. Many ministries are focused on people fulfilling a spiritual ambition through various training efforts, seminars, retreats, and other platforms until that counseling and counseling centers have been diminished in value. It has resulted in successful people who continue to struggle with issues and trauma. Moreover, a false mindset has developed throughout the body of Christ and many professions that counseling is for those with weak character. To reject counseling is to reject a valuable asset that God implemented for us all the way back to Jethro and Moses' interaction. Jesus is the Spirit of Counsel, and Jesus is the Wonderful, Counselor.

Jesus is the Spirit of Counsel, &
Jesus Is the Wonderful, Counselor!

---

[22] Ibid, n.d.
[23] Sara G. Miller. (2016, December 13). 1 in 6 Americans take a psychiatric drug. Retrieved from *Scientific American* website at https://www.scientificamerican.com/article/1-in-6-americans-takes-a-psychiatric-drug/

With many confused, wounded, hurt, and struggling believers, it becomes apparent that we need a paradigm SHIFT. While attending church, Bible study, Sunday school, conferences and so on are informative, they do not contain the dynamics to bring healing. We would not simply attend an informative workshop to address high blood pressure or diabetes. Rather, we would make the appointment, consult a physician, and follow the wellness plan required. Too frequently, well-intended ministries become guilty of tunnel vision. The "that's the way we've always done it" mentality creates a repetitious cycle that can continue for generations. Part of the task at hand for faith-based counseling is to undertake the mission of culture change.

At both the individual and organizational level, there are urgent needs for effective processing, guidance, mentoring, support, and empowerment that will bring revival for destiny. Leaders have to view counseling as a necessity and work toward establishing credible centers so that people can receive help after the altar, after they have gone home and considered their encounter with God, after they have been tempted with the very thing they just got delivered and healed from.

We often ask who strengthens leaders, superstars, public figures, or those who live by giving to others? It is the role models, nurturers, and caretakers who must also see the need for counseling. Counseling serves as a confidential place to:

- Vent without feeling judged for their position, stature or need for breakthrough.
- Be replenished empower, and encouraged,
- Be held accountable to maintaining balance in their schedule, interactions, relationships, and in taking time for themselves,
- Receive deliverance and healing in areas where restoration is needed, and
- Receive wise counsel while exploring direction and accountability to maintaining and achieving personal goals that are essential to their wellness and overall well-being.

Many in high positions rely on other leaders who are too busy, too burned out, or too desensitized to the things of God to provide sufficient accountability and guidance to help heal and restore them to wholeness. Beyond socio-economic status and demographics, the Word of God holds universal solutions, including counseling.

Chapter 7

UNDERSTANDING UNGODLY COUNSEL AND ERROR

There will be situations where counsel may initially appear applicable to the client's life; however, that is not always accurate. All counsel is not of from God's Spirit or of his design.

Proverbs 19:21 *There are many devices in a man's heart; nevertheless the counsel of the LORD, that shall stand.*

Psalm 1:1-4 *Blessed is the man that walketh not in the counsel of the ungodly, nor standeth in the way of sinners, nor sitteth in the seat of the scornful. But his delight is in the law of the Lord; and in his law doth he meditate day and night. And he shall be like a tree planted by the rivers of water, that bringeth forth his fruit in his season; his leaf also shall not wither; and whatsoever he doeth shall prosper.*

Ungodly in Hebrew is *rasa* and means:
1. morally wrong, condemning, guilty
2. ungodly, wicked, criminal
3. hostile to God, guilty of sin against God or man

In this day and age, it is so easy to receive ungodly counsel. It will not be uncommon for a faith-based counselor to be an extension of previous counseling that the client has received. In the past couple of decades, the increase of pharmaceutical advertising has directly impacted the physician-patient relationship as patients often go to their doctor with a preconceived idea about what drugs will alleviate their symptoms. The trend of direct-to-consumer (DTC) advertising influences are still being measured but several studies show a correlation between

DTC and increased pharmaceutical sales.[24] Faith-based counseling must include a process of undoing the errors of secular counseling and the expectations of the client that are built from direct-to-consumer promotions of wellness.

People are prone to adhere to counsel that allows them to fulfill their needs and desires, with no regard to how it impacts them, others, their relationship with God, his will and purpose for their lives or the earth. With the rise of social media and the internet, there are so many opinions and theories available that sound reliable and true but have no biblical bases and are far from with standards, character, and nature of God. The release of the *Diagnostic and Statistical Manual, 5th ed. (*DSM-5) has upped the total number of mental illnesses from the original 106 in 1952 to 297 in 2015. That is a 200% increase in two generations. "The odds will probably be greater than 50 percent, according to the new manual, that you'll have a mental disorder in your lifetime."[25] Unfortunately, much of the faith based counselor's workload entails convincing believers to trust the Word of God more than secular theories. Centuries ago, the prophet Isaiah was compelled to ask a question that rings true for our contemporary society. ***Isaiah 52:1*** *Who has believed our report, and to whom will the arm of the Lord be revealed.*

The Bible cautions us regarding error.

Romans 1:27 *And likewise also the men, leaving the natural use of the woman, burned in their lust one toward another; men with men working that which is unseemly, and receiving in themselves that recompence of their error which was meet.*

Most people assume that this passage of scripture is simply discussing homosexuality. But sexuality is not the primary focus example in this scripture as the revelation is referring to anything that causes a person to turn away from God. The last phrase of that scripture is a bit of tangle with old English. Here is The Message translation, "*And then they paid for it, oh,*

---

[24]Kevin M. Fain and G. Caleb Alexander. (2015, April 1). Mind the gap: Understanding the effects of pharmaceutical Direct-to-Consumer advertising. Retrieved from U.S. National Library of Medicine website at https://www.ncbi.nlm.nih.gov/pmc/articles/PMC4031617/
[25]Robin S. Rosenberg. (2013, April 12). Abnormal is the new normal. Retrieved from *Health and Science* website at http://www.slate.com/articles/health_and_science/medical_examiner/2013/04/diagnostic_and_statistical_manual_fifth_edition_why_will_half_the_u_s_population.html

how they paid for it—emptied of God and love, godless and loveless wretches." Paul's writing to the Romans (and to us) is establishing that operating outside of God's plan brings consequences.

Paul came to the believers in Rome with intentions of helping them separate what was culturally acceptable from what was godly. Rome was a city of nearly 1 million residents with a socio-economic diversity very much like any of our modern cities. It was the hub of politics and government. There are multiple parallels from the demographics of ancient Rome to any 21st-century major city in the U.S. His teachings are relevant and transferable to the contemporary influences of society on those who profess to be believers. The word *meet* at the very end of ***Romans 1:27*** is referring to what is considered necessary, right, or proper. In this case, what was considered socially acceptable was biblically in error. Such error causes people to leave what God has designed as proper and appropriate for their own ideologies or the ideologies of the world. The person begins serving a person or thing with a devotion that belongs to God. This errored counseling causes them to worship creation, what was made, rather than the true and living God. The complexity of this thinking error compels the faith-based counselor to develop expertise in change management theories and then adapt those theories into faith-based theology. Lewin's model of change is a three-step pattern:

Figure 7.1 Lewin's Model of Change

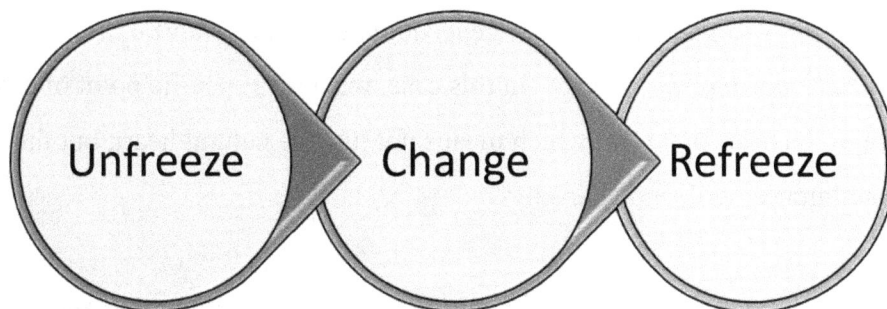

Source: MindTools, 2018

One example is to have a block of ice and want to change it to shaped ice for a party. The steps are to unfreeze the cubed ice, pour the water into molds, and refreeze. The dynamics of change are not to discard all that a client may have received from secular counseling but to show them how to transition (change) those ideas into their spiritual belief system. The level of applicability is to be determined on a case-by-case basis which the counselor will assess and present to the client.

Errored and ungodly counsel promotes behavior that is unseemly. *Unseemly* means *indecent, shameful, unnatural.* In some cases, the client has willingly embraced unwise counsel to justify behaviors that avoid accountability. Such actions do not identify one's authentic self in relations to being created in the image of God or God himself as the sovereign holy being of all creation. Unfortunately, society is consistently working at odds against spiritual counsel with its permeating messages of satisfying a person's sinful nature. This is what the Bible means by *recompense of error.* Recompense is a *reward or requital.* The recompense of error seems to satisfy an appetite or manmade belief system to fulfill various emotional needs and desires; however, its true nature is to promote taking on the characteristics of the sin. According to Paul's teaching, the person begins to look like and be identified by their choices.

The King James Version of *Mark 12:24* records Jesus talking about error. The New King James Version says, *Jesus answered and said to them, "Are you not therefore mistaken, because you do not know the Scriptures nor the power of God?*

Hebrews 3:10 Wherefore, I was grieved with that generation, and said, They do always err in their heart; and they have not known my ways. In this case, we hear a specific point of error that it is taking place in the heart or *kardia* which means not just the natural heart, but the soul as the seat of life, intelligence, will, and character.

Hosea 4:12 My people ask counsel at their stocks, and their staff declareth unto them: for the spirit of whoredoms hath caused them to err, and they have gone a whoring from under their God. In the case of Hosea, God has instructed the prophet to marry a whore for purposes of turning the man into a living demonstration. Much like Paul's message to Rome and our present society, the Old Testament prophet had to deal with a culture permeated with notions of following their thoughts and feelings – their ideologies - rather than keeping a relationship with God and his word.

1 John 4:6 We are of God. He who knows God hears us; he who is not of God does not hear us. By this we know the spirit of truth and the spirit of error. Specifically, from John's epistle, we learn that error results in a person wandering around. When a counselor becomes aware that the client is suffering from influences of error, the first task is to align them to a treatment plan that will serve as a wellness map and disconnect them from the wandering around that is embedded in their character. This spirit can literally cause a person to move from place to place geographically as well as developing a pattern of changing jobs, relationships, housing, and so on. The initial client history should explore these areas of the counselor has any indication of error from their client.

As counselors, we can never provide counseling based on our beliefs, the client's beliefs, or societal standards. We must be careful to recognize that the morals and ethics of the world are not necessarily rooted in the laws and standards of God. Many similarities to godly standards are more coincidental than intentional in our current society that has demanded separation of church and state. It is our responsibility to respect the laws of the land, while making sure people know that our counseling services are rooted in the biblical truths, principles, and standards of God. Any counsel that violates God's principles is ungodly counsel. Clearly then, before becoming a student of counseling theories, we must be a student of God's word.

We must be willing to counsel through the purposes and standards of God even if people choose not to adhere to them. We cannot process people to authentic healing and wholeness if we are mixing ungodly principles or error into the counseling plan. As a faith-based counselor, it is our responsibility to ensure that what is presented to our clients is acceptable counsel. This is a serious profession with weighty responsibilities. The consequences of misleading a child of God are significant, whether by omission or commission. Counselors cannot allow silence to be interpreted as support for choices that pull a client further away from God.

Romans 1:31-32 Without understanding, covenant breakers, without natural affection, implacable, unmerciful: Who knowing the judgment of God, that they which commit such things are worthy of death, not only do the same, but have pleasure in them that do them.

This is a key area of the manual to remind the reader of our diversity and inclusivity statement. God did not deputize Christians to "arrest" people into our belief system. We live in a diversity society that demands we operate with sensitivity and strategy. Jesus demonstrated again and again how to engage and interact with those who have differing understanding of God's presence and what it means to individuals. His commission to the disciples from *Matthew 28:19* to go out into the world and teach is a clear instruction that they needed a skill the modern world calls cultural agility. Likewise, *2 Corinthians 5:20* instructs us to be ambassadors of Christ; therefore, it is necessary to be diplomatic and gracious while interacting with others.

ESSENTIAL QUALITIES OF A FAITH BASED COUNSELOR

A counselor has no magical powers. A counselor is not perfect, but the call to the ministry of counseling places demands on the individual's life that cannot be compromised. As a faith-based counselor, that professionalism exceeds the secular ambition of becoming influential. A faith-based counselor embodies the New Testament ideology of commitment that improving the lifestyle of one improves the greater good for all.

The overall character of a faith-based counselor who professes a calling and not merely a vocation rests under the sevenfold spirit of God, while encompassing the following attributes in the draft below.

Isaiah 11:1-2 A shoot will come up from the stump of Jesse; from his root a branch will bear fruit. The spirit of the Lord will rest on him-the Spirit of wisdom and of understanding, the Spirit of counsel and of power, the Spirit of knowledge and of the fear of The Lord.

Balanced	Godly lifestyle	Equipped
• Stable	• Mature	• Intelligent
• Loving	• Prophetic	• Trained
• Godly	• Discerning	• Educated
• Self-controlled	• Intercessor	• Articulate
• Compassionate	• Enduring	• Communicator
• Kind	• Spiritual gifts	• Reciprocal
• Gentle	• Morally upright	• Strategic
• Meek	• Discerning	• Perceptive
• Blameless	• Perceptive	• Confident
• Practical	• Spirit-filled	• Risk Taker

Let's go beyond this initial list of thirty traits and add some other clusters of qualities that a client may expect from a faith-based counselor. Please remember that these lists are built from over twenty years' experience in the field, innumerable conversations with other professionals and ministers, and feedback from clients. Education is a given, but education without spiritual gifts and maturity can be disastrous. Reading the lists suggests that a faith-based counselor is a believer extraordinaire, but the expectation is the presence of the qualities.

Strategic

- Confrontational
- Diplomatic
- Foresight
- Critiques without criticism
- Inquisitive with compassion

Invested

- Sees the bigger picture
- Maps the journey
- Perceptive
- Punctual
- Dependable

Empowered

- Empowering
- Creative
- Resourceful
- Spiritually gifted
- Believer in miracles, signs, and wonders

Chapter 8

THE COUNSELOR-CLIENT RELATIONSHIP

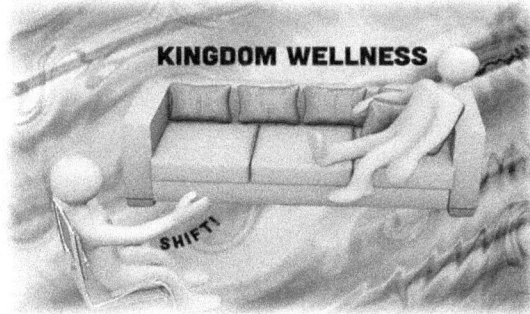

The counselor-client relationship is key to clients effectively processing to wholeness. Imbalance in the relationship can cause consequences for both the counselor and the client, while causing others to steer away from counseling. Let's step briefly away from the topic at hand and interject a business principle. Word-of-mouth (WOM) advertising is the original social media platform and remains the most proven method of reaching consumers. "In a recent study, 64% of marketing executives indicated that they believe word of mouth is the most effective form of marketing."[26] The flip side of that principle is that WOM is also the quickest way to lose business (clients) if there has been a negative experience. Never underestimate the damage that will be done, not only to the client but to your practice. A healthy counselor-client relationship is the central ingredient to your ability to continue as a positive influence.

Let's explore the benefits of a healthy counselor and client relationship.

---

[26]Kimberly A. Whitler. (2014, July 17). Why word of mouth advertising is the most important social media advertising. Retrieved from *Forbes* website at https://www.forbes.com/sites/kimberlywhitler/2014/07/17/why-word-of-mouth-marketing-is-the-most-important-social-media/#35f3530f54a8

Ministry of Endurance

Psalm 84:7 They go from strength to strength, every one of them in Zion appeareth before God.

2 Corinthians 3:18 But we all, with open face beholding as in a glass the glory of the Lord, are changed into the same image from glory to glory, even as by the Spirit of the Lord.

Hebrews 10:36 You need to persevere so that when you have done the will of God, you will receive what he has promised.

Counseling can be viewed as a ministry of endurance as it requires time and processing for deliverance and healing to solidify. Clients have to be committed to their counseling process; otherwise, you cannot sufficiently help them. **They must be willing to do the work. The counselor cannot do the work for them. Neither should a counselor want a client to be healed more than the client wants it. As a counselor, you are not responsible for a client's healing.** To some degree, you are the tour guide that is pointing out features in their journey. If a counselor is involved in the counseling process more than the client, then boundaries have been crossed. The counselor is getting personal needs met through the interaction.

The counselor must be assertive and willing to either reset boundaries or refer the client to a colleague. Secrets birth shame, and shame becomes a weapon in the hands of the enemy. A counselor that needs counseling is not shameful. When there are red flags in the counselor-client interactions, pay attention! Be transparent enough to ask for help. Any other response is a recipe for a tragedy that will affect both parties. Have a self-check-up plan. You are worth it. "What needs to be addressed in training is something called "countertransference," Lopez explains. While client transferring emotions they would have for someone in their outside lives on to their therapist (called "transference") is generally considered a good thing, a therapist transferring emotions on to their client is to be avoided."[27] This is soulish and demonic entanglement that can hinder the process, progress and success of a client.

---

[27]Rose Hackman. (2017, April 19). When therapists also need therapists: 'Suffering is not unique to one group.' Retrieved from *The Guardian* website at https://www.theguardian.com/society/2017/apr/19/therapists-go-to-therapy-prince-harry-mental-health

Enmeshment is an easy side effect for people, especially counselors who are gifted in empathy. Counselors listen to tragic stories with nearly unimaginable levels of pain and brokenness from their clients. It is critical to know if there has been a SHIFT into a fixer mentality. A fixer mentality occurs when a professional has a fixation on fixing others and are validated in their beliefs, actions, and outcomes regarding their impact on the lives and experiences of others. It sounds a bit like a tongue twister or a play on words, but there is nothing humorous about a counselor who has fallen prey to the fixer mentality. It is not only unhealthy, but also the epitome of enmeshment, enablement, and distorted validation.

Let us take a moment to address one of the most severe consequences to enmeshment in both spiritual and legal terms. Effective counseling includes the ability to influence. Too many times in our society, that influence, when misused, has become seductive resulting in sexual victimization of a client. A counselor must be incredibly careful of their physical and emotional boundaries with clients. A client may ask for a hug. Know ahead of time what is appropriate as a counselor regarding physical touch and know what a client can handle. Remember that a client can easily see the counselor as a hero, a savior, or as one who fulfill voids that others in their lives have not, cannot, or refuse to fulfill. **Document, document, document. But most importantly, the counselor MUST maintain boundaries that provide a clear understanding of who they are, who they are not, and who they CANNOT BE.**

Counselors are not fixers. They guide people through God's ordained process where wholeness takes place. SHIFT!

A faith-based counselor's primary guide is the Word of God, and to borrow from a popular bracelet's acronym WWJD, we ask the question, "What would Jesus do?" As we examine the interaction between Jesus and those he healed, we find a diverse set of dynamics. In some cases, the healing came from desperation. *Matthew 15:21-28* records the Syrophoenician woman's despairing plea for her daughter. In other scenarios, faith is in the spotlight (*Luke 7:50*). When we look at the healing of the centurion's daughter, we see honoring authority as the primary focus (*Luke 7:8-10*). While certain stories in the scripture demonstrate healing as a result of intercession, most of the healing stories are a one-to-one interaction between Jesus and the individual. People wanted to be healed, had faith to be healed, and honored the healing process.

Matthew 13:57-58 And they were offended in him. But Jesus said unto them, A prophet is not without honour, save in his own country, and in his own house. And he did not many mighty works there because of their unbelief.

Luke 5:17-20 And it came to pass on a certain day, as he was teaching, that there were Pharisees and doctors of the law sitting by, which were come out of every town of Galilee, and Judaea, and Jerusalem: and the power of the Lord was present to heal them. And, behold, men brought in a bed a man which was taken with a palsy: and they sought means to bring him in, and to lay him before him. And when they could not find by what way they might bring him in because of the multitude, they went upon the housetop, and let him down through the tiling with his couch into the midst before Jesus. And when he saw their faith, he said unto him, Man, thy sins are forgiven thee.

Luke 9:1 But the crowds were aware of this and followed Him; and welcoming them, He began speaking to them about the kingdom of God and curing those who had need of healing.

John 5:5-9 And a certain man was there, which had an infirmity thirty and eight years. When Jesus saw him lie, and knew that he had been now a long time in that case, he saith unto him, Wilt thou be made whole? The impotent man answered him, Sir, I have no man, when the water is troubled, to put me into the pool: but while I am coming, another steppeth down before me. Jesus saith unto him, Rise, take up thy bed, and walk. And immediately the man was made whole, and took up his bed, and walked: and on the same day was the sabbath.

There were times when Jesus asked people if they wanted to be healed. He knew that healing came with responsibility and a willingness to want breakthrough. It is important to remember that clients make decisions based in their belief system. As much as the counselor desires the client to capture what the counselor foresees, it is the client that will ultimately choose to move toward breakthrough or continue in the patterns that brought success to their counseling process. Every teacher has a vision of a whole class of A+ students, but the reality is that students will achieve at varying levels. Because a client grasps (and practices) less than 100% of what the counselor presents does not mean that either the counselor or the client has failed or come short. Remain confident of the seeds that you are planting with your client and know that there are times and seasons that are set by God further maturity and breakthrough.

Ecclesiastes 3:1 To everything there is a season, A time for every purpose under heaven:

1 Corinthians 3:7-8 So then neither he who plants is anything, nor he who waters, but God who gives the increase. Now he who plants and he who waters are one, and each one will receive his own reward according to his own labor.

The task at hand for the counselor is to give 100% of what is to be given through their expertise for a specific time in the client's life. One of my sayings is, "I cannot be more to you than God has assigned, but I promise you that I won't be less." Our responsibility is to wholeheartedly give through the skills that God has developed in us, and to trust that the same God who was patient with us is working in our client.

Remember that Jesus did not simply come to preach the good news of redemption but to offer a cultural and societal SHIFT by preaching the Kingdom of God. Faith based counselors today have that same revolutionary assignment to not merely be another piece of the wellness trend, but to bring kingdom principles that can change lives to the forefront of our profession. Jesus came to make culture. "He came to breathe new life into human beings."[28] As disciples of

---

[28]Ben Witherington III. (2011). *Work: A Kingdom Perspective on Labor*. Grand Rapids, MI: William B. Eerdmans Publishing Compnay

Christ, we are culture makers. ". . . culture is also about what we make of what there is, which is to say, what sense we make of what exists."[29] We are God's co-workers in the earth.

The next three subsections to this chapter have been placed on distinct pages to encourage total focus from the reader to the manual.

1. **Healthy Boundaries**

2. **Nonjudgmental Environment**

3. **Confidentiality and Code of Ethics**

4. **HIPPA Laws**

---

[29]Ibid., p. 103

Counselors must dutifully practice
ethical codes and laws!

Healthy Boundaries

- Boundaries are seen and unseen and are important in any professional relationship.
- Both seen and unseen boundaries must be clearly defined and respected so that the counseling process can remain healthy and progressive.
- Counseling sessions must be completed in a therapeutic setting that promotes the respect of boundaries.
- Sessions completed via video chat, phone, and email should also have specific boundaries.
- The relationship between a counselor and a client is one-dimensional and should always remain that way. Counseling sessions are for the client not the counselor. Counselors should not be getting physical, emotional, or intellectual needs met through the counseling sessions. If a counselor requires counseling, they should receive it through the pursuit of counseling services.
- Counselors should not counsel friends or relatives as this makes it easy to cross boundaries, to be more to the client than one should be, and compromises accountability to the counseling process.
- Counselors and clients should not engage in social interactions as familiarity can cause boundaries to be crossed.
- Sexual contact between counselors and clients is prohibited and is an ethical issue at the deepest level. The consequences of crossing this boundary can destroy a career, either in the present or at some unseen time in the future.
- Counselors must be time conscious in making sure they are not providing more services and time to clients as agreed. The result is enabling and enmeshment that keeps them bound to the counseling process rather than growing through the counseling process.
- Clients should invest financially in their counseling process. Counselors should adhere to their payment standards. This will ensure boundaries where behaviors of offering free or discounted services and expecting other type of monetary payments can occur. If the counselor does choose to discount or offer free services, a written agreement should be made and signed to protect the counselor and the client from false expectations and engaging in unethical behaviors to offset payment for services.

Non-judgmental Environment

- The counseling environment should be compassionate, genuine, trustworthy, and comfortable so the client will feel safe to share and explore their challenges.
- Counselors should provide a listening ear and be attentive in the counseling process so that clients can feel valued and supported in their counseling process.
- Counselors should express empathy, compassion, and genuine concern for clients.
- Clients should be able to clearly discern the love of God for them through the counselor, and his desire for them to be delivered and heal. This love should be demonstrated through the well of compassion and not lust or inordinacy.
- There must be honest and open communication between the counselor and the client. Both must be able to share their concerns, receive constructive criticism, where the counseling environment can continue to mature and manifest the healing clients need to breakthrough to wellness (*Matthew 9:35-36*). Compassion provokes the love of God so counselors can be endued with God's love, pity, and sympathy, to alleviate the suffering of others.
- Counselors must speak godly truth to clients but respect the client's choice to accept or reject those truths. The counselor must be nonjudgmental and display unconditional positive regard for clients. Counselors must resist imposing their beliefs on clients and be respectful of clients' choices and decisions and their right to choose whatever path they desire to take in the counseling process, even if it is not the most beneficial path for them. Proselytizing is not part of counseling. Counselors are not converting clients into client into their image but into the image of Christ, and even then, this is their choice – freewill.
- Counselors provide guidance and direction to clients as God leads, but it is the client's decision on how they utilize the guidance and direction. This guidance and direction should be in the form of choices and not advice, and not such that the client feels obligated to follow it. This way clients cannot blame the counselor when matters do not unfold the way they desire, or clients become too dependent on the counseling relationship where they cannot make decisions independently from the counselor. Counselors are not intermediaries between the client and God. That invites the idolatry of becoming a god to the client.

Confidentiality and Code of Ethics

Counselors must abide by the American Counseling Association (ACA) code of ethics which can be found at counseling.org (24-page document). It is vital that counselors are familiar with these ethics as they provide guidelines, obligations, and responsibilities to counselors for the purposes of protecting the dignity, boundaries, and well-being of clients. They also assist counselors with providing the most effective treatment for clients where the client's best interest is at the center of the counseling process. Clients are able to contact ACA when they have a compliant concerning their counselor or counseling experience. The code of ethics provides guidelines to determine if a client's rights have been violated and what actions should be taken toward a professional and ethical resolution.

It is important for counselors to make clients aware of the code of ethics and how to contact ACA should they have a complaint. Clients should also be informed that the counselor is bound by the code of ethics which places specific stipulations on the counselor-client interactions:

- A counselor has a duty to report if they determine that a client is a threat to himself or others.
- All counseling information and content is bound by privacy and confidentiality unless client gives consent; this may exclude extreme situations where law enforcement is involved or other pertinent matters.

Word of Advice: Like it or not, record keeping is part of the counselor's workload. If this is not one of your strengths, be prepared to hire staff or contract the service in some manner. Consistency is key to successful documentation. If you rely on technology, have a back-up, whether that is a flash drive or using cloud storage.

HIPPA - Health Insurance Portability and Accountability Act

The Privacy Rule, legislated HIPPA laws in 2000 to establish sufficient standards for disclosure rights for clients. HIPPA provides provisions that allows counselors to keep notes and documents confidential. Some ways counselors can keep notes and documents confidential is by keep records locked in a safe cabinet, using clients initials on verbal and written notes and documents rather than their real name, using HIPPA approved computer programs email services that protect the privacy of users.

HIPPA also clarifies when counselors are able to share treatment information with other care providers and with a clients' family members. Counselors have clients sign a confidentiality form with HIPPA standards that clearly define who can have privy to their counseling information. This form is essential because it protects the client in only sharing information with providers and family members the client approves of, while providing consent for counselors so they will not be in violation of sharing information illegally. Though there are more, here is a list of some reasons counselors should have clients sign a HIPPA confidentiality form:

- To establish clear boundaries for what can be shared regarding the counseling process,
- When clients need to partner with deliverance ministries or other services to aide in the counseling process,
- For the purposes of scheduling and rescheduling appointments through family members or loved ones, add family members to counseling sessions, discuss counseling services with family members or loved ones,
- A medical, mental health, or social service agency desires counseling information.

If a client is unconscious, delirious, experiencing psychosis, intoxicated, a threat to self or others, or otherwise incapable of making decisions, then counselors can legally share information under HIPPA law. Counselors should keep abreast of the HIPPA laws so they will know how to maintain confidentiality for their clients and good mental health practice for themselves. Goodtherapy.org along with other reputable websites provide up to date information regarding HIPPA laws.

Chapter 9

THE DISCERNING COUNSELOR

There is no question that the principles of the Bible often collide head-on with concepts that are presented in our society. Inclusion of the concept of discernment comes with the disclaimer of what it is "not." There is a current trend called discernment counseling; however, that is in no way to be confused with a discerning counselor. As a brief sidenote, discernment counseling is specific to ambivalent married couples who are striving to make one of three decisions about their marriage: (1) stay married, (2) leave things as they are, or (3) get divorced. It is an intensive therapy that entails only 1-5 sessions. Once again, there is a continual caution needed when exploring counseling theories grounded in the Bible versus secular theories. Webster's definition of discernment speaks to knowing or recognizing mentally, grasping something that is obscured, or perceiving. Faith based counselors do not operate from secular definition but from spiritual practices. Discernment is essential to operating as a counselor.

Discernment is not the same as instinct or intuition. There is a familiar saying of "trusting your gut" referring to instinct. The American Psychological Association defines an instinct as "an innate, species-specific biological force that impels an organism to do something, particularly to perform a certain act or respond in a certain manner to specific stimuli."[30] For instance,

---

[30]Instinct. (n.d.) Retrieved from American Psychological Association website at https://dictionary.apa.org/instinct

when winter comes, bears hibernate. It is an action that does not require a specific thought process to activate. Humans are genetically pre-wired for instincts. Examples include sucking at the mother's breast, which is innate to all mammals. Another word that is close to instinct and often confused as discernment is intuition. Intuition is formed out of prior experiences and knowledge which allows decision making seemingly with little to no thought. Discernment is not innate nor is it based in known fact or experience. It is the spiritual ability to comprehend the unstated truth of a situation or person.

It is through the counselor's spiritual relationship with God that he or she will receive thoughts, visions, and evidence regarding what is being discerned.

Let's spend a little more time resting with the concept and application of discernment. Particularly for those new to the profession, it is important to note that discernment is a strategic tool for you to assist the client; however, the client will not necessarily (likely not) have any awareness of your use of discernment. Discernment is not something that is intended for confrontation with the client. It should never, ever result in a conversation where you are aggressive or argumentative with the client about something they shared. The presence of discernment is a dynamic between you (the counselor) and God. In our exploration of discernment, the prophet Samuel offers an excellent example in his assignment to anoint David as king.

1 Samuel 16:6 And it came to pass, when they were come, that he looked on Eliab, and said, Surely the LORD'S anointed is before him.

God sent Samuel to Jesse but did not tell the prophet which one of the sons was to be selected king. He only told him that the one chosen would come from the sons. The word *looked* from the verse is *ra'ah* which means to discern. The next verse is an auto-correct, much like a spiritual Siri that says, "Re-routing." Even with the presence of discernment, the counselor needs the checks and balances of God's voice. It is the compass that guides every counseling effort.

1 Samuel 16:7 But the LORD said unto Samuel, Look not on his countenance, or on the height of his stature; because I have refused him: for the LORD seeth not as man seeth; for man looketh on the outward appearance, but the LORD looketh on the heart.

When the Lord spoke to Samuel, the Hebrew translation refers to speaking in his heart as a way of certifying what Samuel knew about Eliab. Can you imagine the spiritual stamina of Samuel to know that son after son after son was NOT the one? Seven times, Jesse presented a son with the hope of being the father of a king, but discernment declined each one. Can you imagine being the prophet who had to ask, "Do you have any more sons?" Operating in discernment requires fortitude, patience, and commitment to what God has revealed to you.

Discernment requires a counselor to lean not to their own understanding, But to trust the spirit of God within them. Proverbs 3:5-6

Diakrisis (Greek) is a *judicial estimation, discern, disputation.* It is the ability to distinguish. The etymology of discern mean *to separate thoroughly, withdraw, oppose, discriminate, decide, hesitate, contend, make to differ, doubt, judge, be partial, stagger, waver.* Discernment is not a feeling; it is knowing. When the counselor is operating in discernment, the voice of

God accompanied by the intention of the understanding of God is present. There is a presence of truth that would not be naturally revealed. God is expressing his truth through our spiritual senses. We are relying on what he is stating is true, not what we want to believe is the truth.

Hebrews 5:14 But strong meat belongeth to them that are of full age, even those who by reason of use have their senses exercised to discern both good and evil.

To grasp the depth of discernment, we must go back to the trichotomy of humanity as body, soul, and spirit. Spiritual senses are exercised through our spiritual self (spirit man). The soul contains the mind, will, and emotions; therefore, discerning through the soul is different than spiritual perceptiveness. Should a counselor feel uncertain about what a client presents, discernment is a tool used to decipher truth. Spiritual discernment separates that which is true from that which is soulish. Remember that the soul is part of the created nature of humankind; however, God never intended for the spirit to be directed by the soul. It is the soul that should be directed by the spirit. The counselor may have questions in their flesh, heart or mind, but our spirit will experience a certainty, surety, or a constant tugging in God's direction because spiritual discernment is a knowing of truth – a spiritual truth – of God's decisive truth.

When we discern through the soul:

- We search for knowledge through our human understanding or our common sense rather than the word of God.
- We tend to question what we feel, believe, or comprehend, rather than accept, trust, and rest in the truth of God.
- Suspicion is the voice we hear, feelings we sense and experience, visions we see, and expressions we ingest. We are hesitant, and reluctant, because we fear being vulnerable or making a mistake as human discernment is subject to human error. It cannot discern the things of the spirit and can waver due to the state, experience, mindset, or impression of the counselor at that time. *1 Corinthians 2:14 But the natural man receiveth not the things of the Spirit of God: for they are foolishness unto him: neither can he know them, because they are spiritually discerned.*

Perceiving through the soul has its place in counseling, only because it allows us to be in tune with a person's fleshly and emotional reaction to a situation. However, the soul is severely out of order when it is used at a time to override what the spirit should be discerning. When the soul tries to discern in place of the spirit, it looks for the spectacular, and for ways and answers to impress, rather than acquiring God's supernatural answer or direction regarding a situation.

If you operate in discernment, that is a statement that God trusts you enough to allow you become a conduit of what He knows about a person flowing into your words or guidance that will align that person to the will of God. Discernment is a heavy responsibility that has nothing to do with building you up but everything to do with serving as a blessing in someone's wellness journey. With the *Hebrews 5:14* standard, we understand that discernment is a practice that is refined with maturity.

Without discernment, the counselor may be offered insights that seem good at first glance, but if not and is accepted as truth, the result can become a stumbling block for both counselor and client. There are moments that discernment can cause an internal struggle as the counselor weighs what is being said versus what God is speaking. When there is a sense of opposition, dispute, contention, doubting, or wavering in your spirit, take time to hear God. Discernment is sometimes a nudge and not always a trumpet to blast off, "Hey, the truth is (fill in the blank)." Sometimes it is best to weigh what God is saying, let the client know you will be praying about the matter and will share what God is speaking when you have more clarity and ability to decider and confer what God is speaking. This wisdom is essential to knowing what to share as you discern the truth of God and the heart of God. And in making sure what is shared successfully contributes to the counseling process.

No counselor becomes so proficient that they dare negate the value of godly discernment.

DISCERNING THROUGH EXPERIENCE

Though we should never become a counselor just because we have lived a challenging life and have overcome difficult experiences, our personal experiences play a vital role in our discernment.

Many parents make this comment about their children, "*I wish they would have listened to me.*" This is the wisdom and common knowledge of experience that helps us to discern the future. The counselor must have a specific purpose to share their experience of discernment. If there is no divine purpose in using one's own experience to help another, then the sharing can be familiar and unfruitful. Moreover, an unhealthy client will use the information at a later date to avoid accountability, confrontation, or avoidance of an issue they may not be ready to address. Using discretion when sharing personal experiences will diminish the likelihood of this occurring. It also helps maintain balance with not sharing too much personal information with someone that is a client and not a personal acquaintance. Behind every experience resides a cause, effect, and purpose or lack of purpose that makes a person become bitter or better. When David stood in face of Goliath, it was experience with a cause that gave him strength to say, "*the Lord that delivered me out of the paw of the lion and out of the paw of the bear, he will deliver me out of the hand of this Philistine*" *(1Samuel 17:32, 34-36).*

DISCERNMENT THROUGH THE WORD OF GOD

The Bible as the Word of God lays the foundation for discernment. Within the Word are key principles, standards, instructions, and skills, engulfed in the character and nature of God. If the counselor does not know the Word, there is no ability to discern accurately. It becomes impossible to teach people how to apply biblical principles and his spoken word to their everyday life. The Word helps us discern the will, plan, path, and fruit of God. It provides the framework for directing the course of counseling. Discerning through the word is not about spectacular revelation. Remember God is simple. It is us who make Him difficult. Look for the simplicities of God. This enables the counselor to discern when God's word is speaking and revealing keys regarding a client's situation.

In *1 Corinthians 12*, there is a gift of discerning the spirits. Notice it does not say "*spirit*" but "*spirits*" which is plural. There are several spirits to discern.

We must be able to discern:

Diagram 9.0 Areas of Discernment

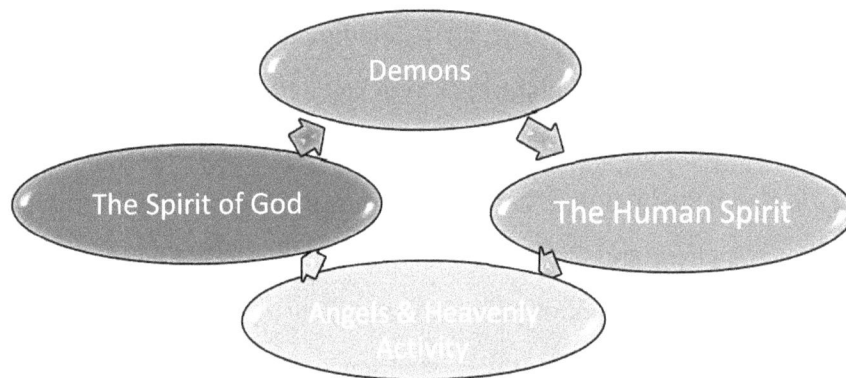

Source: Baker, 2018

Counselors discern the **SPIRITS**, so clients will know which voices are speaking in their lives.

The Human Spirit

The human spirit is the totality of our created being, including:

Diagram 9.1 The Human Spirit

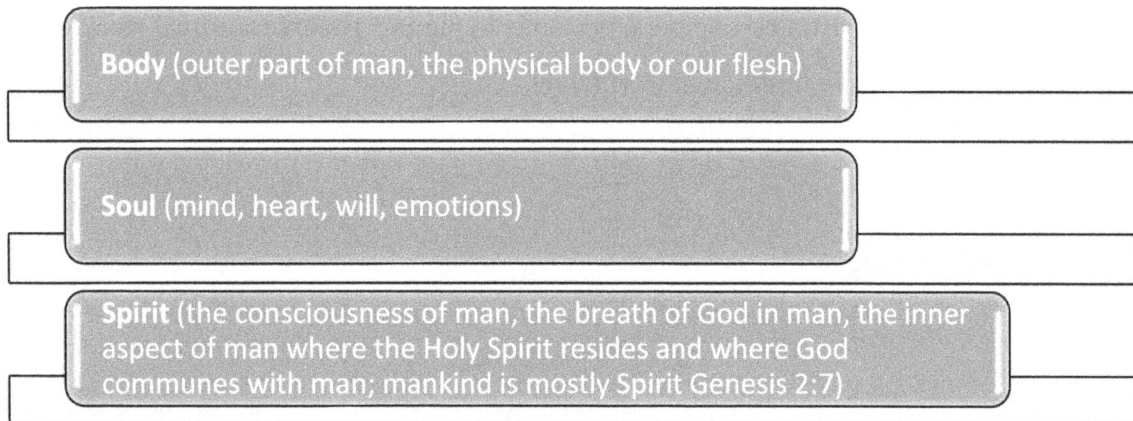

Body (outer part of man, the physical body or our flesh)

Soul (mind, heart, will, emotions)

Spirit (the consciousness of man, the breath of God in man, the inner aspect of man where the Holy Spirit resides and where God communes with man; mankind is mostly Spirit Genesis 2:7)

Source: Baker, 2018

Because there are some things that can only be spiritually discerned, it is important to know the difference between the three parts of our humanity.

Diagram 9.2 Trichotomy

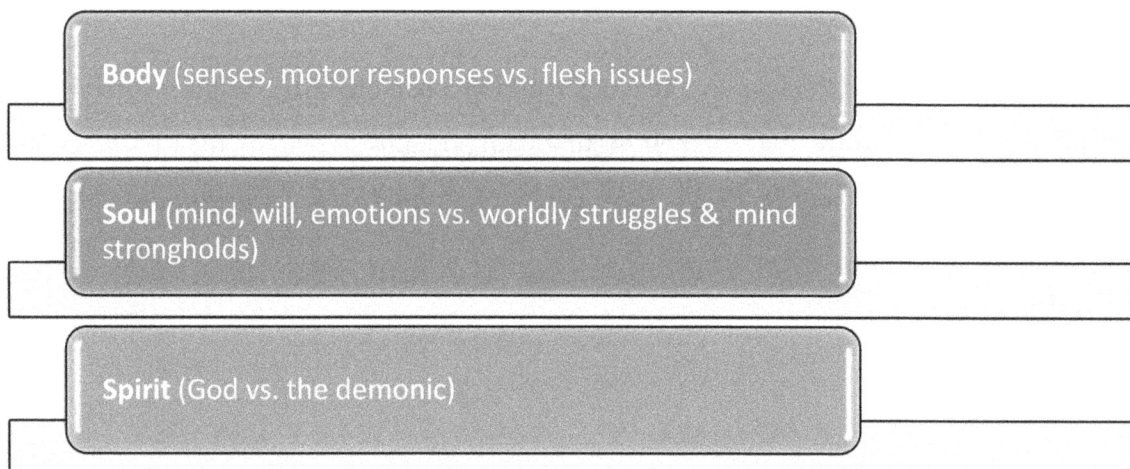

Body (senses, motor responses vs. flesh issues)

Soul (mind, will, emotions vs. worldly struggles & mind strongholds)

Spirit (God vs. the demonic)

Source: Baker, 2018

As a faith-based counselor, you are helping your client to shape a worldview that is based on a spiritual standard. "A worldview is a framework (or "web") of basic assumptions about reality from which people make sense of the world, figure out their place in it, and derive the values that dictate their lifestyle choices."[31] As we consider the human spirit and properly discern its different faculties, we also need to explore the holy trinity versus unholy trinity. The difference of the two demonstrates whether a person is living in a positive spiritual worldview or living through a spiritually destructive worldview.

The Holy Trinity

Diagram 9.3 Holy Trinity

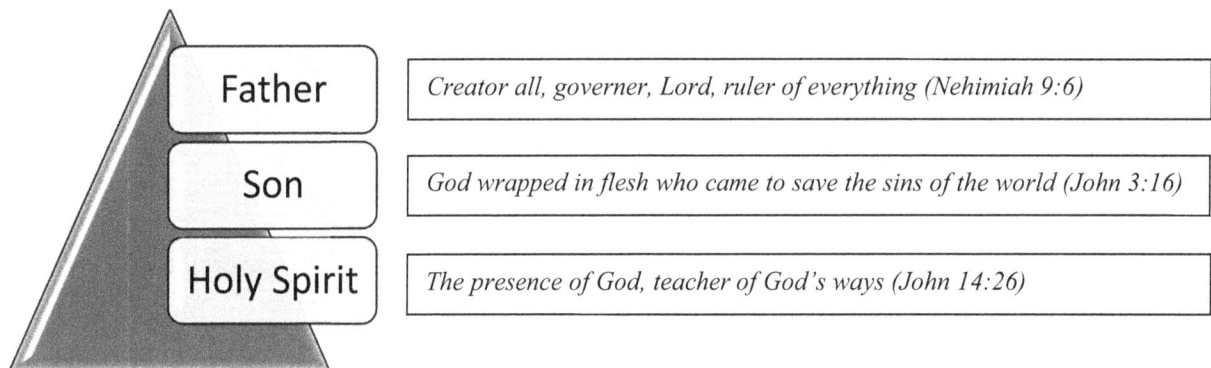

Father	Creator all, governer, Lord, ruler of everything (Nehimiah 9:6)
Son	God wrapped in flesh who came to save the sins of the world (John 3:16)
Holy Spirit	The presence of God, teacher of God's ways (John 14:26)

Source: Baker, 2018

The Holy Trinity should be the kingdom that is governing a person's life. When a person is governed by an unholy trinity, it alters their destiny with potential to destroy their progress and success. (*1 John 5:7, Matthew 28:18-20, John 14:15-26, John 15:26, 1 Corinthians 8:6, Isaiah 9:6*)

---

[31]Jeff Forey. (2016, August 26). Growing in discernment. Retrieved from Biblical Counseling website at https://biblicalcounselingcoalition.org/2016/08/26/growing-in-discernment-part-1/

The Unholy Trinity

Diagram 9.4 The Unholy Trinity

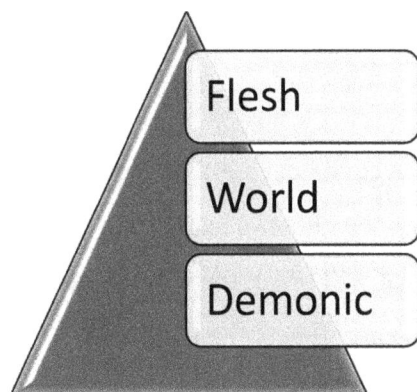

Source: Baker, 2018

Flesh - Sexual immortality, impurity, jealous, discord, rage, selfish ambition, dissension, selfishness, failure, envy, drunkenness, addictions; cannot bind, loose or cast out the flesh; have to crucify it through prayer, fasting, and discipline; flesh has to be killed (disclaimer: not in a literal physical death) because you cannot contend with it (*Matthew 16:24, Mark 8:34, Romans 6:6, 1 Corinthians 6:8, Ephesians 4:22, Colossians 2:5, Galatians 5:20-21*)

World & Systems Of The World - Lust of the flesh, lust of the eyes, and of the things of the world which are the cravings of sinful man; prides of life; anything that entice us to fall to the flesh and to the enemy is the world system working; the world system also entails mixture, idolatry, and a drawing away from God (*Matthew 6:24, 1 John 2:16, John 15:18-21, Romans 12:2, 1 John 2:15-17, James 4:4*)

Demonic Activity - Strongholds, possession, oppression, depression, suppression, snares, infiltrations; the devil seeks to tempt, destroy, afflict, bind, torment, cycle, and hinder (*2 Corinthians 7:15, 2 Corinthians 11:14, 2 Corinthians 12:7, 1 Thessalonians 2:18*)

The unholy trinity is important because all three concepts have some bearing on human behavior. It is easier to discern what your client needs and what goals they need to set if you know what part of the unholy trinity is affecting their worldview. Faith based counseling is a holistic approach that is well able to address concerns from any combination of the three or all three areas collectively.

Here are some preliminary strategies to address these areas:

Set goals with the client to address underlying root issues. If needed, teach prayer techniques and give the client homework assignments about prayer. While the client is learning to use breakthrough prayer, you, the counselor, can initiate prayers that will break the legal rights of demonic strongholds. In some cases, the counselor as intercessor will become the primary force to implement breaking strongholds. Your clients who are non-believers may not understand the intercession process; therefore, that becomes the counselor's responsibility.

This process may need to be repeated as the client progresses and continues to recognize root issues. The counselor's role is to develop a safe space and to provide tools. The overall agenda is always a reconciled relationship with God. Studies show that chronic shame is the root cause of most embedded emotional issues. "Mistrust of God, shame and guilt before God, resulting in no experiences of communion with God, lack of self-acceptance, and mistrust of others, and shame and guilt before them. As a result, one experiences negative emotions "all alone," in a state of emotional abandonment. As a result, one's core identity remains implicitly unrelated to God, regardless of one's explicit beliefs."[32] Faith based counseling is reconstructing the client's life story such that the outcome is harmony with God.

Provide deliverance ministry for the demonic strongholds. This is a sensitive topic as the concept may be foreign to your client. There are various models of deliverance, and it is the counselor's responsibility to know which one fits the client's ability to receive. This is about releasing spiritually negative influences which does not have to be measured by the traditionalist dynamics of volume and dramatic exhibition. Deliverance may include the use of anointing oil, laying on of hands, a prayer team, or recommendation to a specific deliverance

---

[32]Carditive Therapy: A Distinctly Christian Model of Psychotherapy and Counseling. (n.d.) Retrieved from the Christian Psychology website at http://www.christianpsych.org/wp_scp/

ministry that is an extension of your counseling center. Any partner ministries should have a contractual obligation to maintain confidentiality via a signed document that can be submitted to the counselor and the client. Keep in mind that self-forgiveness and forgiveness of others is often the key that will release all ungodly influences for the client. Self-forgiveness restores identity, and identity rejects ideas and behaviors that oppose wholeness. Forgiveness of others release the responsibility of revenge and reprimand into the hands of God and how he decides to intervene regarding a wrong infracted upon an individual. Every counselor should have training in deliverance and have a commitment to knowing that when a demonic stronghold is exposed, counseling is impotent for that level of warfare. (more detail in upcoming chapters on deliverance)

Return to the counseling process and work through the worldly and flesh issues, while providing applicable tools and skills that help clients walk in a healthy lifestyle with Jesus Christ.

Flesh, the world, and demons, are **ALL** subject to the power of God.

SHIFT!

INFLUENTIAL VOICES THAT IMPACT A PERSON'S LIFE

There are all kinds of influential spirits constantly speaking even when we are doing other things not related to that voice, and even when that is not a voice we desire to hear. The voices that people may hear are:

- **God's Voice** – The ultimate voice of our creator that governs our lives.
- **Satan's Voice** – The voice of the devil and demon forces that want to destroy our lives.
- **The Voice of The Flesh (carnal, personal wants)** – Can be a person's own voice at work or the flesh speaking in aches of its own desires.
- **The Voice of Cultural and Family Traditions, Loyalties, And Obligations** - People can be guided by the perceptions of those close to them, e.g. parents, family members. This is where family spirits lurk. Family spirits attempt to have people operating in values and standards that may not necessarily align with the word.
- **The Voice of Society** - These voices consist of ethnic groups, cultural traditions, loyalties, and obligations, trends, pastors, teachers, leaders, friends, acquaintances, etc. These voices tend to operate more through opinion and personal choices that have people choosing their will and desires above God or without considering God and his standards for their lives.

A great percentage of people come to counseling because demonic, fleshly, family, or societal voices have become exalted against the knowledge of God, and have caused confusion, misbeliefs, and/or disorder in the person's spirit and life in general.

2 Corinthians 10:5 *Casting down arguments and every high thing that exalts itself against the knowledge of God, bringing every thought into captivity to the obedience of Christ.*

2 Corinthians 10:5 *We use our powerful God-tools for smashing warped philosophies, tearing down barriers erected against the truth of God, fitting every loose thought and emotion and impulse into the structure of life shaped by Christ. (MSG)*

There has been a change in the narrative of morality in our society, so it is little wonder that the outcome is the struggle both within and from outside of a person striving to align to God's will. People will often have issues of not aligning to certain standards, whether it be their own personal standards, the world's standards, society's standards, or their family/religious/cultural standards. If you can discern where the voices of these standards originate from, you can combat the lies and mind strongholds that people have formed, cast down the lies and strongholds, and SHIFT people forward into their true identity and destiny in God. Remember that God has not called us to "fix" people but to guide people to God's truth about their identity and purpose.

As a counselor committed to walking with your client, this portion of the journey may take a while. Someone said once, "Before you can embrace the truth, you have to release the lie." Releasing false narratives about life will include a grief and loss process. Your role as the counselor is to have a strategy that addresses all of the details of the process without allowing your client to become stuck in any one portion of it. It is definitely a balancing act and one that requires not only your professional knowledge and skills but your spiritual insight. Refer back to the Counseling Paradigm:

Diagram 9.5 Counseling Paradigm

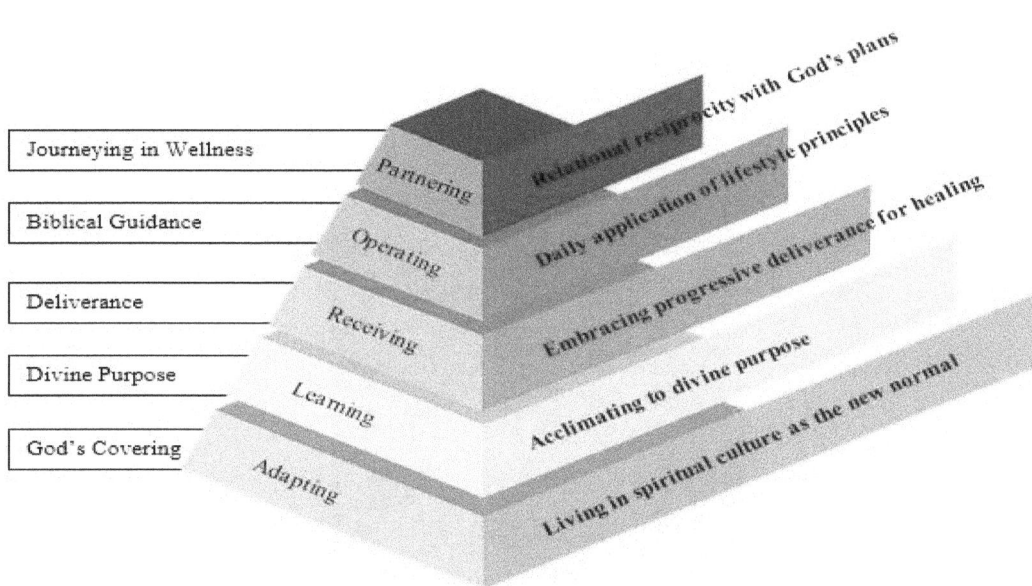

Source: Baker, 2018

Kingdom Wellness Counseling and Mentoring Center

Faith Based Counseling

Manual I

Part 3: Chapters (10 – 14)

Learning Objectives:

- To provide definitive revelation regarding the biblical foundation of deliverance ministry and its benefits to clients and society.
- To provide applicable tools and strategies to maintain deliverance and healing.
- To provide strategic insight on the difference between healing and wholeness, and how to process a client to wholeness.
- To provide clear understanding for the need to process to wholeness and how to help clients rest in God, while working the counseling process.

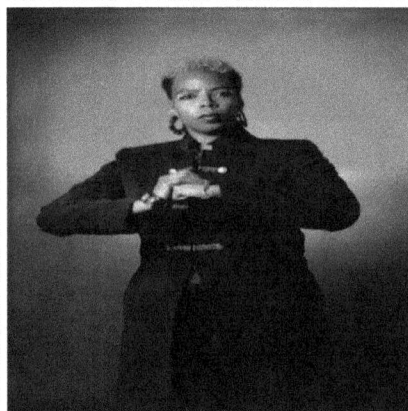

Chapter 10

DELIVERANCE MINISTRY

This may be a difficult chapter for many. Deliverance ministry is not something that is spooky or weird. It is definitely an area of ministry that requires sensitivity and diplomacy. It is not to be imposed by a counselor on a client who does not first have understanding of the process. The potential for deliverance ministry as part of the counseling process must be considered from multiple perspectives, including legally protecting your counseling career. It is recommended that there is a separate deliverance agreement from the general counseling agreement between the client and counselor. Depending on the individual, it may be useful to have a pastoral recommendation for the process. No more than a physician should examine a patient without a nurse present, should a counselor initiate deliverance ministry without a support person present as an accountability witness. The saying is true that wounded people wound people, and you cannot leave your counseling service vulnerable to an indefensible accusation.

If deliverance ministry is a new concept for you, reading this chapter will not equip you to operate at that level. Make the investment in your career and your client's wellness to register for deliverance training. Please contact me if you need a recommendation to a balanced deliverance training ministry. On one hand, we can propose that deliverance is as simple as having the faith to believe that Jesus is a deliverer. On the other hand, deliverance requires skillfulness and strategy to know the timing and situation when it is most beneficial. This chapter is not designed to have you, the reader, feel certified in deliverance ministry, but to demonstrate the necessity of believing that it is an authentic portion of the counseling process. As stated earlier in the book, networking is a professional standard, and there is no reason to discount the value of networking in counseling. Your practice may be partnered with a particular local ministry that is experienced in deliverance ministry. Just as a physician may refer their patient to a specialist, so a counselor may feel that they can best serve their client by including ministry referrals for particular portions of the overall journey.

Deliverance ministry is the practice of cleansing and expelling demonic spirits in effort to resolve problems caused by the presence and manifestations of these entities. Counselors must believe in, understand, know how to conduct, and become advocates of deliverance ministry.

Jesus conducted and ordained deliverance ministry.

1 John 3:8 *He that committeth sin is of the devil; for the devil sinneth from the beginning. For this purpose the Son of God was manifested, that he might destroy the works of the devil.*

The Bible refers to demonic spirits as demons, devils, and unclean spirits. Demonic spirits are actually falling angels that now roam the earth seeking inhabitants (*Isaiah 4 :12-15, 2Peter :4-10*). Demon spirits can possess, depress, oppress, torment, or influence person, place, or thing.

Diagram 10.0 Demonic Spirits

People	Ephesians 2:1-2, Matthew 12:22, Matthew 12:43-45, Mark 1:21-27, Mark 4:1, Luke 22:3-4, 2 Corinthians 4:4, John 8 :44, John l0:l0, 1 John 4:4, James 4:7, 2 Corinthians 12:7
Families	Psalm 106:37-38
Generations	Hebrews 2:14
Animals	Matthew 8:28-34, Mark 5:13, Luke 8:13
Objects	Deuteronomy 7:25-26, Deuteronomy 18:9-13, Isaiah 30:22, Joshua 7:11-13, Joshua 7:20-21
Homes	The Bible speaks of how the devil prowls the earth and how he masquerades as a angel of light - 2 Corinthians 11:14, 1 Peter 5:8. Demons love to prowl around and inhabit whatever is legally available to them.
Locations	When Jesus walked on water the disciples mistook him as a ghost. Jesus did not deny ghosts exists, but he let them know that he was not one - Matthew 14:26. This lets us know that demons prowl as ghostly figures causing fear in people.
Laws/Decrees	Such demonic laws/decrees are used to destroy God's people, his standards, and way of life. Pharaoh ordered the Hebrew male children to be killed, Shadrach, Meshack, and Abednego refused to bow to the king's image - were thrown in the fiery furnace; Daniel thrown in the lions' den due decrees designed to kill him, the beheading of John the Baptist – Exodus 1-2, Daniel 3, Daniel 6, Matthew 14, Mark 6 :14-29
Cultures	Daniel 2:27, Acts 19:17-27, 2 Corinthians 6:14-18
Ethnic Groups	Any ethnic group that serves idol gods have demons at work in them. 1 Corinthians 10:20-21
World Events	John 12:31, Ephesians 6:11-12, Colossians 2:8, Revelation 12:9
Governments	Daniel 10:13, 20
Political Arenas	When laws and political parties do not align with God, they risk demonic infiltration. Proverbs 14:34, Daniel 6, 2 Samuel 15:2-6, Psalm 12:2, Psalm 33:12, Matthew 6:24, Acts 5:29, Titus 3:1-9, Galatians 2:19
Trends	Romans 12:2
Platforms	Matthew 7:14-20, I Timothy 4:1
Agencies	Acts 19:13-16, Revelation 16:14
Waters	Job 3:8, Job 7:12, Job 40:15-41, Job 41:1-34, Isaiah 27:1, Psalm 74:13-14, Psalm 89:9, Ezekiel 9:2-3, Revelations 12:12
Land	Luke 10:19, Psalm 91:13
Atmosphere	Job 4:15, Ephesians 2:2
Regions / Nations **Communities /** **Cities**	Deuteronomy 18:9-12, Deuteronomy 32:8-9, Daniel 10, Acts 16, Ephesians 6, Revelation 12 :9

Source: Baker, 2018

Deliverance ministry may be required at some point during the counseling process to expel demons that are hindering the person's ability to delivered, healed, while processing effectively to a healthy and whole lifestyle.

Jesus gave believers the power to cast out demons.

Matthew 10:1 Jesus summoned His twelve disciples and gave them authority over unclean spirits, to cast them out, and to heal every kind of disease and every kind of sickness.

Matthew 10:8 Heal the sick, raise the dead, cleanse the lepers, cast out demons. Freely you received, freely give.

Mark 3 :13-15 And he goeth up into a mountain, and calleth unto him whom he would: and they came unto him. And he ordained twelve, that they should be with him, and that he might send them forth to preach, And to have power to heal sicknesses, and to cast out devils.

Mark 16:15-18 And he said unto them, Go ye into all the world, and preach the gospel to every creature. He that believeth and is baptized shall be saved; but he that believeth not shall be damned. And these signs shall follow them that believe; In my name shall they cast out devils; they shall speak with new tongues; They shall take up serpents; and if they drink any deadly thing, it shall not hurt them; they shall lay hands on the sick, and they shall recover.

Jesus states that if we cast out devils by the Holy Spirit, the kingdom of God is manifesting in our lives and spheres of influence.

Matthew 12:28 But if I cast out devils by the Spirit of God, then the kingdom of God is come unto you.

Though there are different ranks of demonic spirits, Jesus gave us authority over all the power of the enemy.

Luke 10:19 Behold, I give unto you power to tread on serpents and scorpions, and over all the power of the enemy: and nothing shall by any means hurt you.

Demons affect non-believers and believers:

Ephesians 2:2	Ephesians 6:11-12	Luke 13:10-17
1 Corinthians 5:5	1 Corinthians 10:20	2 Corinthians 11:3,4
Galatians 3:1	2 Peter 2:1-22	1 Timothy 4:1

Possession: If a person is an unbeliever and does not have the Holy Spirit living on the inside, a demon can possess their spirit, along with their body and soul (mind, will, and emotions). This is called demon possession. With possession, the demon will occupy, dominate, or control a person, place, or atmosphere. The man Legion in *Luke 8* and *Mark 5* was possessed by numerous devils.

Jesus called the devils out of him and sent them into pigs.

Demonization: If a person is a believer such that they have accepted Jesus Christ as their personal savior, they possess the Holy Spirit (*Acts 2:23*). A demon cannot possess their spirit but can control or influence their body and soul (mind, will, and emotions). This called demonization. King Saul in *I Samuel 16:15* had the spirit of God within him but was demonized and often troubled by an evil spirit. The bent-over woman in *Luke 13:10-17* was a believer but was demonized with a spirit of infirmity. Jesus laid hands on her and healed her in the synagogue. Other ways in which a demonization manifests is through oppression, depression, or negative influence.

- **Oppression** - To burden, restrain, weigh heavy upon, to put down; press down, subdue, or suppress an atmosphere or the soul, heart, body of a person.

- **Depression** – To make sad or gloomy; lower in spirits; deject, dispirit, to lower in force, vigor, activity, etc.; weaken, make dull, a person or atmosphere.

- **Negatively Influenced** – Cause confusion, discombobulation, double-mindedness, unexplainable weariness, tiredness or sluggardness, irritation, frustration, ungodly thoughts, thought racing within a person or atmosphere.

Legal Entry: Many people believe that the only way for demonic spirits to enter a person's life is through generational curses, sin, abandoning godly standards and practices. Generational issues and sin is one route but not an exclusive route.

Illegal Entry: Demons can enter one's life illegally through spiritual warfare, affliction, the calling of God on a person's life, and demonic association. *Psalm 34:19, Ephesians 6, 2 Corinthians 4 :7-11, 2 Corinthians 6:3-10, 2 Corinthians 12 :1-12*

Spiritual Warfare: Demonic forces wage war with the believers of God in effort to hinder them from:

- Living in the fullness of salvation that Jesus provided through his works and resurrection on the cross;
- Journeying in dominion in the earth, and over the world's and demonic kingdom;
- Believing, proclaiming and drawing souls to Jesus Christ;
- Advancing the kingdom.

Ephesians 6:12 For we wrestle not against flesh and blood, but against principalities, against powers, against the rulers of the darkness of this world, against spiritual wickedness in high places.

The Bible tells us that we will experience contention from the enemy.

Matthew 11:12 And from the days of John the Baptist until now the kingdom of heaven suffereth violence, and the violent take it by force.

Often these contentions are not legal, but about authority, territory, and dominion in the earth. The enemy wants to rule people and the earth and is roaming about to fulfill his demonic mandate in the earth.

John 10 :10 The thief cometh not, but for to steal, and to kill, and to destroy: I am come that they might have life, and that they might have it more abundantly.

1 Peter 5:8 Be sober, be vigilant; because your adversary the devil, as a roaring lion, walketh about, seeking whom he may devour.

Spiritual warfare is a heightened level of prayer and intercession that allows the believer to wage war, contend and overthrow these demonic forces. Just like military warfare, it can fight against attacks designed to bind their lives, families, ministries, business, lands, communities, and regions.

Demonic Association: Demonic association is when a person is in relationship, covenant, or engaging in social interaction with something or someone that is negatively or demonically influenced. Sometimes the person can be demonically oppressed just by being around certain people or in a particular place or area. The person may not be engaging in demonic or negative behavior, but because they are in the environment, the person is impacted.

Strongman: The Bible speaks about how a strong demon can enter and take over a person's house, referring to their body, soul (mind, will, emotions), or life (experiences, situations). Once that demon enters, it controls the house. The only way to be delivered is to spoil – break the powers of – the strongman.

Matthew 12:29 Or else how can one enter into a strong man's house, and spoil his goods, except he first bind the strong man? and then he will spoil his house.

Mark 3:27 No man can enter into a strong man's house, and spoil his goods, except he will first bind the strong man; and then he will spoil his house.

When the strongman is cast out, it roams about looking for another place or thing to inhabit. If it does not find a house, it returns to its previous occupant. If the person or thing is not filled with God, it reenters and invites other demons to occupy the home with it.

Matthew 12:43-45 When the unclean spirit is gone out of a man, he walketh through dry places, seeking rest, and findeth none. Then he saith, I will return into my house from whence I came out; and when he is come, he findeth it empty, swept, and garnished. Then goeth he, and taketh with himself seven other spirits more wicked than himself, and they enter in and dwell there: and the last state of that man is worse than the first. Even so shall it be also unto this wicked generation.

Counseling is essential after deliverance ministry to make sure people fill their homes with the presence of God, so that strongmen and other demons cannot reoccupy.

Understanding demonic rankings is essential to understanding social, regional, economic, political, idolatrous, or world forces that may be influencing a person.

Demonic Rankings: In *Ephesians 6:12* We are provided the rankings of demonic spirits:

- **Principalities** are satanic princes and territorial spirits ruling over a nation, city, region, and community for the purposes of establishing Satan's plan in people's lives and spheres.

- **Powers** are high ranking supernatural demons or demonic influences that cause evil and sin in the world.

- **Rulers of Darkness** are demonic forces that govern deception and manipulative hardships and catastrophes that are generally produced by witchcraft, manipulation of the weather and worldly systems; they operate in cultures and countries such that idolatry and sin reign in the earth.

- **Spiritual Wickedness in High Places** are evil plots and deceptions, and demonic attacks directed in and against the church and God's people for the purposes of hindering, contaminating and demolishing God's will in the earth.

- **Strongholds** are demonically possessed, demonically depressed, demonically gripping clutches, barriers, fortresses, walls, or entanglements that harass, influence, hinder and/or prevent a person from being free to walk in the full salvation for the Lord.
  2 Corinthians 10:3-5, Ephesians 4:22-23, Matthew 16:19, Mark 3:27

Engaging in witchcraft practices or being bewitched can also cause demonic forces and influences to infiltrate a person's life.

Witchcraft is the practice of magic, especially black magic; it is the utilization of spells and the invocation of demons to bind people, families, ministries, businesses, organizations, land, atmospheres, climates, regions, nations. Some people engage in witchcraft for entertainment, curiosity, or due to ignorance. Those that dedicate their lives to it use it to acquire personal success and advancement, power, fame, rank in spiritual realms, spheres, to obtain high ranking positions and platforms in the natural.

Unfortunately, popular culture is probably the most common channel where witchcraft is normalized and presented as acceptable, even to God's believers. Googling "witchcraft apps" brings over 57 million results in .048 seconds.

Diagram 10.1 Sources of Witchcraft

Practices of Witchcraft			
Sorcery	Magic	Witching	Wizardry
Black Magic	White Magic	Candle Magic	Spells
Hexes	Vexes	Hoodoo	Voodoo
Wicca	Mojo	Chants	Demonic Crossroads
Santeria	Yoruba Religion	Hinduism	New Age Practices
Horoscopes	Tarot Readings	Psychic Readings	Chain Letters
Familiar Spirits	Spirit Guides	High Priest/Priestess	Demonic Omens
Necromancy	Yoga	Shamanism	Fortune Telling
Hypnotism	Acupuncture	Psychic Readings	Superstition
Reincarnation	Ouija Boards	Fengshai	Good Luck Charms
Buddhism	Tibetan	Freemasonry	Eastern Stars
Sororities/Fraternities	Psychic Readings	Witchery	Pagan Holidays
Chakras	Kundalini	Astrology	Tarot Cards
Numerology	Dream Catchers	Palm Readings	Fortune Cookies
Popular Games			
Ouija Board	Which Witch	Dungeons and Dragons	Ouija Board
Harry Potter Scrabble	Chronicles of Narnia	Witchcraft Video Games	Harry Potter Scrabble
Popular Television Shows			
Charmed	Bewitched	American Horror Story	Charmed
Witches of East End	Buffy the Vampire Slayer	Supernatural	Witches of East End
Sabrina The Teenage Witch	True Blood	Once Upon A Time	

Source: Baker, 2018

There is no such thing as a good witch or good witchcraft. The Holy Spirit of God is the only good spirit. There is no such thing as a good demonic spirit. God does not desire us to use sorcery, spells, and demonic manipulation to influence anyone's life. Regardless to what is perceived good through the manifestations of witchcraft, its source is rooted in demonic spirits that have now become gateways and influencers in a person's life. Witchcraft activities open doors for other demonic spirits to operate. As bad things happen, other spirits come along and serve as perceived rescuers to keep people tied to the demonic entities. All of this is so the demonic spirits can keep people as a spiritual host and gateway to them operating in the earth realm, as spirits need bodies to effectively complete their demonic assignments in the earth.

Please understand that witches, warlocks, and demons do not have people's best interest at heart. Witchcraft is rooted in self-absorbed, self-idolatrous gain. The witches and demons are always getting something out of being privy to operate in a person's life; whether that is influence, possession, demonic rank, or drawing the life source out of people into themselves for more, energy, power, and strength.

Counselors must be discerning of bewitchment, witchcraft activities and practices, and have honest conversations with clients regarding the negative influence in their lives. Counselors must avoid utilizing witchcraft and new age practices in effort to deliver and heal people. No matter how beneficial this appears, if it is not in alignment with God and his word, it should not be implemented in the counseling process.

If the client is battling with some demonic forces and influences, the counselor should not perform deliverance ministry on the person by themselves. Simply discuss the option of receiving deliverance ministry and make an appointment with them to be seen by the deliverance ministry. As counselor, you are to attend the deliverance meeting if you are available; however, you are to play more of a supportive role rather than actually performing the deliverance yourself unless God leads you to do otherwise. This will help the client to experience God's spirit work through the deliverance team without you providing information you already know about the client. Also, a lot of embarrassing manifestations can occur during deliverance. When manifestation occur, demonic forces behavior or display their presence, personality trait, and character in a person, place, or thing. The counselor operating in more of a support role will strengthen the counseling relationship and help minimize any shame that could result from the process of deliverance.

Manifestations are dependent on how the demon responds to deliverance ministry.

Diagram 10.2 Demonic Exits

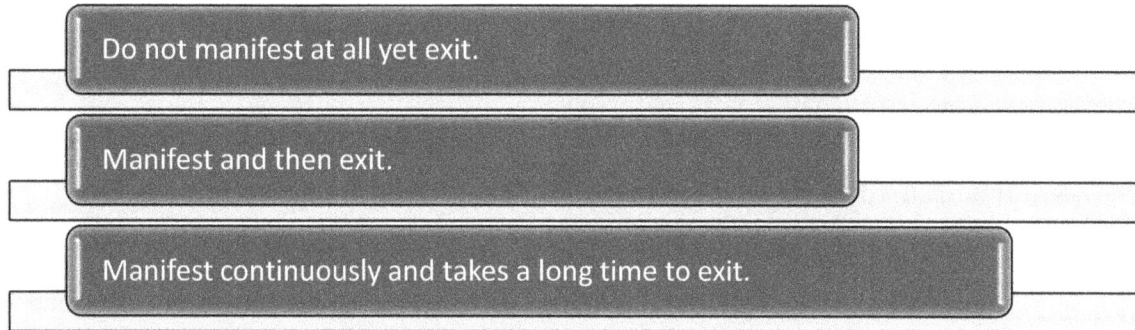

Do not manifest at all yet exit.

Manifest and then exit.

Manifest continuously and takes a long time to exit.

Source: Baker, 2018

Diagram 10.3 Demonic Manifestations

Crying/Whimpering	Belching	Expelling Gas	Regurgitation/Urination/Defecation
Coughing	Choking	Writhing/Body Movement/Tingling	Fighting
Cursing/Vulgar Language	Yelling/Screaming	Yawning/Sneezing/Breathing Out	Laughing
Unusual Eye Movement	Facial Contortions	Babbling/Barking/Growling/Singing	Throwing the Person
Fainting/Falling Out	Rolling/Shaking/Spinning	Physical Pain	Become Unresponsive

Source: Baker, 2018

Sometimes the client has never experienced demons manifesting so they are just as shocked as those working with them. Regardless of the manifestations, it is important to recognize that the person is present and aware of everything that is being said by those working with them and by what is occurring through them regarding the demonic forces. At times, deliverance workers can be cruel to demonic forces without recognizing and acknowledging that if there is yelling, pushing, pointing at, and shoving the demon, the client is also experiencing these things. Deliverance is about operating in the dominion and authority of God. There is no need to manifest crude behavior to get a demon to leave. The deliverance worker should know their authority, assert authority over demonic forces, while remaining considerate of the person who is being delivered. *Matthew 10:1, Matthew 10:8, Mark 3:15, Mark 6:7, Luke 9:1, Luke 10:19*

Counselors should make sure clients are not being mistreated and further traumatized, abused, and misused during deliverance ministry. Counselors should also explain the procedure of deliverance ministry so that clients will know what to expect from themselves, the deliverance ministers, and demonic forces. This will make it easier for them to embrace and cooperate with the deliverance ministry, and to posture themselves in a way where demons can easily expel.

Deliverance ministry often comes after counseling exposes personal, family, or generational strongholds. It will often come as a series of sessions so that there has been an instructional foundation laid for the client followed by the actual deliverance and follow-up that will include further instruction concerning maintaining deliverance and removing any personal habits or practices that might leave the client vulnerable to future demonic attacks. There can also be a fine line between the context of spiritual warfare and demonic oppression or possession. Woven within the maintenance plan is the concept of sanctification. As much as we have proposed that most pastors are not counselors, it is fair to suggest that most counselors are not pastors. It is the counselor's assignment to stay on-task with the client and not attempt to fill every spiritual need for the person. The boundaries and expectations should be reasonably set at the beginning of the interaction and with few expectations, those boundaries stay fixed. It is the counselor's responsibility to carefully and thoroughly understand when deliverance ministry is effective and equally, when it is not needed.

Let us wade a little further into the deeper waters of deliverance ministry. For many decades, churches operated with the best of intention but under the premise that "everything is a demon." Mental illness, learning disabilities, and physical handicaps were often approached as if demonic possession was the root of the issue. A fascinating study about child soldiers and other severely traumatic occurrences resulted in this hypothesis, "Explanations of mental health problems in terms of "possession" have taken many forms over the course of history, and it is a form of explanation that has meant that many who have been suffering debilitating and distressing psychological problems have been persecuted and physically abused rather than offered the support and treatment they need."[33]   Once again, it is important to reiterate the value of an accurate family history (as much as possible) and other influences in the client's life experience as there may be cultural or other social explanations for a behavior or pattern of thinking.

There is a section in the manual with sample forms. A thorough intake will accurately guide the counselor in understanding the process that will best serve the client.

No greater gift than to be delivered God's way!

---

[33]Graham C.L. Davey. (2014, December 31). 'Spirit possession' and mental health. Retrieved from *Psychology Today* website at https://www.psychologytoday.com/us/blog/why-we-worry/201412/spirit-possession-and-mental-health

Chapter 11

DELIVERANCE – THE CHILDREN'S BREAD

It is also important to rely on the Holy Spirit for the timing of including deliverance ministry. Deliverance is being freed from demonic oppression or possession. From a variety of entry points, a demonic spirit has gained legal access to an individual; therefore, deliverance breaks the legal hold and liberates the person to the presence of God. God wants his children to be free. Faith based counselors must have a commitment to deliverance. This is important because:

Diagram 11.0 Deliverance

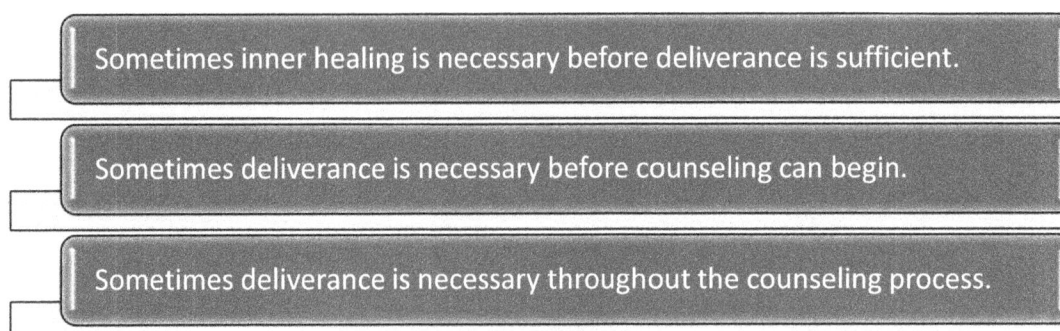

- Sometimes inner healing is necessary before deliverance is sufficient.
- Sometimes deliverance is necessary before counseling can begin.
- Sometimes deliverance is necessary throughout the counseling process.

Source: Baker, 2018

The statement "deliverance is the children's bread" means that deliverance is a blessing that God wants to give, not only to individuals but it can be received through family lines. Your client's commitment to counseling is an open door for their generations to be free of similar issues. The counselor's role is much like the old-fashioned telephone operator who was responsible for plugging wires into a switchboard to connect callers and calls. The counselor plugs the appropriate principles into the client's life that will benefit a particular wellness plan. Deliverance should be approached and presented as an essential need of a believer's daily life.

We see an example in *Matthew 15* where a woman was seeking deliverance for her daughter from a demonic spirit.

Matthew 15:21-28 *Then Jesus went thence, and departed into the coasts of Tyre and Sidon. And, behold, a woman of Canaan came out of the same coasts, and cried unto him, saying, Have mercy on me, O Lord, thou Son of David; my daughter is grievously vexed with a devil. But he answered her not a word. And his disciples came and besought him, saying, Send her away; for she crieth after us. But he answered and said, I am not sent but unto the lost sheep of the house of Israel. Then came she and worshipped him, saying, Lord, help me. But he answered and said, It is not meet to take the children's bread, and to cast it to dogs. And she said, Truth, Lord: yet the dogs eat of the crumbs which fall from their masters' table. Then Jesus answered and said unto her, O woman, great is thy faith: be it unto thee even as thou wilt. And her daughter was made whole from that very hour.*

In this passage of scripture, we see Jesus comparing deliverance to his "*children's bread.*" His children represent those who believed in and followed him, and though this woman sought his grace and mercy, she was not yet a believer. She argued with Jesus that even the crumbs from the table were a sufficient meal from the master's table. This woman understood the value of receiving deliverance from Jesus and was willing to liken herself into a dog to receive it.

Examining the story from Matthew 15 gives us other details about deliverance.

Matthew 15: 22-28 *From there Jesus took a trip to Tyre and Sidon. They had hardly arrived when a Canaanite woman came down from the hills and pleaded, "Mercy, Master, Son of David! My daughter is cruelly afflicted by an evil spirit." Jesus ignored her. The disciples came and complained, "Now she's bothering us. Would you please take care of her? She's driving us crazy." Jesus refused, telling them, "I've got my hands full dealing with the lost sheep of Israel." Then the woman came back to Jesus, went to her knees, and begged. "Master, help me." He said, "It's not right to take bread out of children's mouths and throw it to dogs." She was quick: "You're right, Master, but beggar dogs do get scraps from the master's table." Jesus gave in. "Oh, woman, your faith is something else. What you want is what you get!" Right then her daughter became well. (MSG)*

The mother is identified as a Canaanite woman which means she was not only not one of God's chosen people of Israel, but she was an outsider to Jesus' ministry. The woman is a role model for persistence and refusing to be discouraged. As a counselor, it is your role to hear the unspoken details of your client's story. What theme continues to come up in your sessions? What stories does your client want to repeat? Your responsibility as a Faith based counselor is to have a Christ-like character and be willing to hear issues that you did not foresee as critical to your client's wellness. Jesus affirmed the woman for having faith when faith was a concept she had never even attempted to grasp. Faith based counselors have to operate in positive affirmation and building up their clients with life-giving words. That is deliverance, and it is the children's bread!

The concept of the *"children's bread"* reveals that deliverance from oppressive and possessive spirits is something a believer should literally eat - feast upon. It should be like daily manna for believers, and we should seek and consume deliverance to be free of the vexing of the enemy. For this reason, deliverance should be considered a daily part of the believers' walk with God and should be as natural to us as eating bread - partaking of daily food.

Matthew 6:11 *Give us this day our daily bread.*

Deliverance is essential to inner healing as some healings cannot occur without the freedom of demonic oppression and possession. A counselor must be discerning and sensitive to the leading of the Holy Spirit of knowing when deliverance is needed to further advance the counseling process. This is essential because a demonic spirit can block, hold up and even control the process. If the counseling is not discerning, countless hours can be spent unnecessarily in striving to bring inner healing and wholeness to a person. We hear a lot that everything is not a demon, and this is indeed true. Sometimes curses are in operation that can cause a hinderance to both healing and wholeness. Educate yourself to the difference between curses and demonic presence. At the simplest level, many recurring issues in your client's life can be attributed to bad habits and lack of discipline or commitment. Those individuals will become repeat clients. When the client's profile is complete, watch for previous counseling history as a clue. Some individuals are addicted to the attention given by counseling and ministry. It is acceptable to recognize the pattern (if present) and choose not to become part of the client's enmeshment cycle.

Painful life experiences that require a series of discussions to heal the root cause of life challenges is the main culprit to which someone would need counseling. There are six primary ways a person can become demonized:

Diagram 11.1 Demonization

Sins of the ancestors
3, 4, or 10 generations

Conception in sin
Fornication, adultery, incest

Rejection in the womb
Attempted abortion, unwanted

Birth
Anethesia, trauma

Before the age of accountability
Sin against innocent child

Age of accountability
Sin by accountable adult

Source: Moody, n.d.[34]

There are many other gates that open a person to demonic influence. Some of those include word curses, vows, the occult, and many more. Networking with other faith-based counselors and members in these organization are both valuable tools for the counselor, particularly for a beginning counselor. Whatever gate has been opened in your client's life, remember that deliverance is the children's bread. We serve a God who wants us to know complete freedom.

---

[34] Gene Moody. (n.d.). Deliverance Manual 1.1. Retrieved from Deliverance Ministries website at www.gbmoody.com

Chapter 12

MAINTAINING DELIVERANCE AND WELLNESS

This chapter provides the counselor with strategies for equipping the client with tools to sustain their deliverance and continue in wellness. Because the counselor has a responsibility to align their counseling style to biblical principles, they are obligated to find scriptural support. Matthew records a conversation between Jesus and the disciples where Jesus not only instructs them to heal, cleanse, raise, and cast but reminds them that they have to also received from that level of ministry. Remember Jesus healing Peter's mother-in-law? Lazarus? Those who followed Jesus had first-hand experience of how his ministry changed their lives. As counselors, remember that you are equipped to bless others because Jesus first did a work in your life. Freely you have received so freely give hope to others that they can also be healed, cleanses, raised, and delivered.

Matthew 10:8 *Heal the sick, cleanse the lepers, raise the dead, cast out devils: freely ye have received, freely give.*

Spiritual Cleansing – The discipline of purging and purifying the mind, body, and soul of impurities that cause a plethora of negative influences. While there are multiple styles of including this practice, every faith-based counselor is equipped to support the client in spiritual cleansing. The New Testament language of origin is Greek. The word leprosy is *leora* which refers to scaliness (or the skin); an offensive and dangerous cutaneous (akin) disease that will eventually pervade the entire body. Cleanse is *katharizo* which means to make clean or in a moral sense, to free from defilement and faults, to purify from wickedness, or to consecrate.

Leprosy is an infectious disease that causes disfiguring sores, nerve damage, and progressive debilitation. In the Bible, lepers were outcasts because of its highly contagious nature. It is intriguing that leprosy begins on the surface (skin) and then works its way to the internal organs, eventually resulting in death. Many of the issues that will bring clients to your counseling service may, on the surface, seem no more than an irritant. It is your responsibility to understand the potential devastation that issues that seem to be on the surface have toward your client's destiny.

Lepers are isolated, in part, because of how others react to them. The way the disease physically alters a person, the fear others had about the disfigurement, and fear of contracting leprosy were factors in the isolation. Judaism includes laws to mandate separation.

Leviticus 13:45-46 And the leper in whom the plague is, his clothes shall be rent, and his head bare, and he shall put a covering upon his upper lip, and shall cry, Unclean, unclean. All the days wherein the plague shall be in him he shall be defiled; he is unclean: he shall dwell alone; without the camp shall his habitation be.

Numbers 5:1-3 And the LORD spake unto Moses, saying, Command the children of Israel, that they put out of the camp every leper, and every one that hath an issue, and whosoever is defiled by the dead: Both male and female shall ye put out, without the camp shall ye put them; that they defile not their camps, in the midst whereof I dwell.

God gave Moses clear instructions about lepers and the necessity of separating them from the community.

Let's take a moment to explore the comparison between leprosy and sin:

- Sin causes us to be unclean, impure, unhealthy.
- Our sin contaminates and influences others; it pollutes society and the world at large.
- We think people cannot see our sins, but sins can be seen in our presentation, disposition, personality, clothing, conversation, perceptions, communication, interactions, relationships, how we handle situations, and how we live our lives (*Proverbs 4:23*).
- Sin causes a separation from God's presence and his plan for our lives.
- Sin defames God and tarnishes his reputation, especially when we are living a life of sin while contending that we serve God.

When considering the concept of cleansing the lepers or shall we say, cleansing sins, it is important to cleanse the infection and cleanse what is causing the infection.

Matthew 8:1-4 When he was come down from the mountain, great multitudes followed him. And, behold, there came a leper and worshipped him, saying, Lord, if thou wilt, thou canst make me clean. And Jesus put forth his hand, and touched him, saying, I will; be thou clean.

And immediately his leprosy was cleansed. And Jesus saith unto him, See thou tell no man; but go thy way, shew thyself to the priest, and offer the gift that Moses commanded, for a testimony unto them.

For many individuals, willpower is their primary strength used to stop sinning. When using will power the person is operating through self-control. The person is striving to control their impulses and choices. But if one cannot keep themselves from engaging in the sin, how can he or she stop themselves from never doing it again? A person needs more will power. God has provided us with Holy Ghost power!

A positive attribute of leprosy is its appreciation for pain.

> "References to leprosy have a different emphasis in the New Testament. They stress God's desire to heal. Jesus freely touched people with leprosy. While people with leprosy traditionally suffered banishment from family and neighbors, Jesus broke from the tradition. He treated lepers with compassion, touching and healing them.
>
> Although we can't know all the reasons that God allows disease into our lives, biblical leprosy is a powerful symbol reminding us of sin's spread and its horrible consequences. Like leprosy, sin starts out small but can then spread, leading to other sins and causing great damage to our relationship with God and others."[35]

Ephesians 3:16 *He would grant you, according to the riches of His glory, to be strengthened with power through His Spirit in the inner man.*

God's Holy Ghost power empowers a person to grow strong, so he or she can withstand against sins and worldliness. The Holy Spirit instills a sensitivity to negativity.

May He grant you out of the rich treasury of His glory to be strengthened and reinforced with mighty power in the inner man by the [Holy] Spirit [Himself indwelling your innermost being and personality]. (AMP)

---

[35] Allen L. Gillen. (2007, June 10). Biblical leprosy: Casting light on the disease that shuns. Retrieved from *Answers in Genesis* website at https://answersingenesis.org/biology/disease/biblical-leprosy-shedding-light-on-the-disease-that-shuns/

Even if the person uses their own will to stop sinning, they are still unclean if they do not allow God's Holy Ghost power to cleanse them from sin.

In *Matthew 8:1-4*, Jesus laid hands on the lepers and they were made clean. This is miraculously awesome and is a form of deliverance and healing that many have experienced when encountering Jesus. Even with this miraculous cleansing, the leper still had to make a lifestyle change to remain clean.

- He could not return to the leper camp as he would risk being contaminated again.
- If his leprosy was a sin issue, then he had to reframe from that sin to maintain his deliverance and healing.
- Even as the leper's community had changed, his relationships and interactions had to be changed.

The leper's identity and lifestyle had to change to maintain his healing. Such a change requires a processing to wholeness. This requires relationship with God beyond just the initial encounter of deliverance and healing. A person must journey with him in a lifestyle change, learn his plan for maintaining healing, and walk that plan out in as a daily lifestyle.

This brings us to this scripture:

Isaiah 64:6 But we are all as an unclean thing, and all our righteousnesses are as filthy rags; and we all do fade as a leaf; and our iniquities, like the wind, have taken us away.

Unclean is *tame* in Hebrew and means:
1. to be unclean, become unclean, become impure, regard as unclean
2. to be or become unclean, to defile oneself, be defiled
   a. sexually
   b. religiously
   c. ceremonially
   d. by idolatry
3. to profane (God's name)

Filth is *ed* in Hebrew and means:
1. to set a period, the menstrual flux, soiling, filthy
2. menstruation
   a. a filthy rag, stained garment

b. figuratively of best deeds of guilty people

For we have all become like one who is unclean [ceremonially, like a leper], and all our righteousness (our best deeds of rightness and justice) is like filthy rags or a polluted garment; we all fade like a leaf, and our iniquities, like the wind, take us away [far from God's favor, hurrying us toward destruction]. (AMP)

Even the righteousness of a person needs cleaning in God's eyes. Just like we cleanse our physical body, it is necessary to cleanse the inner person. When we cleanse our physical bodies, we are detailed in making sure we clean every part of our bodies. We even purchase the correct hygienic products to ensure that we remain clean. When we find a product that does not work, we move onto to different products until we find out what work best. We need this same standard for our spiritual lives. And because our righteousness is filthy, we should be cleaning our soul, hearts, minds daily just like we do our physical bodies. For even when we think we are clean, to God there are still areas that need cleansing.

Let's explore the Holy Spirit equipping you with deliver and healing techniques sufficient for cleansing the life of those you will counsel.

Soaking Prayer & Cleansing – Sometimes in order for an item to get cleaned, it has to be soaked for a period of time. Depending on the composite of the stain and the item that is stained, an item may require lengthy soaking and continuous soaking and purifying before the stain is removed. This is the same for our body, souls, minds, will, identity, personality, emotions, etc. Soaking prayer and cleansing denote a time of intimate prayer, meditate, resting, and communing with the Lord. It is a focused time of being with the Lord and allowing him to build relationship or to cleanse stubborn and difficult areas of a person's life. While the terminology may be new for many, the concept is likely something that is already a spiritual practice. As you learn the tools and strategies below, you will learn that you can teach clients to use some of these tools such as the blood of Jesus, the Glory of God, fire of the Holy Spirit, word of God, etc., during their intimate time of soaking, to deliver, heal, purge, and cleanse themselves of ungodly or unhealthy attributes, infestations, manifestations, and strongholds.

- **Psalm 4: 4** *Meditate within your heart on your bed, and be still.*
- **Psalm 16:11** *Thou wilt shew me the path of life: in thy presence [is] fulness of joy; at thy right hand [there are] pleasures for evermore.*
- **Psalm 27:8** *My heart has heard you say, "Come and talk with me." And my heart responds, "LORD, I am coming.*
- **Psalm 51:7** *Purge me with hyssop, and I shall be clean: wash me, and I shall be whiter than snow.*
- **Psalm 51:7** *Soak me in your laundry and I'll come out clean, scrub me and I'll have a snow-white life. (MSG)*
- **Psalm 145:18** *The LORD [is] nigh unto all them that call upon him, to all that call upon him in truth.*
- **Jeremiah 29:13** *And ye shall seek me, and find [me], when ye shall search for me with all your heart.*
- **Luke 11:9** *And so I tell you, keep on asking, and you will receive what you ask for. Keep on seeking, and you will find. Keep on knocking, and the door will be opened to you.*
- **Matthew 11:28-30** *Come to Me, all you who labor and are heavy laden, and I will give you rest. Take My yoke upon you and learn from Me, for I am gentle and lowly in heart, and you will find rest for your souls. For My yoke is easy and My burden is light.*

Infilling of the Holy Spirit (***Acts 1-2, Acts 13:22*** *And the disciples were continually filled with joy and with the Holy Spirit*). All of us receive the Holy Spirit upon us when we accept Jesus as our personal savior. When I speak of infilling, I am referencing speaking in tongues where God's voice and power speaks through us and empowers us as believers. When God's power flows through us, his voice equips us with greater heavenly sound and power to annihilate the enemy. There are some things the enemy will not respond to in our voice, but he will if we speak in our heavenly prayer language of tongues. If a person does not speak in tongues, witness to them about the infilling of the Holy Spirit. Additionally, encourage them to begin to study the purpose of doing so, while asking the Holy Spirit to manifest his voice through them. If the person does speak in tongues, encourage them to pray in their prayer language for a period of time each day. I encourage people to speak in tongues while in the shower or driving to work. These are perfect times, because the person is generally alone, and can focus. Let the person know that they do not

have to know what they are saying or even have a prayer focus. The more they speak in tongues and just focus on being empowered in God, the more they will know what they are saying and praying, and the more the Holy Spirit will guide them in knowing what to pray for, against, and how to use their prayer language to cleanse themselves of the filth of the enemy. (*John 16:13 Howbeit when he, the Spirit of truth, is come, he will guide you into all truth: for he shall not speak of himself; but whatsoever he shall hear, that shall he speak: and he will shew you things to come).*

Spirit of Lord – Empowers the believer with the wisdom, revelation, knowledge, counsel, understanding, and guidance needed to handle one's daily affairs and journey in a destiny lifestyle with the Lord. (*Isaiah 11:2 And the spirit of the LORD shall rest upon him, the spirit of wisdom and understanding, the spirit of counsel and might, the spirit of knowledge and of the fear of the LORD).* Encourage clients to study the attributes of the spirit of the Lord, seek God for the importance of these attributes as it relates to their deliverance and healing, and declare continually that they are consumed in the spirit of wisdom, revelation, understanding, etc. until they become part of their identity. Refuse to accept and cleanse all confusion, ignorance, foolery, witchcraft, bewitchment, mind control, mind blinding/binding, lack of knowing, lack of guidance, etc. Encourage them to assert their right to have the spirit of the Lord teach them all things and to practice living by his leading. (*John 14:26 But the Comforter, which is the Holy Ghost, whom the Father will send in my name, he shall teach you all things, and bring all things to your remembrance, whatsoever I have said unto you).*

Fruit of God – Fills, restores, produces, reproduces (*Galatians 5:22-23 But the fruit of the Spirit is love, joy, peace, long suffering, gentleness, goodness, faith, Meekness, temperance: against such there is no law).* Teach clients to cleanse themselves of all defiled, demonic, and unhealthy fruit that does not represent the character and nature of God, while filling themselves up with spiritual fruit that represents his character and nature.

Blood of Jesus – Purges, purifies, redeems, reconciles, sanctifies, sanitizes, forgives, heals, and frees a person from death (*Ephesians 1:7 whom we have redemption through his blood, the forgiveness of sins, according to the riches of his grace).* We hear a lot about pleading the blood, but the blood is an application. Jesus applied his blood to our sins and sicknesses, and through his perfected blood, we were redeemed, and made whole. Believers can apply the blood of Jesus to their soul, heart, mind, thoughts, personality, character, identity, righteousness, body, and command redemption, life, and wholeness to come. Believers can soak themselves in the blood of Jesus until they see breakthrough in these areas, or as a daily application of being cleansed and free in the redeeming blood power of Jesus.

Binding, Loosing & Casting Out Devils – Delivers the person from demons, and strongholds (***Matthew 16:19*** *And I will give unto thee the keys of the kingdom of heaven: and whatsoever thou shalt bind on earth shall be bound in heaven: and whatsoever thou shalt loose on earth shall be loosed in heaven*). Bind means "*to knit, chain, tie, and to fasten, put under subjection, to forbid, prohibit, declare to be illicit.*" Loose means to "*loosen, cast off, break (up), destroy, dissolve, (un-)loose, melt, put off, to declare unlawful, to overthrow.*" Believers possess the power to bind demons and demonic kingdoms and forbid them to remain inside of them and others. Believers can bind themselves, others, their ministry, their atmosphere, the land and region to God and his kingdom. Believers can also loose themselves from demonic powers, and forbid and overthrow their working in their lives, lives of others, their ministry, the atmosphere, the land, and region.

Casting Out Devils – Deliverance ministry is a part of our right and health as believers of Jesus Christ. It is the believer's daily manna and authority to be free of demons and their demonic stronghold. Jesus has given us power over all the power of the enemy. *Cast out* means to "*eject with violence, drive (out), expel, leave, pluck (pull, take, thrust) out, put forth (out), send away.*" Use the chapter on deliverance ministry to teach clients to cast the devil out of their lives and to be free of demonic fruit, filth, oppression, depression, and possession.

- ***Matthew 10:8*** *Heal the sick, cleanse the lepers, raise the dead, cast out devils: freely ye have received, freely give.*
- ***Luke 10:19*** *Behold, I give unto you power to tread on serpents and scorpions, and over all the power of the enemy: and nothing shall by any means hurt you.*
- ***Luke 11:20*** *But if I with the finger of God cast out devils, no doubt the kingdom of God is come upon you.*

It is important to assert power and authority over the enemy because he is always trying to claim rights to the believer and what belongs to us. The devil is not passive and is always seeking to possess, devour, and destroy what is ours. Counselors must teach clients to be offensive and aggressive in letting the devil know that he cannot have their lives, families, ministries, atmosphere, land, regions, nations.

Breaking Curses – A curse is a solemn utterance intended to invoke a supernatural power to hinder blessings, inflict harm, judgment, or punishment, on a person, group of people, generational line, place, situation, or thing. Curses can enter a person's life:

- **Word Curses** – Words carry power. We can curse ourselves by what we speak and others can speak words that inflict curses in our lives.

    - *Proverbs 12:18 The words of the reckless pierce like swords, but the tongue of the wise brings healing. (NIV)*
    - *Proverbs 13:3 Be careful what you say and protect your life. A careless talker destroys himself. (GNT)*
    - *Proverbs 18:21 NIV The tongue has the power of life and death, and those who love it will eat its fruit. (NIV)*
    - *James 3:10 Out of the same mouth proceedeth blessing and cursing. My brethren, these things ought not so to be.*

- **Generational Curses** – Curses are passed down through the family line from one generation to the next, due to sin, transgressions, ungodly or unhealthy behavioral cycles, patterns, and customs. When parents and older family members do not reject or conquer these issues, the children and other family members become susceptible to them or have a propensity for them. These curses must be verbally broken and triumphed over, for the fullness of salvation to operate in a person's life and in their family line.

    - *Exodus 34:7 - Keeping mercy for thousands, forgiving iniquity and transgression and sin, and that will by no means clear [the guilty]; visiting the iniquity of the fathers upon the children, and upon the children's children, unto the third and to the fourth [generation].*

- *Numbers 14:18* - *The LORD [is] longsuffering, and of great mercy, forgiving iniquity and transgression, and by no means clearing [the guilty], visiting the iniquity of the fathers upon the children unto the third and fourth [generation].*
- *Deuteronomy 5:9* - *Thou shalt not bow down thyself unto them, nor serve them: for I the LORD thy God [am] a jealous God, visiting the iniquity of the fathers upon the children unto the third and fourth [generation] of them that hate me.*

- **Witchcraft/Occult Curses** – Curses are released by witches, warlocks, and those involved in witchcraft and/or occult practices. Such people engage in witchcraft, satanism, new age religions, magic, psychic powers, occult activities, while releasing curses via rituals, spells, hexes, incantations, jinxes, sorcery, bewitchment, telepathy, demonic prayers, love potions, and other demonic activities. They may also use demonic spirits to aide them in carrying out their curses or demonic assignments.

  - *Deuteronomy 18:10-11* *Let no one be found among you who sacrifices their son or daughter in the fire, who practices divination or sorcery, interprets omens, engages in witchcraft, or casts spells, or who is a medium or spiritist or who consults the dead.*
  - *Numbers 22-24* *Balaam refused to speak what God did not speak and would not curse the Israelites, even though King Balak of Moab offered him money. People will actually higher those who operate in witchcraft and occult practices to curse others.*
  - *Ephesians 5:16* *Above all, taking the shield of faith, wherewith ye shall be able to quench all the fiery darts of the wicked.*

Provide personal, generational, regional, cultural freedom from negative words spoken over the person's life, sent to them, or curses implemented due to personal and generational sins, and occult practice (*Galatians 3:13* *Christ hath redeemed us from the curse of the law, being made a curse for us: for it is written, Cursed is every one that hangeth on a tree*). Teach clients how to:

- Identify curses and where they are originating from.
- Repent for personal, generational, regional, and cultural strongholds.
- Break curses and loose the blood of Jesus to cleanse the curse and all filth associated with it.
- Bind and cast out any spirits operating behind the curse.
- Declare their freedom through Jesus Christ (*2Corinthians 3:17* *Now the Lord is that Spirit: and where the Spirit of the Lord is, there is liberty*).

o   Fill themselves back up with the fruit, promises, prophecies and blessings of God.

The most powerful book I ever read and worked through regarding breaking curses was, "Repentance Cleansing your Generational Bloodline," Natasha Grbich. I highly recommend to you as a counselor and to your clients.

Word of God – Discerns, divides what is of God and what is not of God, cuts out, does surgery, instills God's truth, will, and plan (*Hebrews 4:12 For the word of God is quick, and powerful, and sharper than any two-edged sword, piercing even to the dividing asunder of soul and spirit, and of the joints and marrow, and is a discerner of the thoughts and intents of the heart*). Teach clients to:

o   Use the word of God to divide what is of God in their lives from what is not of him.
o   Use the word of God to extract what is not of God from their soul, heart, mind, body, and spirit.
o   Use the word of God to overthrow every lie that the enemy uses to keep them bound to demons.
o   Use the word of God to cut out any word, character trait, hurt, pain, and flaw that keeps them bound to demons.
o   Spend time studying, meditating on, and soaking themselves in the word of God. Allow God's word to go inside of their (heart, mind, soul, identity), and cleanse everything that is contrary to the word of God for their lives.
o   Study and meditate on God's word and be refilled in his truth concerning their identity, purpose, destiny, and who he is as daddy God, Lord and savior, ruler and king of their lives.

Fire of God – Burns out, fuses, refines, purges, purifies, consumes, and tests (*Malachi 3:2-3 But who may abide the day of his coming? and who shall stand when he appeareth? for he is like a refiner's fire, and like fullers' soap: And he shall sit as a refiner and purifier of silver: and he shall purify the sons of Levi, and purge them as gold and silver, that they may offer unto the Lord an offering in righteousness*). Sometimes when demons are cast out, their deposits, residue, and attributes are still lodged in the person. The fire of God can be used purge and burn out these demonic deposits. A person can also be purified and refined with the fire of God. Demons hate the fire of God and the blood of Jesus. Fire is judgment to demons. The fire of God can be used to torment demons and send them fleeing from a person's life, blood line, ministry, land, atmosphere, and region. (***Revelations 20:10*** *And the devil that deceived them was cast into the lake of fire and brimstone, where the beast and the false prophet are, and shall be tormented day and night for ever and ever*).

Fullers' Soap – Entails a washing by trampling, treading, stamping, scrubbing. It is likened to trampling or scrubbing something hard until it is clean. (***Malachi 3:2-3*** *But who may abide the day of his coming? and who shall stand when he appeareth? for he is like a refiner's fire, and like fullers' soap: And he shall sit as a refiner and purifier of silver: and he shall purify the sons of Levi, and purge them as gold and silver, that they may offer unto the Lord an offering in righteousness*). When there are things in a person that require deep cleansing, the fuller soap of God can be used to scrub and trample them out.

Power of God – Delivers, overthrows demonic powers and governments, releases the virtue and government of God, releases miracles, signs, and wonders (***Acts 1:8*** *But ye shall receive power, after that the Holy Ghost is come upon you: and ye shall be witnesses unto me both in Jerusalem, and in all Judaea, and in Samaria, and unto the uttermost part of the earth*). Teach clients to use the power of God to annihilate the powers of the enemy (***Luke 10:19*** *Behold, I give unto you power to tread on serpents and scorpions, and over all the power of the enemy: and nothing shall by any means hurt you*). Encourage clients to study the power of God so they will know their authority and ability to recreate and create body parts, birth forth things that they need, bring excellency to their heart, mind and soul, release virtue into their lives, and annihilate the power of the enemy, such that it brings transforming deliverance and healing.

Glory of God – Much of what the believer needs and desires from God is inside his glory. The Glory refreshes, fills, refills, fulfills, creates, recreates, revives, renews, makes whole, establishes the presence of God, draws us into intimacy and relationship with God, while instilling God's character, nature, truth, knowledge, revelation, and pleasures forevermore (***Psalm 16:11*** *Thou wilt shew me the path of life: in thy presence is fulness of joy; at thy right hand there are pleasures for evermore*). Every believer should be living inside the presence of God. This is where the believer's direction of life is revealed. As the believer walk in alignment with God, continual fulness of joy and pleasures of God should be evident in their lives. If the believer is living in the glory of God, they should be living a fulfilled life no matter what trials and tribulations may occur. Teach your clients to seek God for revelation on how to build a relationship with him where they abide in his presence. Teach them how to engage his presence to be refreshed, fulfilled, and filled and encourage them to continually cultivate their lives and atmospheres in his presence so they can be true glory carriers of the Lord (*John 15:4 Abide in me, and I in you. As the branch cannot bear fruit of itself, except it abide in the vine; no more can ye, except ye abide in me*).

Rivers of Living Water – Stirs, replenishes, breeds life, vitality, beauty, youthfulness, creativity, strength, efficiency, and releases what is inside of them to whatever you are sending it to (*John. 7:38 He that believeth on me, as the scripture hath said, out of his belly shall flow rivers of living water*). It is important to encourage clients to spend time cleansing and stir the rivers that are inside of them, such that their inner wells so that they are encouraged and incite pure waters as whatever is in them will be released into the things God has granted to their hands.

Pluck Out – Roots out, pulls down, destroys, and throws down (*Jeremiah 1:10 See, I have this day set thee over the nations and over the kingdoms, to root out, and to pull down, and to destroy, and to throw down, to build, and to plant*). Some demonic spirits and ungodly attributes are imbedded in a person's foundation and need to be uprooted. They can be a root that has been there for years or can be rooted generationally, so keep that in mind. Teach clients to:

- o Pluck out demons.
- o Command demons and strongholds that are lodged deep within to come up out of the by the root.
- o Cut the root in pieces then pull them out.

A person may have to pull down an ideation or attribute, such as pulling down strongholds, imaginations, and prideful spirits that have exalted themselves above God and have exalted themselves as idols in their lives.

Please let clients know that they cannot be nice to demons and or compromise with wickedness. Our mission as believers has to be to destroy the forces of darkness just like they want to destroy us. The devil understands he is in a fight and will do whatever necessary to gain entry and control to a believer's life. Believers must be warriors and be willing to pluck up, root out, toss, trample, etc., to assert authority over demons and their powers. The process of plucking up may require a constant contending to uproot demons and their contaminations out of the believer's life.

Hammer Down – Walls, barricades, barriers, hindrances, and blockages, have to be hammered down (***Jeremiah 23:29*** *Is not my word like as a fire? saith the LORD; and like a hammer that breaketh the rock in pieces?*) Sometimes these fortifications are made by the believer, sometimes the words and ideologies of others cause these walls and barriers, and sometimes they are made by the devil. Either way they need to come down. Teach clients to use the hammer of God to break down walls and barriers that have been erected to hinder their breakthrough.

Run Through Troops – Blast through troops that keep you bound or that may be blocking your breakthrough (***Psalm 18:30*** *For by thee I have run through a troop; and by my God have I leaped over a wall*). If you read ***Psalm 18:30-51***, you will determine that it is the power of God that enables you to do this. When you find yourself in tough life situations, ganged up on by demons or you come up against a stronghold that does not want to budge in your life, ask God to empower you to run through troops. Then as you pray and deal with these situations in your natural life, use your faith, power and authority to blast through these bondages.

Resist the Devil – Stand against, oppose, withstand, set against the devil and all that concerns him (***James 4:7*** *Submit yourselves therefore to God. Resist the devil, and he will flee from you*). Before demons and filth will leave the believer, they must fall out of agreement with it. The devil and his filth cannot stay if there is nothing in the believer wanting or aiding him to remain. Teach your clients to break every covenant with it, divorce it, hate it, dread it being in you, and resist it from being a part of their lives. Teach them to spend time breaking covenants with the devil, sin, pleasures of sin, mindsets, errors, and anything that keeps them in relationship with the enemy and his filthiness.

Breaking Soulties – Soulties can be godly or ungodly in nature. In the same way generational curses are passed down, soulties are transferred from one person to the other person and vice versa. Soulties can be formed through close friendships and interactions, covenants, vows, commitments, promises, physical intimacy, etc. A person can also have a soultie by having an unhealthy attachment to something or someone that has taken the place of God in their lives or that has become an addiction in their lives. A person's soul, heart, mind, and body can be intertwined, bound, knitted, or in covenant with that person, place, or thing. In addition, a person can exchange parts of themselves with the person they are in a soultie with. Parts of their personality, soul, heart, thoughts, mindsets, character, nature, and other deposits, infuse them and begin to influence and live in the person and vice versa. Also, whomever they have had relationship with and have not cleansed themselves of, is being passed on to those two people.

Visualization of a Knot

A soul tie is a knotting together. Consider the visualization. A piece of rope has a beginning and an ending that are each easy to identify. A person is free to choose which end is which because it won't matter UNTIL the person decides to put the piece of rope to work.

Now look at it again.

Once the rope has been knotted, it is not a simple task to identify the beginning and the ending.

Did you know that rope is made by taking multiple fibers called slivers and twisting those into strands until there is a continuous and unified piece? Rope has something called tensile strength which is the maximum capacity to carry weight and stretch. Adding a knot will increase the strength of the bond by at least fifty percent. Have you ever had a knot in a shoestring? Have you ever used the point of something to get into the knot to loosen it? In a soul tie, it often takes something sharp to get in between the knot and loosen.

- *Hebrews 4:12 For the word of God is quick, and powerful, and sharper than any twoedged sword, piercing even to the dividing asunder of soul and spirit, and of the joints and marrow, and is a discerner of the thoughts and intents of the heart.*

What does all this have to do with helping a client understand a soul tie?

A person is free of knots until they are tied to someone. Suddenly what was simple and clear is complex and difficult and its presence strengthens a bond that can be empowering and challenging. That is why many people who know they are in a soul tie and admittedly want out of the soul tie still have such a struggle to be free. With soul ties, the more entangled the soul tie becomes, the more difficult it becomes to tell where one person starts and the other ends and vice versa.

Soul ties are often provoked by external circumstances that feel uncontrollable by those effected, so the distorted attempt to address the issue is the cause of the knotting and entangling. The more knotting occurs, the less room there is for anyone else to be involved. The cycle continues to deepen and is dependent on isolating those in the soul tie to believe that the solution can only happen if the other person is involved. That is why women who are victimized by domestic violence continue to return to, "Nobody will love you like I love you." It is what keeps believers in unhealthy church settings with the voice of leadership saying, "But God assigned you to this ministry." It becomes a covenant of soulish perversion. If you leave a rope knotted for a lengthy period of time, the friction of the rope in the knot will discolor the rope and cause fraying of the material. The longer a person stays in a soul tie, the more alteration takes place within the original nature of the person(s) which is why there is a great need for deliverance, counseling, and submission to the healing process

Godly Soulties – Soulties can be godly and healthy. They possess the fruit and nature of God and empower a person's life, ministry, purpose, and destiny. A healthy soultie has God's character, nature, fruit, will, and plan for their lives, a person can be tied to good things, but they may not necessarily be God's design.

- ***1Samuel 18:1*** *And it came to pass, when he had made an end of speaking unto Saul, that the soul of Jonathan was knit with the soul of David, and Jonathan loved him as his own soul.*

<u>*Knit* is *qâšar* in Hebrew and means:</u>
1. to tie, physically (gird, confine, compact) or mentally (in love, league)
2. bind (up), (make a) conspire (-acy, -ator), join together, knit, stronger
3. work (treason). to bind, tie, bind together, league together, conspire
4. to bind, confine, to league together, conspire
    a. to be bound, be bound up
    b. to bind onto, bind fast to, bind, tie to, bind to oneself
    c. robust, vigorous (participle), to conspire

When souls are knitted, there is an actual tying together that occurs. This knitting girds like a belt and is robust and vigorous in nature. The soul tie is conspiring to be strong where people are locked together such that they love and uphold one another as one soul. SHIFT!

- ***Ecclesiastes 4:9-12*** *Two are better than one, because they have a good [more satisfying] reward for their labor; For if they fall, the one will lift up his fellow. But woe to him who is alone when he falls and has not another to lift him up! Again, if two lie down together, then they have warmth; but how can one be warm alone? And though a man might prevail against him who is alone, two will withstand him. A threefold cord is not quickly broken. (AMP)*

Threefold cord is equated to a covenant agreement between parties. The concept that a threefold cord is not quickly broken confirms that there is a binding together that can occur between two or more people or between two people and God that can be so strong that it is not easy to break. It is a unifying that is so strong, it can literally hold the weight of a person up within the relationship. The threefold cord asserts that each person can be sustained, empowered, built up, and held up by the other person and by God within the relationship; that even in the weakness of one person, the cord can pull that person up just by the mere vigorous power of the binding cord that connects their souls, hearts, spirits, and lives together.

The word *fall* is *nasal* in Hebrew and means:
1. to fall, lie, be cast down, fail, to fall (of violent death)
2. to fall prostrate, prostrate oneself before, to fall upon, attack, desert
3. fall away to, go away to, fall into the hand of, to fall short, fail, fall out
4. turn out, result, to settle, waste away, be offered, be inferior to, to lie, lie prostrate

As we consider the power of a knitted cord between two or more people, it will take more than just the separation of the relationship to break it.

The word *together* in Hebrew is *šâkab* and means:
1. a primitive root - to lie down (for rest, sexual connection, decease or any other purpose)
2. at all, cast down, ((lover-)) lay (self) (down)
3. (make to) lie (down, down to sleep, still with), lodge, ravish, take rest, sleep, stay

Heat in Hebrew is *ḥâmam* and means:
1. a primitive root - to be hot (literally or figuratively)
2. enflame self, get (have) heat, be (wax) hot, (be, wax) warm (self, at)
3. to become aroused, inflame oneself with, passioned, to be or grow warm

Prevails in Hebrew is *taqap* and means, *"to prevail over or against, overcome, overpower."* Within our physical bodies are mechanisms in our metabolism and hormone levels that produce natural heat as two people lie together to keep warm. This same heat is possible as our souls are knitted in friendship and in companionship. Because friendships and companionships are knitted through our hearts, souls, emotions, and spirits, the knitting is even more infused as these areas of respond to the laws of the spirit and the soulish realm and the principles of God that he established in the earth when he created it. Heat automatically leaves when our physical bodies depart, but the heat remains when our hearts, souls, emotions, and spirits are knitted. Your body walks away, but the other parts of you is still knitted by the prevailing power of the soul tie that was form in the soulish and spiritual realm.

- *Matthew 18:19 Again I say unto you, That if two of you shall agree on earth as touching any thing that they shall ask, it shall be done for them of my Father which is in heaven.*

- ✓ When we touch, we are saying we are giving an account regarding that person, place, or thing.
- ✓ We are giving our approval that we want the knitting or manifestation that is taking place.
- ✓ We are giving our agreement that we want covenant or prevailing with that person, place, or thing.

Marriage Soulties – When people get married, their lives are knitted in covenant with their spouse and they become one with one another. They are no longer individuals, but the two become one when married.

- ***Genesis 2:24*** *Therefore shall a man leave his father and his mother, and shall cleave unto his wife: and they shall be one flesh.*

- ***Matthew 19:5*** *And said, For this cause shall a man leave father and mother, and shall cleave to his wife: and they twain shall be one flesh?*

Cleave is *dâbaq* Hebrew and means:
1. a primitive root; properly, to impinge, i.e. cling or adhere
2. figuratively, to catch by pursuit
3. abide fast, cleave (fast together), follow close (hard after)
4. be joined (together), keep (fast), overtake, pursue hard, stick, take

Cleave is *proskollaō* in Greek and means:
1. to glue to, i.e. (figuratively) to adhere
2. cleave, join (self), cleave oneself to, stick to

The cleaving of godly covenant marriage bonds a couple together like glue. When two people are not married but operate as married or engage in marital relations, their words, life posture, and soul, is leaving and cleaving. This is an illegal leaving and cleaving, but everything about their life is become one soul with that one another, and the sexual relations makes the cleaving even stronger.

Ungodly Soulties – An ungodly soultie is any knitting of a person with a person, place, or thing that is not of God or that is not God's will and plan for their lives. God will not have a person bond to sin, idolatry, unhealthiness, unfruitfulness, or bondage. He will not have a person engage or remain in a relationship that is a transgression against his word, will and plan for their lives. God will not have a person tie to something that is going to deplete them rather than build them in him and in their identity, purpose, and destiny.

- *1 Corinthians 6:16 What? know ye not that he which is joined (Hebrew word Kollao meaning glue, cement, fasting) to an harlot is one body? for two, saith he, shall be one flesh.*

- *Genesis 34:1-3 And Dinah the daughter of Leah, which she bare unto Jacob went out to see the daughters of the land. And when Shechem the son of Hamor the Hivite, prince of the country, saw her, he took her, and lay with her, and defiled her. And his soul clave unto Dinah the daughter of Jacob, and he loved the damsel, and spake kindly unto the damsel. Verse 8 And Hamor communed with them, saying the soul of my son Shechem longeth for your daughter: I pray you give her him to wife. Sexual involvement can form such entangling tentacles of soul ties that it is extremely hard to break off the relationship.*

- *Proverbs 5:20-24 And why wilt thou, my son, be ravished with a strange woman, and embrace the bosom of a stranger? For the ways of man are before the eyes of the Lord, and he pondereth all his goings. His own iniquities shall take the wicked himself, and he shall be holden with the cords of his sins. He shall die without instruction; and in the greatness of his folly he shall go astray.*

- *Psalm 1:1 Blessed is the man that walketh not in the counsel of the ungodly, nor standeth in the way of sinners, nor sitteth in the seat of the scornful*

- *2 Corinthians 6:14-18 Be ye not unequally yoked together with unbelievers: for what fellowship hath righteousness with unrighteousness? and what communion hath light with darkness? And what concord hath Christ with Belial? or what part hath he that believeth with an infidel? And what agreement hath the temple of God with idols? for ye are the temple of the living God; as God hath said, I will dwell in them, and walk in them; and I will be their God, and they shall be my people. Wherefore come out from among them, and be ye separate, saith the Lord, and touch not the unclean thing; and I will receive you, And will be a Father unto you, and ye shall be my sons and daughters, saith the Lord Almighty.*

Soulties With A Place – A person can be tied to a place, and it can become a high place in their life, where they do not want to leave it or cannot leave it. In the scripture, a high place is referring to a place of idolatrous worship. A high place can be any place that has exalted itself above God in a person's life. A person can be tied to a place where God has brought them out of, but the tie keeps pulling them back in. Spiritually the person is free, but their soul is bound to it. Lot's wife had a soultie with Sodom and Gomorrah. God was destroying the city because of the perversion, idolatry, lewdness, and lawlessness. God only allowed so many to live and allowed them time to get out of the city before he destroyed it. As they were walking out, Lot's wife looked back and turned into a pillar of salt.

- *Genesis 19:23-26 Then the Lord rained upon Sodom and upon Gomorrah brimstone and fire from the Lord out of heaven; And he overthrew those cities, and all the plain, and all the inhabitants of the cities, and that which grew upon the ground. But his wife looked back from behind him, and she became a pillar of salt.*

Even though God had graced Lot's wife with deliverance, her eyes and heart had regard for what she was leaving behind. Because her soul was still knitted to Sodom and Gomorrah, God caused her to perish with it. Being tied to something that God is freeing the person from will deplete their life and even bring destruction upon them.

Agreement with God's will for the relationship along with healthiness is important in a Godly Soultie.

- *Amos 3:3 Can two walk together, except they be agreed?*

- *Do two people walk hand in hand if they aren't going to the same place? (MSG)*

When the agreement is unhealthy, it makes for an ungodly soultie. Regardless to whether the person agrees or not, if a soultie is formed, it has to be broken in order for them to be free of whatever was knitted and transferred through that tie. This is vital, as rape, incest, abuse, mind control, religious sects, erred beliefs, etc. are ties that form without their agreement, out of ignorance, fear, or lack of knowledge, depending on the circumstance. When they are not broken, whatever the offender deposited lives in the person. Some people result in manifesting traits of their offender, while others live in the false identity of what was deposited. This is a particularly sensitive area of counseling when dealing with a victim of childhood sexual abuse. Be sure that you, as the counselor, are fully equipped to address the complexities of a client with a history of victimization. Otherwise, the counselor runs the risk of becoming one more offender in the person's life. It is better to refer the client to someone with expertise than to do further harm.

When a person experience divorced, it is best to break soulties with the now ex-spouse. Many people have a difficult time moving forward because their souls are still tied to their ex-spouse. The covenant of marriage must be repented for and broken in the spirit realm, and soulties must be cleansed and broken so the person can be free from all that was deposited and shared while married.

Teach clients the following regarding breaking soul ties:

- Spend time before the Lord identifying every ungodly soultie they have in their lives.
- Confessing and repenting for their role in the soultie, even if it was just giving into the lies and false identity of their offender.
- Forgiving the person they had a soultie with and forgiving themselves for engaging in the soultie.
- Breaking and removing the soultie. The client is to address and call out every person's name they have a soul tie with; go through these steps, and break and remove each tie.
- Using the blood of Jesus and the fire of God to cleanse themselves of all ungodly deposits, and command any parts of their soul, heart, mind and identity to be restored back to them.
- Occasionally spend time cleansing any unhealthiness in their Godly soultie relationships, and any deposits that may have come from misunderstandings, miscommunication, taking one another for granted, being more to one another than God was saying, or becoming lax, fleshy or imbalanced in your interactions.

Do not hesitate to provide these cleaning tools as homework assignments to your client. Teach them to invest in their wholeness journey and utilize these tools at future times in their lives.

teach your client to cleansing tools so they can sustain in destiny!

Chapter 13

THE PROCESS TO WHOLENESS

Consider the word *process*. Jesus performed a lot of miracles. Most of those miracles involved swift healing and immediate deliverance. Our tendency is to expect and desire "*a quick work*" and do not like that there are times and seasons where we are processed for healing and wholeness. We must be cautious that when we say we believe in miracles, signs, and wonders we are not unconsciously trying to control the means by which God answers prayer. Especially as counselors, we need this introspection as a checkpoint. The miracle can be the process itself or can manifest at some point in the process journey.

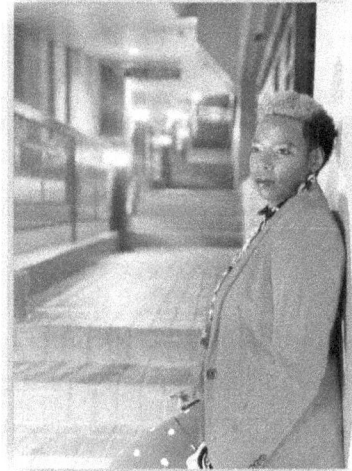

Dictionary.com defines *process* as:
1. a systematic series of actions directed to some end
2. a continuous action, operation, or series of changes taking place in a definite manner
3. a series of actions that produce something or that lead to a particular result

2 Corinthians 3:17-18 Now the Lord is that Spirit: and where the Spirit of the Lord is, there is liberty. But we all, with open face beholding as in a glass the glory of the Lord, are changed into the same image from glory to glory, even as by the Spirit of the Lord.

Glory is the Greek word *doxa* and means, "*honor, renown, glory, splendor, an especially divine quality, the unspoken manifestation of God, dignity, opinion, judgement.*"

When a client SHIFTS from glory to glory, they SHIFT from honor to honor, splendor to splendor, revealing quality after quality of God's divine nature. The client displays manifestations of who God is that have not been exposed, whether in the earth, a region, a city, or personally. There is a unique manifestation of God in an individual that the world needs and that only can reveal to the world. As the client SHIFTS from glory to glory, *doxa* also reveals their opinions and judgments which speaks for their character and nature. As they mature in *doxa*, their opinions and judgments should align and resemble God's precepts until looking at them is like looking in a mirror (glass) at the likeness of Jesus.

The word *changed* in this scripture means "*metamorphose*." Per dictionary.com, metamorphosis denotes "*a profound change in form from one stage to the next in the life history of an organism*." Basically, the client is being transfigured as they enter each stage of life development. According to the scripture, the process in any given season should be as follows:

Diagram 13.0 Stages of Life Development

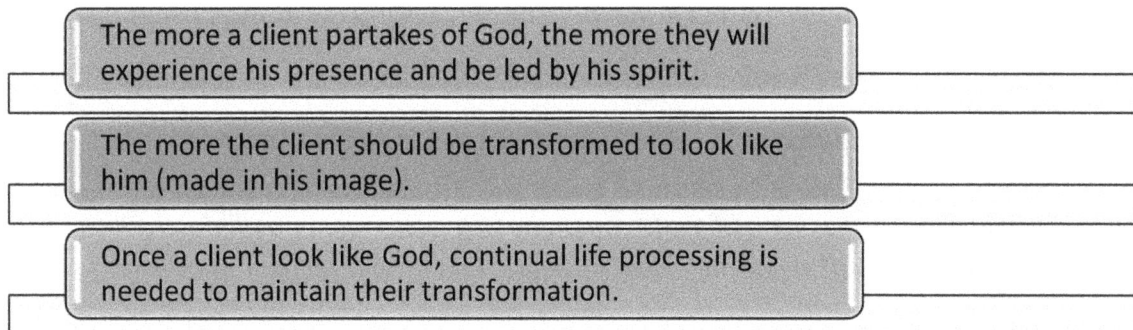

The more a client partakes of God, the more they will experience his presence and be led by his spirit.

The more the client should be transformed to look like him (made in his image).

Once a client look like God, continual life processing is needed to maintain their transformation.

Source: Baker, 2019

> *All of us! Nothing between us and God, our faces shining with the brightness of his face. And so we are transfigured much like the Messiah, our lives gradually becoming brighter and more beautiful as God enters our lives and we become like him. (MSG)*

> *And all of us, as with unveiled face, [because we] continued to behold [in the Word of God] as in a mirror the glory of the Lord, are constantly being transfigured into His very own image in ever increasing splendor and from one degree of glory to another; [for this comes] from the Lord [Who is] the Spirit. (AMP)*

Transfigured in Greek is *metamorphoo* and means to:
1. to change the appearance of something or someone
2. to give a new and typically exalted or spiritual appearance to transform outwardly and usually for the better

3. synonyms see transform are as followed: convert, altar, apply appropriate, commute, download, interchange, make, modify, remodel, reorganize, restyle, revise, switch, translate, transmute, transpose, turn

Many of your clients will want to control the process but transfiguration is guided by the Spirit of God. This word *Spirit* in this scripture refers to the *Holy Spirit*. *Spirit* is *pneuma* in Greek and means "*breath*." Just like a person cannot live without breathing, they cannot live without being processed from glory to glory in God. It is vital to a person's life process.

Jesus was on a mission, and though he had the spirit of counsel (***Isaiah 11:2, Isaiah 9:6***), he did not use counseling to the level we use it today. However, Jesus did state the following:

John 14:26 *But the Comforter, which is the Holy Ghost, whom the Father will send in my name, he shall teach you all things, and bring all things to your remembrance, whatsoever I have said unto you.*

Comforter is *paraklētos* and means "*an intercessor, consoler, advocate, comforter.*"

John 16:13 *But when he, the Spirit of truth, comes, he will guide you into all the truth. He will not speak on his own; he will speak only what he hears, and he will tell you what is yet to come.*

Guide is *hodēgeō* and means "*to show the way (literally or figuratively (teach)), guide, lead, to give guidance.*"

John 14:16 *And I will pray the Father, and he shall give you another Comforter, that he may abide with you for ever.*

Jesus knew that we would need comfort, counseling, and guidance which was the main reason for giving us the gift of the Holy Spirit. The Holy Spirit is our first counselor and is the best role model in knowing the aptitudes of a counselor.

Counseling falls under the gifts of healing and the working of miracles. Counseling is one of the ways God manifests his healing power in our lives and it is also a manner by which he works miracles.

1 Corinthians 12:9:10 To another faith by the same Spirit; to another the gifts of healing by the same Spirit; -- To another the working of miracles; to another prophecy; to another discerning of spirits; to another divers kinds of tongues; to another the interpretation of tongues.

<u>*Working*</u> is *energeo* in Greek and means:
1. effectual fervent (devout, earnest, zealous)
2. to be operative, be at work, put forth power

<u>Dictionary.com defines *operative* as:</u>
1. a person engaged, employed, or skilled in some branch of work, especially productive or industrial work, worker
2. a detective
3. a secret agent; spy
4. operating, or exerting force, power, or influence
5. having force; being in effect or operation
6. effective or efficacious
7. engaged in, concerned with, or pertaining to work or productive activity

The Greek word *energeo* speaks to being energetic or having to exert energy. This lets us know that the working of miracles can be instantaneous or the process of working in a series of steps towards that miracle. Though the disciples saw Jesus perform miracles and Jesus used them to perform miracles, aside from being rescued from danger or hardship, rarely were they the recipients of personal miracles. Much of their deliverance and healing came through being mentored by Jesus and being processed to wholeness. The following interchangeably uses the pronoun "you" as referring to your client but also referring to you as the counselor. We are all evolving in what God has planned for us. As counselors, we cannot serve others with something that we have not submitted to in our own walk. As we consider the disciples, we can conclude the following:

❑ Processing is an indication that God desires more than interaction with a person or that which he wants the person to attain. He desires relationship with the person to a covenant level that will give favor to all he desires for them.

❑ Processes create a solid foundation that helps to sustain progress and success.

❑ The main goal in every season of processing is for the person to become more like God and to further unveil the uniqueness of who a person is in him.

❑ Because the steps in a process are chain linked, avoiding or bypassing steps can hinder the success of the process. This can also frustrate a person's progress and what they have sacrificed in the process.

❑ It takes vulnerability and a relinquishing of control to be processed to breakthrough.

❑ The process is not designed for the person to know everything, do everything, or to figure everything out. The process is intended for the person to be in a posture of humility and attentiveness to the voice and direction of God and those he has ordained to walk in the process with you.

Proverbs 3:5-6 *Trust in the Lord with all thine heart; and lean not unto thine own understanding. In all thy ways acknowledge him, and he shall direct thy paths.*

Hebrews 13:17 *Obey them that have the rule over you, and submit yourselves: for they watch for your souls, as they that must give account, that they may do it with joy, and not with grief: for that is unprofitable for you.*

❑ If the person cannot give up control then they are trying be God or the leader in the process, and since they are in the wrong position, the process will be unnecessarily challenging and possibly aborted.

❑ The more a person seek to be God by trying to control the process or remain prideful in being unwilling to be vulnerable in the process, the longer it will take them to actually begin or establish within that season of processing.

❑ A person can abort or stagnate their progress when they rush the process.

❑ Quick fixes can equal temporary results. Process equals skills and knowledge that produce lasting results.

❑ The process is not intended to withhold healing and knowledge. The fact that a person battles this wrong thinking while experiencing hope deferred, is proof that processing is needed. The outcome is that the person will mature in their relationship and understanding of God and even in appreciating the processes of life. *Proverbs 13:12* *Hope deferred maketh the heart sick: but when the desire cometh, it is a tree of life.*

❑ The inability to submit to the process exposes deeply rooted issues within a person's soul and heart. Dealing with root issues is a process all its own, as it takes energy and time to dig up roots. At times when dealing with underlying roots, it can feel and be like being processed within a process. The twofold processing can be intense and progressively painful. That is because digging up roots is gutting out parts of a person's identity that do not reflect God's image. The person is literally being separated from parts of a person that are not beneficial to who a person is and where they are going in God. Anytime a person loses parts of themselves, whether good or bad, it hurts. But the twofold processing of gutting out roots is worth it. It is best to sustain in the original process, while dealing with roots, so a person does not prolong this season of processing. Setting oneself aside in consecration can be beneficial to maintaining progress during seasons of twofold processing.

❑ When there is a lack of submission and obedience to the process, God and/or those who are helping the person begin processing the person as if they were babies drinking bottled milk and being spoon fed. Where a person should be able to receive, retain, attain, and maintain sufficient knowledge and revelation that keeps the process unfolding effectively, they result with receiving just enough to keep them in the process. Yet the focus is more about breaking a person's will where they become submitted to God's will, more so than about the process itself.

> *Isaiah 28:10* *For precept must be upon precept, precept upon precept; line upon line, line upon line; here a little, and there a little.*

> *Psalm 51:17* *The sacrifices of God are a broken spirit: a broken and a contrite heart, O God, thou wilt not despise.*

> *Hebrews 5:13-14* *For everyone who continues to feed on milk is obviously inexperienced and unskilled in the doctrine of righteousness (of conformity to the divine will in purpose, thought, and action), for he is a mere infant [not able to talk yet]! But solid food is for full-grown men, for those whose senses and mental faculties are trained by practice to discriminate and distinguish between what is morally good and noble and what is evil and contrary either to divine or human law. (AMP)*

❑ Focusing on being perfect or focusing on a person's lack of perfections will hinder and even abort the process, as the process is designed to expose what is of God and what is not of God. If a person cannot handle truths about their imperfections, it will be difficult to relinquish control of the process to God where he can deliver and heal them.

Psalm 138:8 *The Lord will perfect that which concerneth me: thy mercy, O Lord, endureth for ever: forsake not the works of thine own hands.*

Clients must be taught and empowered so they can mature in identity and destiny.

Counselors teach your clients the following processing tools:

1. Counseling does not mean the client is weak or helpless. It demonstrates strength, wisdom, and responsibility to obtain a success in life.

2. Counseling is a process. This must be reiterated throughout the counseling process so the client can stay the course and finish strong and successful.

3. The process is part of a client's destiny journey with God and therefore, should be embraced and valued.

4. A client's entire life is being processed from level to level and glory to glory with God. Counseling ensure success through difficult seasons of one's journey.

5. Even as destiny is its own process, there are seasons of life where there is in-depth needful processing within the process.

6. Clients much learn to discern potential threats that can hinder or abort there counseling and destiny process.

7. A client's unresolved issues are enemies to the process and should never be given control of the process.

8. Each client is a unique blueprint of God. Though they may have similar experiences as other people, their process will be different and have its own distinct pattern.

9. God provides the processing blueprint and guides the process.

10. Everyone will not understand a client's process. Yet the process will speak for itself as God's word always manifests with signs following.

11. The client will lose some things, people, and pleasures as they journey in the process, but none of it is comparable to the healing and restoration they will gain as they complete the process.

12. The client's investment in the process is key to their success of being well and sustaining their healing and destiny journey.

In a brief sidebar, lets clarify that the goal is to become spiritually developed which is not one and the same with the notion of being religious. Religion is a social sphere, while spirituality is an individual domain.

> "Religion is defined as an, "organized belief system that includes shared and institutionalized moral values, beliefs about God, and involvement in religious community," and spirituality is defined as, "an internal set of values - a sense of meaning, inner wholeness, and connection with others." Spirituality is focused on connection with others and contains three main components: connection to someone or something beyond oneself, sense of compassion for others, and desire to contribute to the good of others."[36]

Experts agree that the level of spirituality in an individual is a correlation to stress levels and coping skills. Even within the secular counseling world, most clients want to discuss their religious and spiritual beliefs as part of explaining personal history and optimism about resolution. How much more then should the faith-based counselor assist a client in delving into their spiritual nature as an essential piece of the process?

---

[36] Tiffany Nickels. (2011). The role of religion and spirituality in counseling. Retrieved from California Polytech State University website at https://digitalcommons.calpoly.edu/cgi/viewcontent.cgi?referer=https://search.yahoo.com/&httpsredir=1&article=1024&context=psycdsp

The process of triumphing over issues is a miracle that God gives the client through the counselor.

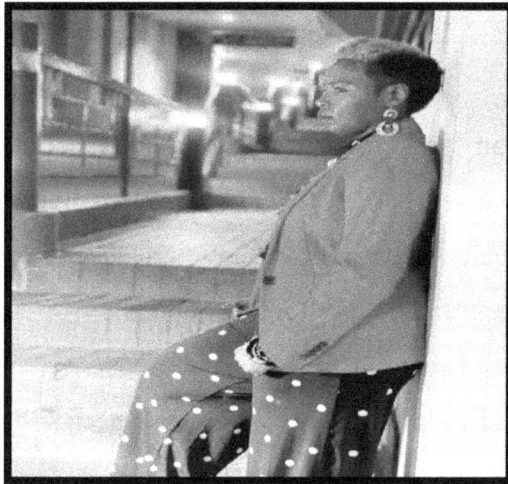

DIFFERENCE BETWEEN HEALING & WHOLENESS

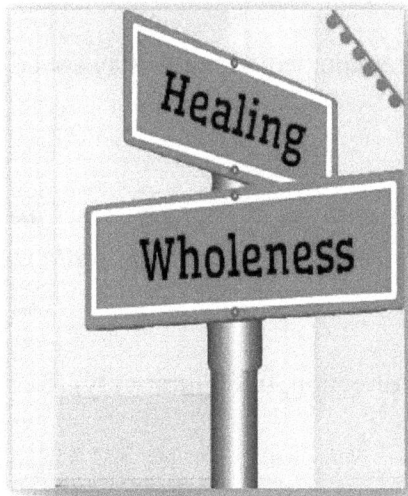

There is a difference between healing and wholeness. Healing can be conditional which is why Jesus admonished people to go and sin no more. Wholeness is when a person has SHIFTED from maintaining healing to sustaining in a lifestyle of wellness. When a person is whole, the deliverance and healing is sustained and eternal. Similarly, the person is empowered with clear tools and strategies (godly truths), for how to process someone else to wholeness.

John 5:1-6 - After this there was a feast of the Jews; and Jesus went up to Jerusalem. Now there is at Jerusalem by the sheep market a pool, which is called in the Hebrew tongue Bethesda, having five porches. In these lay a great multitude of impotent folk, of blind, halt, withered, waiting for the moving of the water. For an angel went down at a certain season into the pool, and troubled the water: whosoever then first after the troubling of the water stepped in was made whole of whatsoever disease he had. And a certain man was there, which had an infirmity thirty and eight years. When Jesus saw him lie, and knew that he had been now a long time in that case, he saith unto him, Wilt thou be made whole?

"Whole" in Greek is *hygiēs* and means, *"healthy, i.e. well (in body); figuratively, true (in doctrine), sound, whole."*

Wholeness is when a person has SHIFTED from maintaining healing to sustaining in a lifestyle of wellness.

The impotent man was on the side of the pool waiting to be healed. His healing was based on whether someone could put him in the pool. Jesus, however, came by and offered him wholeness. The only condition to his wholeness was his willingness to come into agreement with God releasing it to him. He had to do nothing but receive it. If the impotent man would have become healed by entering the pool, he most likely would not have had the instruction Jesus gave him regarding remaining healed:

Verse 14 *Afterward Jesus findeth him in the temple, and said unto him, Behold, thou art made whole: sin no more, lest a worse thing come unto thee.*

Through these instructions, the man was not only able to remain healed but to stay sound in his healing.

1 Peter 5:10 - *But the God of all grace, who hath called us unto his eternal glory by Christ Jesus, after that ye have suffered a while, make you perfect, stablish, strengthen, settle you.*

<u>*Stablish*</u> in Greek is *stērizō* and means:
1. to set fast, i.e. (literally) to turn resolutely in a certain direction, or (figuratively) to confirm
2. fix, (e-)stablish, stedfastly set, strengthen
3. to make stable, place firmly, set fast
4. fix to strengthen, make firm to render constant, confirm, one's mind

Counseling offers the added advantage of not just being healed, but being sound, firmly rooted, and grounded, eternally fix in one's healing - made whole.

Counseling provides keys, tools, and strategies that clients can use after the counseling process has ended to remain healed so they can walk in wholeness. Counselors must have a mindset not just to heal, but to SHIFT a client to a posture of wholeness.

Be thou made whole!

Chapter 14

THE GRACE OF THE PROCESS

One of the biggest mistakes made in the faith based community is when people come for prayer or counsel, especially during altar calls, they are often stripped of their walls of protection, identity, and supports, without adequately filling these areas of their lives where they can maintain in deliverance and healing. The efforts by altar workers or prayer ministers is well intended but can result in more harm to the person. There are also instances where scriptures, principles, and cliches, are used, while expecting people to know how to implement them in their lives with no equipping, process to wellness, skills development, or building. A person is then rebuked for being lost, confused, lukewarm, backslidden, stagnant, slow to progressing, and unable to mature in the Lord. It is essential to:

- Recognize when a person needs a processing to wholeness and connect them to counseling services so they can begin that process.
- Have grace as people process to wholeness.
- Discern if you are the counselor that is to process that person to wholeness and connect

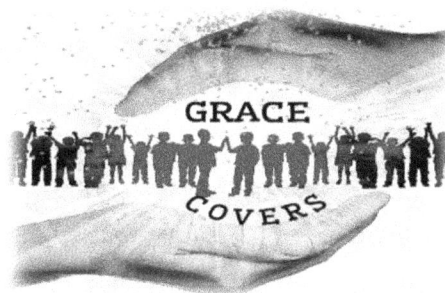

them with the correct counselor who has the grace for their healing process.

Recognize when processing is necessary.

Sometimes people will come for prayer and may not be ready for the level of deliverance necessary to SHIFT them to healing and even wholeness. They may have walls of survival that keeps them from experiencing deep levels of pain, depression, or digression. As laborers in the gospel, ministries must be wise in recognizing when they are not capable of relinquishing those walls in that moment, and refer them to counseling where they can process to wholeness, while still maintaining their ability to survive and progress in their day to day life. When the drive to feel needed, deliver or heal someone, validates a labor man's own worth or overrides the needs of that person, they have become reckless and damaging to that soul. When a personal or professional agenda takes over, there is a lack of demonstrating the love and grace of God needed to draw another person out of darkness and into the salvation with the Lord.

It takes grace to process people to wholeness.

It is important to have grace for people as they process to wholeness. Sometimes, the laborers do not have the patience to work with different types of people and unique situations. Sometimes a counselor may not have the grace to work with certain clients. It is important to discern this and create partnerships with other counselors in case you need to refer a client to someone who is more suitable for their needs.

Ephesians 4:1-2 *I therefore, the prisoner of the Lord, beseech you that ye walk worthy of the vocation wherewith ye are called, with all lowliness and meekness, with longsuffering, forbearing one another in love.*

Forbearing means to suffer, labor, endure, and hold a person up against oneself. It means to help a person sustain until they can maintain their progress and journey with the Lord independently. I am personally called to difficult cases where people have experienced severe trauma. It may take months and even years to unravel the hurts and pains they are intertwined in, heal, and learn new tools and skills to sustain in life. If you are a counselor who is not called to these types of cases, refer them to someone who has that calling. Though we would love for people to be immediately set free and able to sustain it, that is not always the case. In these instances, the counselor must consider the soul of the person as a priority over the counselor's zealousness by connecting the client with counseling services where they can be delivered and healed.

Choosing the correct counselor may mean that it isn't you.

Just because a counselor is saved does not mean they are the best match for every person. Counselors can have various graces of wisdom and expertise. Sometimes this can be a factor in providing adequate services to a client and can be a hinderance when a counselor is counseling for counseling sake but not through the grace of the calling that is on their lives. My counseling expertise needs to include a reality check on whether I am the best choice for a particular issue, e.g. sexual addiction or substance abuse. Sometimes a person who has experienced traumatic abuse may need a counselor with that expertise, which may include the gender, age, or ethnicity of the counselor. These factors must be taken into consideration. We want people to have the best chance at restoration and healing. These considerations motivate us to offering the best avenues for making that happen.

Counselors Homework Activation

When examining your grace as a counselor, consider the following:

1. What types of people or situations are you drawn too? For example, I am drawn to more severe cases of trauma, mental health challenges, and deep spiritual issues that hinder destiny. I am drawn to ages 16 to 40. I have counseled clients younger and older but understand that this is not my grace. I, therefore, seek God as to whether I am the correct fit, and refer when I believe another counselor is more sufficient.

2. What reasons are you drawn to certain types of clients and cases? I have the gift of counseling for the cases I mentioned. I have a gift to be able to spiritually explore their experience with God and provide strategy and keys for how to break them through to healing and wholeness. I enjoy these types of clients and find it draining and difficult to work with client's outside of this metron. This has nothing to do with my life experiences but everything to do with my skill set and the spirit of counsel on my life. Spend time searching God and your experiences for what your true skill set is, and where the spirit of counsel works best through you. Even if it is like your life experiences, make sure the grace to counsel such clients rest upon you (***Luke 4:18***).

3. What clients and cases are efficient in working with? Knowing this is just as important as knowing your grace. I am not good with clients who come to counseling out of obligation, are not committed to the counseling process, and who are looking for quick fixes. I inform clients of this during the initial consultation, and that such actions are subject to me ending the counseling relationship and referring them to another counselor. I am no good to a client if I am being drained and dragged through the counseling process. I am unmotivated and waned in my compassion and ability to hear God from this posture. Because I recognize this about myself, I learn to discern such clients at consultation, and avoid taking them as clients. If the counseling process results to this posture, I do what is best for myself and the client by referring them to a more capable counselor. Though I work well with severe trauma clients, I do not have the expertise or grace to work with many substance abuse clients. Also, though I have a master's degree emphasis on marriage, children, and families, and have a spiritual grace in this area, with some marriage couples, I add another married or prophetic counselor to the process. I find that married couples respond better to my wisdom and

the counseling process when a married or prophetic counselor is confirming and adding insight to what God is leading me to speak and do within the counseling journey. I understand my grace and my spiritual mantle of counseling and I am at peace that I am not called to everyone. How would you handle a client that you know you did not have the grace to counsel?

4. What clients and cases you least enjoy working with? This is just as important as understanding the grace and spirit of counsel that is on your life. Certain cases will be particularly challenging. Enjoying what you are doing as a counselor to help transform a client is vital to you being effective in operating through compassion, love, and hearing God for his will and purpose in the counseling journey. Having a lack of joy can reveal a plethora of things. It could mean the counselor:

   ✓ Is tired and burnout is setting in.
   ✓ Is not the right match for the client.
   ✓ Does not have the grace for the client.
   ✓ Has exhausted their ability to help the client and another counselor may be needed to assist the client further in their counseling journey.
   ✓ May not like the client. It is the truth anyhow!!! It is okay as long as you are able to provide adequate services to the client. But if it is waning your joy in a manner that impacts your ability to provide sufficient services, it is time to refer the client. Hurting people can be challenging. They are not always the most pleasant and can say and do some very hurtful things, even to their counselors. The counselor can say and do everything right and still clients will have to process from hurting others, to trusting and demonstrating love and appreciation for others. Some clients who receive counseling like prisoners, murderers, sex offenders, etc., may not be initially likeable or may not ever be likeable. This is the reason knowing your grace and mantle is important. If you do not possess grace to have empathy for these clients beyond their actions, you will not enjoy counseling them. Wisdom and guidance are great but can only take the counseling process so far. When a faith-based counselor relies on this only, they have yielded to secular counseling. They have resorted to only being able

to counsel in measure, rather than the fullness of the counsel of God that is on their lives. Again, what clients do you enjoy counseling?

5. How would you handle a client you knew well who was adamant about you counseling them? As a counselor, you will always be sought after for your expertise. At times, you will provide when people do not want to hear it. This is because counseling is rooted in your identity. It is who we are. Get ready to hear "don't be trying to psychoanalyze me," as it will be a saying that will follow you for the rest of your life. I do not recommend counseling those you are familiar with. They will claim to feel safe and comfortable with you and this may be true, but there are points in the counseling process where vulnerability and accountability goes beyond familiarity. Many people are not able to triumph these areas of the process because they do not want to expose themselves or they do not want to be accountable to the transformation needed to SHIFT further in the counseling process. Save yourself some time and energy by not placing yourself in these situations where the counseling process is aborted due to these factors. Be mindful of what types of situations tug on your heart, so you will not find yourself volunteering to counsel those you are familiar with. You are not the savior. You are the guide to the savior. Observe those in your life who need counseling and journal reasons it would be better to refer them to a counselor rather than counseling them yourself. Then journal a statement you can stand on when people close to you ask you to counsel them. Practice using this throughout your counseling career to maintain boundaries with those you love but know that it would be best for another counselor to journey with them.

6. List at least seven standards you can live by to protect your grace and maintain healthy boundaries as a counselor. Counseling can be an exciting career, especially because you are able to discern and provide wisdom for people at will. But I have learned that there must be balance with such a gift. People will always want to know your perspective and how you would handle a matter. If not careful, a counselor could literally be counseling 24 hours a day as folks seek to draw from the grace on your life. I have learned not to rescue, not to feel obligated to provide counsel for every situation and every conversation I hear, when to start the day and to shut the day down. I have learned that my health and sanity is just as important as my clients. When I allow

people to make me savior, I become unhealthy. When I become unhealthy, my grace and ability to operate in the spirit of counsel is hindered. This is because I am no longer operating in grace, I am operating in my own will and strength. What I am giving is from my humanity and not my gift of counseling. As a counselor, people will be angry with you for not being all things to them. They will be angry with you for withholding wisdom that they deem is rightfully needed for their lives. They will be angry with you for not being an ambulance service for them. Someone once told me, "for you to be an educated counselor, you never have any answers for me when I call you." This person was messy and only called to draw me into drama. To speak any counsel would have given this person cause to use my name in her mess. It would have then appeared as if I were confirming the drama she was stirring. I therefore remained a listener when she called and never felt obligated to be anything else. The truth is, a counselor that is truly called, only releases counsel at the Lord's leading. Being able to counsel and being guided by God to counsel are two different things. You must know the difference and protect your own health so you can sustain in your calling. For this reason, I have made it a lifestyle principle to only counsel when the Lord is leading me and to only enter a counsel process when directed by the Lord, to counsel on specific days of the week and during specific times, to stick to my rules regarding who I have the grace to counsel and when to refer a client when the process is not progressing. I have other standards, but these are just a few to give you an idea of what you should be exploring and practicing while maintaining healthiness as a counselor. People treat you in the way you allow them. Do not allow people to abuse you or your counseling mantle.

Counselor, know your grace and live it!

Kingdom Wellness Counseling and Mentoring Center

Faith Based Counseling

Manual I

Part 4: Chapters (15 – 16)

Learning Objectives:

- To provide definitive revelation regarding the authenticity of identity.
- To provide insight on the different between true, false, unhealthy, and distorted identities.
- To provide biblical proof of God versus man or demonic identity.
- To provide strategic insight on helping clients identify true God identify and ho to maintain a healthy identity.

Chapter 15

HEALTHY IDENTITY VERSUS UNHEALTHY IDENTITY

Identity is about who you are - your authentic self. You are your real, actual self, an original origin of yourself. You are authentically you. You are not a copy of someone else and you are not a facade.

We are identified by who made us. God created us. He identifies us (*Genesis 1:27, Genesis 5:1-2, Genesis 9:6, Psalm 139:14*). For us to identify ourselves or to decide we do not want to be who our Creator made us to be, we either have to reject God or we have to distort God's identity to fit our own. We then SHIFT from the role of the created to the creator, where we attempt to redefine ourselves into what we want (*Romans 1:28-32*).

It is problematic for the creation to decide that we do not want what our Creator designed and determined for us. The chair cannot decide suddenly that it wants to be a desk. No matter how much a person can squat down and use the seat of a chair to write, it is still a chair. Though it can function in another manner, it is still a chair.

NO MATTER

How the chair is used,
  What setting it is used in,
    Who sits in it,
      How much the chair cost,
        How it feels when used for another task,
          How much it tries to deny it is not a chair,
            How much it tries to change its original state . . .

IT IS STILL A CHAIR

Though our thoughts and feelings can help to construct our identity, they cannot change the true nature of who we are.

Diagram 15.0 Who we are

Our nature is the reality of who we are	Our nature is the bottom line foundation of who we are	Our nature is the essence of who we are	Our nature is the origin, constitution (laws and principles), and inherited character of who we are

Source: Baker, 2019

Though many have tried, we cannot change the character of who we are. Character is the collection of features and traits that forms our nature.

Referring to our chair example, whatever collection of elements went into making the chair is what made it a chair. The plastic molding, the metal legs, the screws, and other elements collectively shaped together gave it the identity of a chair. Even if those elements are the same as a desk, once it is molded into a chair, then that is its nature. For the desk to become a chair, it must be created all over again. That means it must be broken all the way down to its lowest form where it is no longer identified as a chair, and then recreated into a desk. But after it is formed, it will no longer be identified as a chair because it is now created anew as a desk.

Though humans attempt to recreate themselves, clone themselves, recalibrate themselves, there is no way to change our character and nature without dying. No matter how much we add on, take away, reject, deny, or rename our authentic selves, we are still who we were created to be because the Creator patterned us into a self. A lot of faith believers like to tell those who feel differently than who they are to be born again (*John 3:5-6, 1 Peter1:3*). Being born in Jesus Christ is not going to change a person's identity, it however, does purify and heals the perception of their identity so they can live in the truth of who they were created to be. In order for being "born again to work," a person has to want to be who God created them to be. If a person try to be born again and still try to reshape, take on, claim, another identity, they will still be rejecting the creator, rejecting the true nature and character of who they are, and rejecting truth. And without these three principles, a person cannot be adequately be "born again" through Jesus Christ.

After we try to learn and educate ourselves, in order to change our identity. Knowledge, wisdom, and education was never intended to reinvent who we are. These attributes can only enhance, cultivate, revolutionize, and further evolve who we are so that we can use our identity to create other things. Yet such powers cannot and do not create life - create humans. So when we use these tools to reinvent ourselves, we have stepped into the role of being our own creator which is idolatry because we are now using different ideas, formulas, parts, and behaviors, to create who we want to be. When we become our own creator, we -

- Reject our creator
- Reject our original design
- Chastise our creator for getting it wrong
- Exalt ourselves in believing we can do it better

We then have to operate in deception, denial, or delusion, in order to live in our recreated self-made identity. Technically this is called a facade. Facades can be difficult to keep up with. Facades are the illusion of truth but not the reality of truth. The struggle one thought they were ridding themselves of by recreating themselves, is now compounded in trying to continually live in and keep up theirs new identity. The resulting conflict is that underneath the illusion,

- Authentic identity is still there,
- The true nature and character is still there,
- The reality of the original creator is still there,
- The reality of who and what you were created to be is still there.

This is the reason there is no real peace in living through a false identity. Underneath the misperceived (incorrect) - misconstrued (exaggerated) contentment resides a truth that cannot be altered or changed.

The American Psychological Association frames identity as,

> *An individual's sense of self defined by (a) a set of physical, psychological, and interpersonal characteristics that is not wholly shared with any other person and (b) a range of affiliations (e.g., ethnicity) and social roles. Identity involves a sense of continuity, or the feeling that one is the same person today that one was yesterday or last year (despite physical or other changes). Such a sense is derived from one's body sensations; one's body image; and the feeling that one's memories, goals, values, expectations, and beliefs belong to the self.*[37]

We can use that as a foundational definition; however, the fulness of the term identity is manifested once the spiritual lens is applied. There is no true identity until God is involved and the spiritual perspective is applied.

Many try to accept their true identity while pursuing what makes them happy. This pursuit of happiness is based on thoughts and feelings that make them feel good, results in self-validation, or brings pleasure. The challenge is, once you accept your identity, you have to examine the reason and purpose you were created the way you were, so that these areas can be fulfilled. When we have no relationship and continual dialog with our Creator, then we are allowing our thoughts and feelings to guide us. The result is being led astray by self-will. We reject being guided by the one who made us - who knows what we need to be pleased, validated, and fulfilled.

Thoughts and feelings are a part of who we are, but they can also be influenced by external factors. Even in the womb, our thoughts and feelings can be affected by:

---

[37] APA Dictionary of Terms. (N.D.) Retrieved from American Psychological Association online dictionary at https://dictionary.apa.org/identity.

- Our mother's thoughts, feelings, experiences,
- Environmental factors (what is in the environment, things being said and done in the environment),
- How we were cultivated in the womb,
- Whether our life was valued and validated,
- The kind of care we received in the womb.

All this and more can impact our thoughts and feelings, as well as impact how we feel about our identity. Yet it does not change our identity.

It is important to help clients identify their true identity, while dismantling false identities.

Identity Theft

Identity theft is when a person's identity has totally been stolen and is used by someone who is not who they portray themselves to be. The enemy has stolen a person's uniqueness when he has caused confusion, distortion, brokenness, idolatry, delays, immaturity, stagnation, etc., within a person's identity. *John 10:10* says, *"The thief cometh not, but for to steal, and to kill, and to destroy: I am come that they might have life, and that they might have it more abundantly."*

- *Steal* means to take way,
- *Kill* means to sacrifice, immolate (suffer, victimize, kiss goodbye, yield, crucify, annihilate, asphyxiated, assassinate, do away with),
- *Destroy* means to render useless, perish, devote, or give over to eternal misery in hell, ruin, put out of the way entirely, mar, demolish.

Anytime there is a deviation from who God has called a person to be, they have experienced a form of identity theft. The enemy has stolen, killed, and destroyed, part of their individuality that is essential to them achieving their life's purpose and sustaining in their destiny journey.

> *"It has long been a curiosity to me why there is a combination of steal, kill, and destroy. Most thieves want to grab the goods and get away. I thought about the many crime shows where the detectives say, "This was a crime of passion." The devil has a penetrating hatred toward us. It is not enough for him to steal from us, but he wants to kill AND destroy us. It is a crime of passion."* Dr. Kathy Williams

Job is an example of one who experienced identity theft by Satan. Job was a perfect and upright man who appeared to have a healthy identity. Job had a close relationship with God. His life manifested God's blessings. He had a successful, godly family, and a wealthy lifestyle. He had God's hedge of protection around him to the point that Satan knew Job was untouchable. After Satan had a conversation with God about testing the identity of Job, God allowed Satan to wreak havoc in Job's life. Satan stripped Job of his life's worth, family and blessings.

Initially, Job remained strong as all these things that appeared to be his identifiers were stripped away from him. After seven days of sitting with his friends in silent grief and mental anguish, he began to question his purpose for being born (*Job 3*). Job SHIFTED into hating and cursing the day of his birth. Then his friends began questioning his perfection and uprightness. They concluded that Job must have sinned and should own up to it so God could spare him further hardship. Having accusations of self-righteousness caused Job to begin to question who God was in his life (*Job 4-7*). The more Job attempted to defend himself, the more he began to stray from his true identity in God and who God was to him (*Job 5-37*).

While Job's identity became distorted and confused while dialoguing with his friends who could not help him, he still sought answers from God. Job welcomed rebuke, correction, and understanding. He accepted what his friends said or what Satan wanted him to believe as truth about his identity. Job continued dialoging with God in effort to understand what was happening to him, the purpose for it, and how could God allow this to occur.

Job's greatest lesson was realizing that his identity was not in family, material things, blessings, wealth, acceptance, and the perceptions of people, but in and through God. When a person's identity is in God, the enemy can test it, people can judge and misperceive it, Satan and people can try to get the person to take on an alternate identity. It can only be stolen, killed, or destroyed if they succumb to an alternate truth. Job continually dialogued with God, while accepting rebuke, correction, deliverance, and healing. He was willing to receive truth. God restored his identity and life greater than what it was before Satan attempted to strip him of it (*Job 37-42*).

The challenge for many is when the enemy seeks to steal, kill, and destroy, they become stuck in identity challenges, create a new contaminated identity, and let unqualified folks give them a new altered identity. Let's explore ways a person's identity is high jacked by the devil.

Identity Confusion

The person's identity has been confused, contaminated and they waver between who God says they are, who they want to be, and/or who people, society, or the demonic forces desire them to be. The person is tormented and/or frustrated by who they believe they are to be and who they want to be, or who others want them to be or say they are. The person's identity is unclear, indistinct, and confounded. Their identity is blurred between two or three belief systems competing and battling for hierarchy in their lives, and often cause disorder in their relationships and interactions. Though not always the case, their identity can also affect their education, job duties, and relating in society. This is because the confusion, conflicts, misunderstandings, and drama, seem to follow them. Some of them can be aggressive and manipulative in effort to assert justice for themselves. Moreover, there are instances where they are the victim or perceive themselves as the victim. Because of continual conflicts surrounding identity confusion, they feel no one understands them and is against them. Truly, it can be difficult to describe, understand and engage the person because they fail to properly distinguish who they are, and there is a perplexity about them that is bewildering. A biblical example is how frequently the Israelites were challenged with identity confusion.

Distorted Identity

The person's identity tends to be a false or untrue identity that is more rooted in fantasy, lies or misrepresentations than truths.

Twisting of Truth

The person tends to embellish stories, tell lies, or present facts that are not true and do not align with their life experiences, abilities, or the presentation, of who they are. These facts do not represent what loved ones and/or the counselor, know about the person, and what they present regarding themselves. The person's identity can appear twisted and confusing because it is mixed with lies and truths or misperceptions.

The person can also perceive, feel, or believe themselves to be one way but really be another way. For example, body image struggles cause a person to feel fat while in reality they are slender, experience gender distortion, see themselves as the victim while operating as an offender, see their life as hopeless when really it is hopeful.

Fantasy Life

The person tends to live and operate within twisted truths, fantasies and/or false reality. They will be challenged with accepting the reality of who they are because the perceptions, feelings, and thoughts, of the distorted identity can be tormenting where they begin to favor the distorted reality over truth. The fantasy life can be seducing, risk taking, enjoyable, and, in some ways, more fulfilling than their true identity. A person begins to favor the distorted identity over their real identity. Sometimes the distorted identity can cause a person to hate and reject their true identity. They resist and reject acknowledging and accepting their true selves and the changes they need to make within themselves and in life that would enable them to enjoy, love, and value, their true self.

Sometimes the person has become so engulfed in their fantasy life that they do not know what is real or true about themselves anymore. This can cause great torment in the person's soul, heart, mind. It can also cause challenges in the person's relationships and societal interactions. They will have a difficult time engaging people and life situations, feeling loved or like they belong.

Shun Responsibility

Sometimes the shunned person does not want to take responsibility for life decisions or for change, so they will live in their fantasy world, and act as if the responsibilities do not exist. Procrastination, stagnation, self-sabotage tends to steal their progress and success. They tend to do just enough to survive but not enough to make changes that progress their lives. Because of the interference and interaction of the fantasy world, sometimes, it will take them years to accomplish what they are capable of accomplishing in a few weeks or months.

Twisted Morals & Values

There are instances where the person with a distorted reality will know right from wrong, but will depart from the right, normal, or usual, course of their lives or of what they have been taught or know is right. They will know the truth or what is morally correct, but will deviate from those truths and morals.

- Often this is to satisfy voids and needs for love and belonging as they are seeking self-fulfillment even if it is temporary fulfillment.

- Sometimes it is because they are operating through their distorted identity where morals and values are blurred or mixed with misperceptions.
- Sometime, they have become mentally unstable or have a lapse in their mental state because they are living in the distorted reality that makes them feel they do not have any consequences to their actions or what they are doing is okay or justifiable.

Identity Deformity

The person has lived in a distorted personality for so long where their identity becomes deformed and thus has taken on the form of that false identity. The natural shape of their identity has become disfigured and they begin to completely identify themselves and live through the distorted identity. The distortion causes the person to behave and even look like an entirely different person than who God created them to be. This deformity is often warped, strange, and odd. The person appears and behaves crippled, contorted, and mangled in their identity, as there is a misshaping of their true selves. They are attempting to transform their nature to birth forth their desired identity which is impossible to do as the nature of who a person is can never be changed. Many people who experience a confused identity strive to change their entire lives based on what they feel or believe about themselves, SHIFT to living through a deformed identity.

Broken Identity

The person's identity has been fractured, breached, split, compromised, or mishandled by some challenging experiences. Because of the experience, the person has a difficult time,

- Accepting who they are to be,
- Dealing with the pain and challenges surrounding who they are to be or having to become due to that experience,
- Pain, rejection, and or rebellion is now ruling the identity and the person begins operating through different personalities of who they are and who they have become rather than a healthy identity.
- Biblical Examples: Tamar, Moses.

Undeveloped Identity

The person becomes stuck at a certain age or developmental state. Multiple studies have proven that a person who is incarcerated becomes stuck in the age relevant to their conviction as opportunity is lacking for normal social development. When a person is imprisoned mentally, emotionally, or spiritually, the same paradigm applies.

Erikson's psychosocial theory of development considers the impact of external factors, parents and society on personality development from childhood to adulthood. According to Erikson's theory, every person must pass through a series of eight interrelated stages over the entire life cycle.

Diagram 15.0 Erik Erikson: Stages of Psychosocial Development

Erikson's Stage Theory in its Final Version			
Age	*Conflict*	*Resolution or "Virtue"*	*Culmination in old age*
Infancy (0-1 year)	Basic trust vs. mistrust	Hope	Appreciation of interdependence and relatedness
Early childhood (1-3 years)	Autonomy vs. shame	Will	Acceptance of the cycle of life, from integration to disintegration
Play age (3-6 years)	Initiative vs. guilt	Purpose	Humor; empathy; resilience
School age (6-12 years)	Industry vs. Inferiority	Competence	Humility; acceptance of the course of one's life and unfulfilled hopes
Adolescence (12-19 years)	Identity vs. Confusion	Fidelity	Sense of complexity of life; merging of sensory, logical and aesthetic perception
Early adulthood (20-25 years)	Intimacy vs. Isolation	Love	Sense of the complexity of relationships; value of tenderness and loving freely
Adulthood (26-64 years)	Generativity vs. stagnation	Care	Caritas, caring for others, and agape, empathy and concern
Old age (65-death)	Integrity vs. Despair	Wisdom	Existential identity; a sense of integrity strong enough to withstand physical disintegration

Source: Google images, 2019

These eight stages, spanning from birth to death, are split in general age ranges. Sometimes (not always the case), we can recognize when people are experiencing an undeveloped identity when their personalities fluctuate between identity stages. For example, an adult may act like a child at times, even to the point of throwing tantrums, or an adult may behave like a teenager who is just learning how to be responsible for life choices. The person will fluctuate between being an adult and being a kid or teen. Parts of their personality may be stuck at a specific age or due to a split in their personality. They go back and forth between their true age and being a child or teen. When exploring what need the person is striving to have met based on Erikson's chart, you as counselor, can most often discern what age a person is operating in. Moreover, you can ask that person if they had a challenging experience in childhood or adolescence and can discern what parts of their personality are stuck or underdeveloped, based on the time of that experience.

The reason I say sometimes is because sometimes, a person can revert to an age where they attempted to deal with an experience. The actual experience may have happened in childhood; however, the person may be stuck in their teen years where they tried to deal with that childhood trauma. It is therefore best not to make assumptions but ask lots of questions. It is also essential to seek God for knowledge and revelation on what the person is dealing with. This may be exceptionally true when dealing with a client who has experience childhood sexual trauma.

1 Corinthians 3:11 When I was a child, I spake as a child, I understood as a child, I thought as a child: but when I became a man, I put away childish things.

Seasonal (Time) Identity Challenges

Experiences that happen at different times in a person's life that cause an underdeveloped or non-progressing identity.

- If it was a good season, the person may fear moving on and even failing, so they remain stuck in that place.
- If it was a bad season, the person has some unhealed pain or root issues that need to be dealt with. These challenges are hindering them from maturing in their identity
- Society, people or life itself, has changed but the person -
    o Is stuck in a time warp,
    o Is rebelling against changing with the times,
    o Fears moving with the times (may think they will lose memories, fulfillment, or comfortability), or
    o Lacks the knowledge to move with the times resulting in stagnation.

Ecclesiastes 3:1 To every thing there is a season, and a time to every purpose under the heaven.

Situational or Needs-Based Identity Challenges

An underdeveloped identity can also be caused by a lack of life needs being met. According to Abraham Maslow, we all have basic needs that must be met in order for us to develop properly into healthy functioning individuals who can self-actualized in life. *Self-actualization* is the attainment of a person's complete potential or capability through creativity, independence, spontaneity, and achievements, as they seek to conquer their life's destiny. Maslow believes we must develop and receive these basic needs before we can become self-actualized. Though I do not agree with how some people and/or societies meet these needs as my belief standards are based on biblical principles, I do agree that most of these needs are essential to people having a healthy identity. People need to eat, drink, have shelter, sleep, have sex if they are married, feel safe, have a support system, and a sense of belonging, etc.

Diagram 15.1 Maslow's Expanded Needs Hierarchy

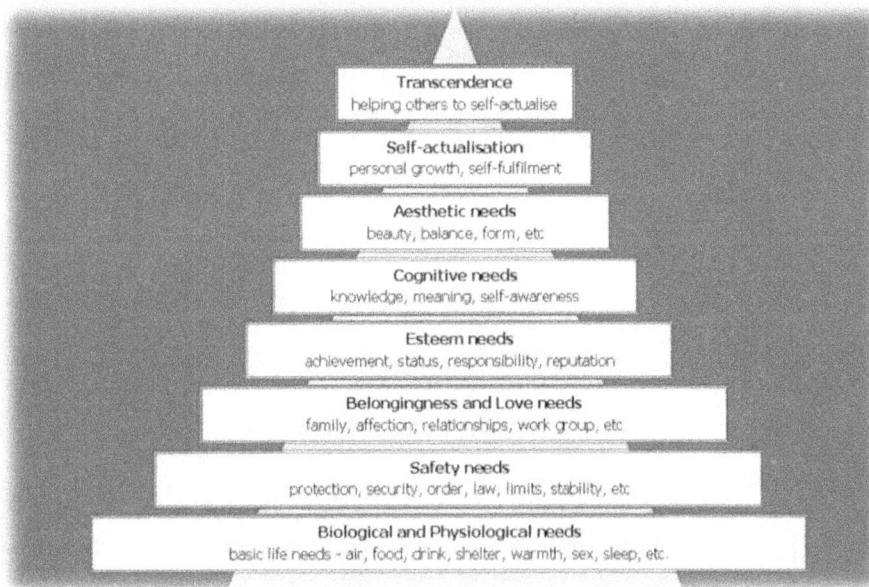

Source: Google images, 2019

James 1:27 Pure religion and undefiled before God and the Father is this, To visit the fatherless and widows in their affliction, and to keep himself unspotted from the world.

Many times in the church, we either want people to deny these needs, sacrifice them, or we only want to meet them one time and call that a testimony of how we evangelized and helped people. We do not want to provide avenues where people can be fulfilled and sustained in these needs, so we can assist them with maturing in their identity.

We also have the challenge where we want to strip people of their identity, especially if many of their needs are being met in an unhealthy manner. However, we do not provide pathways or process people to wholeness where they build their identity through:

- God's provisional means,
- Who God says they are to be,
- Healthy relationships and interactions,
- Destiny oriented successes,
- Skills and training that sustain personal and generational success and inheritance.

We expect people to accomplish this independently and without adequate counseling, mentoring, and equipping. This is the main reason people return to sin habits, cycling patterns of deliverance, and backsliding, or think that God and the church has no power to deliver and heal.

Philippians 2:3-5 Do nothing from factional motives [through contentiousness, strife, selfishness, or for unworthy ends] or prompted by conceit and empty arrogance. Instead, in the true spirit of humility (lowliness of mind) let each regard the others as better than and superior to himself [thinking more highly of one another than you do of yourselves].

Let each of you esteem and look upon and be concerned for not [merely] his own interests, but also each for the interests of others. Let this same attitude and purpose and [humble] mind be in you which was in Christ Jesus: [Let Him be your example in humility:] (AMP)

Ephesians 4:11-16 And he gave some, apostles; and some, prophets; and some, evangelists; and some, pastors and teachers; For the perfecting of the saints, for the work of the ministry, for the edifying of the body of Christ: Till we all come in the unity of the faith, and of the knowledge of the Son of God, unto a perfect man, unto the measure of the stature of the fulness of Christ: That we henceforth be no more children, tossed to and fro, and carried about with every wind of doctrine, by the sleight of men, and cunning craftiness, whereby they lie in wait to deceive; But speaking the truth in love, may grow up into him in all things, which is the head, even Christ: From whom the whole body fitly joined together and compacted by that which every joint supplieth, according to the effectual working in the measure of every part, maketh increase of the body unto the edifying of itself in love.

Perfecting is *katartismos* in Geek and means to "*completely furnish or equip.*" This means the church is responsible for building up the entire person's identity. Not just parts of it that benefit our churches, our agendas, or our egos.

Identity Inferiority

This is where the person feels inadequate about who they are so they either under compensate or overcompensate in their behaviors in effort to define and assert their identity. The person fluctuates between these two extreme personalities due to a lack of self-esteem, thoughts and feelings of self-security or self-sufficiency, or due to a lack of self-confidence. One minute they are prideful and haughty, and the next they are inferior and helpless. Psychiatry calls this an identity or interiority complex. Biblical Example: Saul

Rejection. Individuals who struggle with having an inferiority complex struggle to find a place to "fit in." Over time, the result is a pattern of rejection that builds a defense system of rejection. These individuals often struggle to maintain friendships or relationships because they have internalized a need to reject others before experiencing the rejection they feel is inevitably coming. They will sabotage relationships without having a clear understanding of why they are taking that course which embeds the identity inferiority even deeper.

Humor. It is not uncommon to find that comedians or individuals who are known for their humor are struggling with identity inferiority. The humor becomes a mask to wear for their performance of gaining approval from others, yet there is always the dark undercurrent of wondering if they are "enough." Many will think that they are merely struggling with depression or anxiety, but those diagnoses are not reaching the core of the issue that is driving the humorous personality.

Idolatrous Identity

The person think they are God or desires to be God. The person tends to worship creation rather than the creator. The worship tends to be of themselves, their ideas and perceptions or an idol god. It may seem farfetched, but there are religious practices that construct an altar of worship in the person's mind and invite various deities to come and worship. The deity that comes is the one that also becomes that person's identity.

Though this is not always the case, sometimes a person with an idolatrous identity, may not know they have become their own idol or that they are requiring others to idolize them. They may become upset if God or a person suggests this to them. Yet a person with an idolatrous identity tends to be right in their own eyes. They have a difficult time accepting constructive criticism, rebuke, and acknowledging ungodly or unhealthy behaviors.

Some people with idolatrous identities can be narcissistic. Narcists have an obsessive, grandiose, erotic, absorbed interest, and focus on themselves. Most if not all their decisions are rooted in self-centered benefits. Even when they perform good acts, there is an ulterior motive of personal benefit. They gain pleasure, gratification, and even arousal (for some) from how their actions, whether positive or negative, impact others. They may feel entitled to use and abuse people for their personal pleasure and gain.

Narcissists have a profound impact on people with a confused or inferior identity. They can control these types of people by isolating them, and further stealing and stripping them of their identity. Biblical Examples: Jezebel, Athaliah, Satan

Healthy Identity

The world would say that identity is being one's authentic self. I define healthy identity as being who God created us to be. Biblically, identity means being created in the likeness and image of God, as *identity* began in the garden with Adam and Eve.

Genesis 1:26 And God said, Let us make man in our image, after our likeness: and let them have dominion over the fish of the sea, and over the fowl of the air, and over the cattle, and over all the earth, and over every creeping thing that creepeth upon the earth.

God spoke: "Let us make human beings in our image, make them reflecting our nature So they can be responsible for the fish in the sea, the birds in the air, the cattle, And, yes, Earth itself, and every animal that moves on the face of Earth." (MSG)

<u>*Image* is *şelem* in Hebrew and means:</u>
1. to shade; a phantom, i.e. (figuratively) illusion, resemblance
2. hence, a representative figure, especially an idol
3. image, vain shew

<u>*Likeness* in Hebrew is *dmut* and means:</u>
1. resemblance; concretely, model, shape; adverbially, like
2. fashion, like (-ness, as), manner, similitude

<u>Dictionary.com defines of *likeness* as:</u>
1. a representation, picture, or image, especially a portrait
2. the state or fact of being like
3. the semblance or appearance of something; guise
4. correspondence in appearance; something that corresponds

God's Image - God Likeness				
Affinity	Agreement	Alikeness	Carbon	Clone
Copy	Dead Ringer	Depiction	Double	Fashion
Illusion	Model	Likeness	Model	Photocopy
Photograph	Picture	Replica	Representation	Reproduction
Resemblance	Sameness	Study	Uniformity	Xerox

<u>Dictionary.com defines *identity* as:</u>
1. the state or fact of remaining the same one or ones, as under varying aspects or conditions
2. the condition of being oneself or itself, and not another
3. condition or character as to who a person or what a thing is
4. the state or fact of being the same one as described
5. the sense of self, providing sameness and continuity in personality over time and sometimes disturbed in mental illnesses, as schizophrenia
6. exact likeness in nature or qualities
7. an instance or point of sameness or likeness

My question to the world is, *"How can someone identify who they are or be their authentic self if they do not acknowledge who created them, who their creator is, and seek knowledge of who they are through him?"*

Healthy identity is birthed through relationship with God. We have a healthy identity when we understand:

- Who God is and is not (our creator and ruler)

- Who we are and are not (our identity and purpose)

- We can actively live in our authentic self-based on who God is and who we are through God (our destiny and generational inheritance)

When Satan stole Job's identity, he experienced a season of seeking answers for what was occurring with him. God addressed Job by reminding him of the following truths:

1. He is a sovereign God of supreme authority and power (*Job 38*).

2. He is the creator of everything (*Job 38-39*).

3. Only God knows everything and how and why things operate or evolve in the way they do (*Job 39*).

4. Everything was created for the glory of God (*Job 38-42*).

5. All of creation received its identity through him (*Job 40:15-24*).

    Verse 15-16 Behold now behemoth, which I made with thee; he eateth grass as an ox. Lo now, his strength is in his loins, and his force is in the navel of his belly.

    The word *strength* and *force* speak of the identity of behemoth - its capacity ability, fruit, power, generative (creating) power, wealth, produce, fruit, vigor, mighty, success, goods, etc. As we consider this definition, we can ponder further the concept that God gives us identity.

6. No one can instruct, or judge Him, for he is God.

    Job 40:1-2 Moreover the Lord answered Job, and said, Shall he that contendeth with the Almighty instruct him? he that reproveth God, let him answer it.

7. When we seek to instruct or judge God we are in error, in pride, have exalted ourselves above him, and have become idolatrous.

    Job 40:8-13 Wilt thou also disannul my judgment? wilt thou condemn me, that thou mayest be righteous? Hast thou an arm like God? or canst thou thunder with a voice like him? Deck thyself now with majesty and excellency; and array thyself with glory and beauty. Cast abroad the rage of thy wrath: and behold every one that is proud, and abase him. Look on every one that is proud, and bring him low; and tread down the wicked in their place. Hide them in the dust together; and bind their faces in secret. Then will I also confess unto thee that thine own right hand can save thee.

8. We cannot obtain pure truth, knowledge, or revelation outside of God.

   Job 38:1-4 Then the Lord answered Job out of the whirlwind, and said, Who is this that darkeneth counsel by words without knowledge? Gird up now thy loins like a man; for I will demand of thee, and answer thou me. Where wast thou when I laid the foundations of the earth? declare if thou hast understanding.

9. We cannot save, deliver, and heal ourselves (*Job 41*).

10. Repentance and humility is key to restoring a stolen identity.

    Job 42:1-6 Then Job answered the Lord, and said, I know that thou canst do every thing, and that no thought can be withholden from thee. Who is he that hideth counsel without knowledge? therefore have I uttered that I understood not; things too wonderful for me, which I knew not. Hear, I beseech thee, and I will speak: I will demand of thee, and declare thou unto me. I have heard of thee by the hearing of the ear: but now mine eye seeth thee. Wherefore I abhor myself, and repent in dust and ashes.

11. Only God can restore our identity when it has been stolen (*Job 42:10-17*).

12. God will humble and judge those who alter, speak against our true identity and against who he is in us (*Job 42:7-9*).

13. Trusting him is what solidifies and fulfilled his identity and life's purpose (*Job 42:10-17*, full in *verse 17* means abounding, satisfying, and satiating).

Counselors help clients fulfill identity through God.

The truths of Job can be traced back to the garden with Adam and Eve. This is where our true identity began yet became tainted through interaction with the serpent.

Genesis 3:1-3 *Now the serpent was more subtle than any beast of the field which the Lord God had made. And he said unto the woman, Yea, hath God said, Ye shall not eat of every tree of the garden? And the woman said unto the serpent, We may eat of the fruit of the trees of the garden: But of the fruit of the tree which is in the midst of the garden, God hath said, Ye shall not eat of it, neither shall ye touch it, lest ye die.*

<u>Touch</u> is *nâga'* in Hebrew and means:
1. lay the hand upon (for any purpose; to lie with a woman)
2. to reach (figuratively, to arrive, acquire); violently, to strike (punish, defeat, destroy, etc.)
3. beat, (be able to) bring (down), cast, come (nigh), draw near (nigh), get up, happen, join, near, plague, reach (up), smite, strike, touch

God knew that eating from the tree would strike down (lessen), and kill man's image of self, the image of God as God, and the image of who God created the person to become.

Verse 4 *And the serpent said unto the woman, Ye shall not surely die: For God doth know that in the day ye eat thereof, then your eyes shall be opened, and ye shall be as gods, knowing good and evil. And when the woman saw that the tree was good for food, and that it was pleasant to the eyes, and a tree to be desired to make one wise, she took of the fruit thereof, and did eat, and gave also unto her husband with her; and he did eat.*

Even in this conversation, the serpent was able to change the perception of Eve regarding the tree just by making her think it would provide more knowledge of herself, God, and the world, than what she already had.

Verse 7-11 *And the eyes of them both were opened, and they knew that they were naked; and they sewed fig leaves together, and made themselves aprons. And they heard the voice of the Lord God walking in the garden in the cool of the day: and Adam and his wife hid themselves from the presence of the Lord God amongst the trees of the garden. And the Lord God called unto Adam, and said unto him, Where art thou? And he said, I heard thy voice in the garden, and I was afraid, because I was naked; and I hid myself. And he said, Who told thee that thou wast naked? Hast thou eaten of the tree, whereof I commanded thee that thou shouldest not eat?*

That word *told* in Hebrew also means "*expound*." In other words, God was saying "*who enlightened or gave you a different revelation of yourself that is outside of what I have told you? Outside of my presence?*" To this point, Adam and Even were only communing with God while taking walks with him. God was building them up, letting them know their worth and authority, and teaching them how to live a life of dominion and destiny.

👉 **God was saying, "*Who enlightened or gave you a different revelation of yourself that is outside of what I told you? Outside of my presence?*** I needed to say that again so you, the counselor, could ponder it a bit.

Verse 13 *And the man said, The woman whom thou gavest to be with me, she gave me of the tree, and I did eat.*

Because of this act of disobedience, God judged the serpent, Adam, and Eve, for their rebellious acts towards his word (***Genesis 3:13-19***).

As you finish reading the story in this chapter, you will find that a new life plan was put in place. It was Plan B. It was a plan that distorted the original plan of God for us to live in the image (identity of God) such that we may accede to his distinctive blessings.

As we discern from this story, all of us possess a likeness of God because we were created in his image. It is impossible to be created by someone and not have a strand of who they are in us. We can deny God, deny his existence, deny his rulership over our lives, but that will never change the fact that he created us. It is indisputable that a facet of his image resides in us. We see this in:

Romans 1:18-20 *For the wrath of God is revealed from heaven against all ungodliness and unrighteousness of men, who hold the truth in unrighteousness; Because that which may be known of God is manifest in them; for God hath shewed it unto them. For the invisible things of him from the creation of the world are clearly seen, being understood by the things that are made, even his eternal power and Godhead; so that they are without excuse.*

In this passage of scripture, God confirms that even if we do not want to know Him or that He exists, WE KNOW! He has made His existence noticeably clear in the world around us and has put a knowing inside of us. We can choose to suppress it and even deny it but we know. We can choose to ignore it or even wrestle with it, but we know. We can build and live in our own little fantasy world, but the knowing is still there. Even the devil knows God exists and knows what God likes and dislikes. Satan may rebel against it, BUT HE KNOWS, and makes it clear in his war against all mankind, that he understands God creates and God rules.

With this knowledge inside and around us, also comes some truths about what God sees as righteous and unrighteousness. The knowledge of righteous and unrighteousness helps us distinguish God's character and nature from what is evil, defiled, worldly, and demonic. It is that little voice or twinge inside of us that causes us to question our actions and behavior. It is at this point we must assert power to choose God's righteousness over our own pleasures or desires.

Ephesians 1:18 The eyes of your understanding being enlightened; that ye may know what is the hope of his calling, and what the riches of the glory of his inheritance in the saints,

Eyes is "*ophthalmos*" in the Greek and means, "vision, the eyes of the mind, the faculty of knowing."

The eyes of your understanding are what we see that is palpable to God's existence. It is also the voice or innate twinge on the inside of you. God has already equipped us to know Him, to know what is of Him, and to know more about Him. In **Romans 1:18-20**, God says, you know me and know what is of me, so you have no excuse.

But God shows his anger from heaven against all sinful, wicked people who suppress the truth by their wickedness. They know the truth about God because he has made it obvious to them. For ever since the world was created, people have seen the earth and sky. Through everything God made, they can clearly see his invisible qualities—his eternal power and divine nature. So they have no excuse for not knowing God. (NLT)

This is the reason God wanted us to praise his works from one generation to the other. He knew that doing so would establish his presence in the family line and ensure relationship with him where identity could be instilled in us from the womb.

Psalm 78:1-8 GIVE EAR, O my people, to my teaching; incline your ears to the words of my mouth. I will open my mouth in a parable (in instruction by numerous examples); I will utter dark sayings of old [that hide important truth]—Which we have heard and known, and our fathers have told us. We will not hide them from their children, but we will tell to the generation to come the praiseworthy deeds of the Lord, and His might, and the wonderful works that He has performed. For He established a testimony (an express precept) in Jacob and appointed a law in Israel, commanding our fathers that they should make [the great facts of God's dealings with Israel] known to their children,

That the generation to come might know them, that the children still to be born might arise and recount them to their children, That they might set their hope in God and not forget the works of God, but might keep His commandments And might not be as their fathers—a stubborn and rebellious generation, a generation that set not their hearts aright nor prepared their hearts to know God, and whose spirits were not steadfast and faithful to God. (AMP)

Psalm 145:3-7 Great is the Lord, and greatly to be praised; and his greatness is unsearchable. One generation shall praise thy works to another and shall declare thy mighty acts. I will speak of the glorious honour of thy majesty, and of thy wondrous works. And men shall speak of the might of thy terrible acts: and I will declare thy greatness. They shall abundantly utter the memory of thy great goodness and shall sing of thy righteousness.

Luke 1:50 And his mercy is on them that fear him from generation to generation.

If we are going to restore healthy identities in our generational line and in society, it is important to understand and instill the truth, revelation, wisdom, honor and fear of the Lord into our children from the womb, such that as they grow up, they mature in the image of the Lord.

Psalm 22:10 I was cast upon thee from the womb: thou art my God from my mother's belly.

Psalm 139:13-14 For thou hast possessed my reins: thou hast covered me in my mother's womb. I will praise thee; for I am fearfully and wonderfully made: marvellous are thy works; and that my soul knoweth right well.

Jeremiah 1:5 Before I formed thee in the belly I knew thee; and before thou camest forth out of the womb I sanctified thee, and I ordained thee a prophet unto the nations.

Isaiah 49:1 Listen, O isles, unto me; and hearken, ye people, from far; The LORD hath called me from the womb; from the bowels of my mother hath he made mention of my name.

Biblical Example: David

David remained stable in who he was and who God was despite life challenges, obstacles, personal sins, failures. triumphs and successes. He was always extremely convicted when he engaged in behaviors that he knew were not God or lessened who he was in God. David had a healthy sense of who he was and was not, and who he was called to be. He stood confidently in his office and position. He served those who did not recognize who he was, belittled who he was, wanted to kill who he was, and who he would one day replace and rule over. David would experience times of making decisions through his own flesh and desires. He even had prideful, foolish, or ignorant moments. But despite these decisions, his identity was not distorted. He was not confused about his identity. David knew very well who he was. David was rooted and grounded in his relationship with God. He received corrections and consequences for his action and remained in destiny covenant with God. God was always David's source of provision, security, confidence, successes, restoration, revelation, rejuvenation, renewal of character and integrity, maturity, and growth. God called him a man after his own heart and chose him as king. Not because he was perfect, but because David was clear that he could not live without God, was a representation of God, and wanted the life that God ordained for him.

1 Samuel 13:14 But now thy kingdom shall not continue: the LORD hath sought him a man after his own heart, and the LORD hath commanded him to be captain over his people, because thou hast not kept that which the LORD commanded thee.

Our hearts are a representation of our inner man which consist of our mind, will, heart, soul, and understanding. Our hearts are also a reflection of what we think about ourselves, God, others, and the world around us. Within our hearts reside our appetite, emotions, thoughts, the seat of our courage. David sought God's heart, so even in his own imperfection, he was able to reflect and continuously be restored into the image of God.

Biblical Example: Daniel

Daniel was part of the royal family of the throne of David. When Jerusalem was besieged, Daniel was placed in captivity by Nebuchadnezzar of Babylon. He was made to serve the king and his successors. Despite being an imprisoned slave, David maintained and lived through his true God identity that allowed him to shine, receive favor, and be highly preferred in a sphere that was meant to demoralize and strip him of his identity.

Daniel 6:3 *Then this Daniel was preferred above the presidents and princes, because an excellent spirit was in him; and the king thought to set him over the whole realm (kingdom).*

But Daniel, brimming with spirit and intelligence, so completely outclassed the other vice-regents and governors that the king decided to put him in charge of the whole kingdom. (MSG)

<u>*Excellent*</u> in the Hebrew is <u>*yatiyr*</u> and means:
1. very exceeding(-ly), excellent, pre-eminent, surpassing
2. extreme, extraordinary, exceedingly, extremely

<u>Dictionary.com define *excellent*</u> as:
1. possessing outstanding quality or superior merit; remarkably good
2. extraordinary; superior

Daniel's identity of royalty radiated so that he was given governmental rulership over a kingdom that was meant to enslave him. He was so secure in being himself, that he outclassed those who had positions of power and authority over him.

When someone possesses God identity yet lives in a place of poverty, slavery, misfortune - where the odds are stacked against them, their God identity can still unveil, evolve, while making provision and pathways for them to excel. This is vital information for a counselor. They can use this insight to empower clients who are less fortunate or have extreme challenges, by helping them to evolve in God identity so they can flourish despite life obstacles.

As we explored Daniel's life, we read the president and prince said they could find no fault – no corruption in Daniel. They sought to strip him of the very thing that gave him his identity, which was prayer and relationship with God. The presidents and princes convinced the King to sign a decree that if anyone prayed to any other god outside of the king, they would be put in the lion's den.

Verse 4-9 Then the presidents and princes sought to find occasion against Daniel concerning the kingdom; but they could find none occasion nor fault; forasmuch as he was faithful, neither was there any error or fault found in him. Then said these men, We shall not find any occasion against this Daniel, except we find it against him concerning the law of his God. Then these presidents and princes assembled together to the king, and said thus unto him, King Darius, live for ever. All the presidents of the kingdom, the governors, and the princes, the counsellors, and the captains, have consulted together to establish a royal statute, and to make a firm decree, that whosoever shall ask a petition of any God or man for thirty days, save of thee, O king, he shall be cast into the den of lions. Now, O king, establish the decree, and sign the writing, that it be not changed, according to the law of the Medes and Persians, which altereth not. Wherefore king Darius signed the writing and the decree.

Daniel continued to pray to God and ended up in the lion's den.

Verse 10 Now when Daniel knew that the writing was signed, he went into his house; and his windows being open in his chamber toward Jerusalem, he kneeled upon his knees three times a day, and prayed, and gave thanks before his God, as he did aforetime.

Verse 16 Then the king commanded, and they brought Daniel, and cast him into the den of lions. Now the king spake and said unto Daniel, Thy God whom thou servest continually, he will deliver thee.

Daniel had so much favor with the king that he dread putting him in the lion's den. He arose early in the morning to check on Daniel. God had shut up the mouths of the lions that no harm came to Daniel. Daniel told the king that innocence was found in him.

Verse 20 -23 Then the king arose very early in the morning, and went in haste unto the den of lions. And when he came to the den, he cried with a lamentable voice unto Daniel: and the king spake and said to Daniel, O Daniel, servant of the living God, is thy God, whom thou servest continually, able to deliver thee from the lions? Then said Daniel unto the king, O king, live for ever. My God hath sent his angel, and hath shut the lions' mouths, that they have not hurt me: forasmuch as before him innocency was found in me; and also before thee, O king, have I done no hurt. Then was the king exceedingly glad for him, and commanded that they should take Daniel up out of the den. So Daniel was taken up out of the den, and no manner of hurt was found upon him, because he believed in his God.

That innocence was the pure, transparency, guiltlessness, liberation, and unadorned identity of the Lord in Daniel. Daniel was solid in who he was and his way of life. He lived the image and purpose of the Lord. Not even the threat of losing his life swayed him in his identity and trust of the Lord.

King Darius realized that nothing could kill God's identity. King Darius made a decree regarding the sovereign of Daniel's God, and how God is a deliverer of those who live in and through him.

Verse 26-28 I make a decree, That in every dominion of my kingdom men tremble and fear before the God of Daniel: for he is the living God, and steadfast for ever, and his kingdom that which shall not be destroyed, and his dominion shall be even unto the end. He delivereth and rescueth, and he worketh signs and wonders in heaven and in earth, who hath delivered Daniel from the power of the lions. So this Daniel prospered in the reign of Darius, and in the reign of Cyrus the Persian.

God identity lives through eternity. The signs and wonders that God will perform through his identity in us, will live on forever and ever – throughout generations - even into eternity.

Counselor, nothing can kill God' identity. Generations will celebrate your client's God's identity, as you process them to wholeness!

Chapter 16

MAINTAINING A HEALTHY IDENTITY

Maintaining a healthy identity requires a lifestyle of reverenced fear and honor for the Lord. Canadian psychologist James Marcia extended the previously cited model (Chapter 15) of identity developed by Erik Erickson. Consider his four-part Identity Statuses, particularly in light of our prior consideration that many adults are fixed in an adolescent developmental phase:

- ***Identity Diffusion*** *– The status in which the adolescent does not have a sense of having choices; he or she has not yet made (nor is attempting/willing to make) a commitment.*

- ***Identity Foreclosure*** *– The status in which the adolescent seems willing to commit to some relevant roles, values, or goals for the future. Adolescents in this stage have not experienced an identity crisis. They tend to conform to the expectations of others regarding their future (e. g. allowing a parent to determine a career direction) As such, these individuals have not explored a range of options.*

- ***Identity Moratorium*** *– The status in which the adolescent is currently in a crisis, exploring various commitments and is ready to make choices, but has not made a commitment to these choices yet.*

- ***Identity Achievement*** *– The status in which adolescent has gone through an identity crisis and has made a commitment to a sense of identity (i.e. certain role or value) that he or she has chosen.*[38]

The stages listed are not sequential. A person can experience one or more of these stages. 2Timothy 2:22 advocates that we flee youthful lusts which speaks to our ability to make choices that are grounded, mature, and a reflection of stability. It is not uncommon to have a client who may be extraordinarily successful in their life, yet have a particular area where growth is still needed. It is essential for the counselor to consistently affirm that having areas of life that needs processing and deliverance, does not devalue the other parts of a person's accomplishments. Neither do the successful portions of a person's life extinguish (or balance)

---

[38]James Marcia. (1966). Development and validation of ego-identity status. *Journal of Personality and Social Psychology*, 3(5), 551.

their need for healing in another area. David, Job, John the Baptist, and others who became role models for identity in the scriptures had honor and reverence for the Lord. None of those characters were without flaws, but the scripture allows us to see the bigger picture of their processing. David struggled with lust but is remembered as a man after God's own heart. Job struggled with pride but ultimately became a man blessed with a double portion. John the Baptist questioned whether Jesus was truly the Messiah, but he is known for his commitment to decrease while Jesus' reputation increased. Reverence is a feeling or attitude of deep respect tinged with awe, veneration. Dictionary.com contends that when we revere someone it is outward manifestation of our feeling. It a gesture indicative of deep respect; an obeisance, bow, or curtsy. Reverencing God is recognizing that our life plan is designed by him, and we trust him enough to put our energy into finding our way into that plan. In other words, we are developing competence through reverence. Using biblical characters aligns to the modeling phase of self-efficacy theories.

Self-efficacy theory, when actualized, is an effective strategy for defeating learned helplessness and for restructuring locus of control. The counselor's role begins with setting reasonable goals for skills mastery, utilizes modeling, followed by assisting the client with reinterpreting their response to various cues and symptoms, and finally persuasion cements the efforts of the process into a healthy identity. Unlike coping or social support theories that lack advocacy for resolution, self-efficacy aligns to the biblical model of deliverance and healing.

Diagram 16.0 Self-efficacy theory

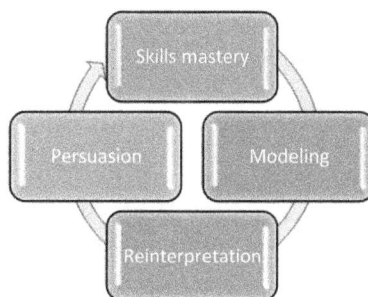

Source: Gonzalez, Goeppinger, and Lorig, 1990[39]

---

[39] Virginia M. Gonzalez, Jean Goeppinger, and Kate Lorig. (1990). Four psychosocial theories and their application to patient education and clinical practice. Retrieved from Wiley online library at https://onlinelibrary.wiley.com/doi/pdf/10.1002/art.1790030305

Honor is when we display high respect, as worth, merit, or rank for someone. It is manifested respect, high public esteem; fame; glory for that person. We are privileged to be associated with that person, group, organization, etc. Human beings are made with the instinctive need to honor their Creator. When we put that honor on anything but God, we are not only operating in idolatry but are missing out on the wonderful blessings that come with healthy relationship through healthy identity.

Honor and reverence are what helps us keep a right perspective of who God is so that we understand that he is the all-powerful sovereign God who reigns in supreme authority. When we no longer honor and reverence God we become:

- lukewarm to the consequences of our actions,
- compromising in our morals and standards,
- wavering in our decision making and actions,
- while opening the door for the devil, people, and society, to come in and steal our identity.

Proverbs 1:7 *The fear of the LORD is the beginning of knowledge: but fools despise wisdom and instruction.*

Proverbs 9:10 *The fear of the LORD is the beginning of wisdom: and the knowledge of the holy is understanding.*

Psalm 111:10 *The fear of the LORD is the beginning of wisdom: a good understanding have all they that do his commandments: his praise endureth for ever.*

Fear of God invokes wisdom in our lives where we can humble ourselves to the Lord and receive the revelation we need for a successful life. When we do not fear God, our decision making is paralleled to a fool.

Fool is ewîyl in Hebrew and means:
1. from an unused root (meaning to be perverse)
2. (figuratively) silly - fool(-ish) (man)
3. be foolish, foolish

4. one who despises wisdom, of one who mocks when guilty
5. of one who is quarrelsome, of one who is licentious

Dictionary.com defines *licentious* as:
1. sexually unrestrained; lascivious; libertine; lewd
2. unrestrained by law or general morality; lawless; immoral
3. going beyond customary or proper bounds or limits; disregarding rules

When we lack fear for the Lord, we risk engaging in behaviors that are contrary to our identity. We succumb to beliefs, laws, and standards, that are contrary to God and contrary to who we are in him.

1 Chronicles 16:17-20 Glory and honour are in his presence; strength and gladness are in his place. Give unto the Lord, ye kindreds of the people, give unto the Lord glory and strength. Give unto the Lord the glory due unto his name: bring an offering, and come before him: worship the Lord in the beauty of holiness. Fear before him, all the earth: the world also shall be stable, that it be not moved.

Give is yâ*hab* in Hebrew and means:
1. to give (whether literal or figurative)
2. generally, to put; imperatively (reflexive)
3. come: — ascribe, bring, come on, give, go, set, take

Ascribe means "to credit or assign, to impute, charge, attribute one as the cause or source of something."

Dictionary.com defines *scribe* as:
1. a person who serves as a professional copyist, especially one who made copies of manuscripts before the invention of printing
2. a public clerk or writer, usually one having official status
3. an interpreter
4. a writer or author, especially a journalist

When you ascribe glory and honor your words are literally writing in the atmosphere, in the region, into the person to which you are giving it to. As a scribe you are serving as an authority figure that is set in position to be able to author the glory and reverence of God.

In this instance you are ascribing that God is *"majestic, grand, beautiful, goodly, excellent, bold, vigorous, strong, mighty, splendid, honorable, worth honoring, all powerful, all knowing."* Remember that God said he desires truth to be in our inward parts (**Psalm 51:6**). That is speaking to truth in the hidden recesses or the secret part of our being.

When you lack honor and reverence for God, your identity is not in a place to fully possess the authority to ascribe him glory and honor. Your ascribing becomes fictional work as you are speaking of a God through your imagination, through imitation and deceit, but what you are scribing is not the truth of your heart or life. It is the fictitious creativity of your mind, a delusion of glory and honor. You are not a demonstration of the true facts needed to ascribe him glory and honor.

Psalm 45:1 *My heart is inditing (composing, prescribing) a good matter: I speak of the things which I have made touching the king: my tongue is the pen of a ready writer.*

This is the reason many people speak of God, but he continues to be defamed as their lives do not proclaim who he is. We can praise and worship him on Sunday but not live a life of praise, worship, and righteousness, in our day-to-day life. What we are scribing is not being written in us, in our households and families, in our atmospheres and regions, so there is nothing to sustain us from one situation to the next.

Many are living an imagined life of glory and honor, but because their identity is confused, distorted, etc., the authority to ascribe glory and see God be established and manifested in one's life is simply vain glory. When a person writes a book of fiction, it is often for their own fame. Now one is receiving credit for their fictional character but them. That person is receiving some type of success, respect, accolade, and gratitude, yet the fictional work is just a form of imagination or what could be considered truth. So its reflection is based on ideas and fantasies, but does not have a tangible factual identity. God is not fiction. He is a real tangible God with factual truths of his existence.

Our fictional imaginations can take us places that are way outside of God's standards and truths. We succumb to acts and behaviors that have nothing to do with him, yet we will contend they are of and for the glory of God. Only when we know who we are and who we are not can we then properly differentiate between spiritual fact and personal fiction. Once there is clarity about who God is and is not, what his purpose is in our lives, can we live in those truths that will adequately ascribe him glory and honor. Living in these truths helps us to maintain a healthy identity that is rooted in honor and reverence for him.

1 Chronicles 16:17-20 *Honor and majesty are [found] in His presence; strength and joy are [found] in His sanctuary. Ascribe to the Lord, you families of the peoples, ascribe to the Lord glory and strength, Ascribe to the Lord the glory due His name. Bring an offering and come before Him; worship the Lord in the beauty of holiness and in holy array. Tremble and reverently fear before Him, all the earth's peoples; the world also shall be established, so it cannot be moved. (AMP)*

Reverence Declaration: We esteem, respect, admire, defer to, look up to, appreciate, value, cherish, adore; reverence, revere, venerate, worship, distinguish, recognize, show privilege to, glory, yield kudos, reign prestige, merit, give all the credit to, pay homage, declare undeniably importance to, declare noteworthy, bestie favor, tremendously bless you, Lord Jesus.

Kingdom Wellness Counseling and Mentoring Center

Faith Based Counseling

Manual I

Part 5: Chapters (17 – 19)

Learning Objectives:

- To provide definitive revelation regarding maintaining biblical standards.
- To provide counseling samples for assisting clients with defining and living through their god ordained standards.
- To provide insight on self-worth, godly value, and how to overcome inferiority and inadequacy.
- To provide counseling samples for assisting clients with exploring self-worth and inadequacy issues and rebuilding their self-esteem.

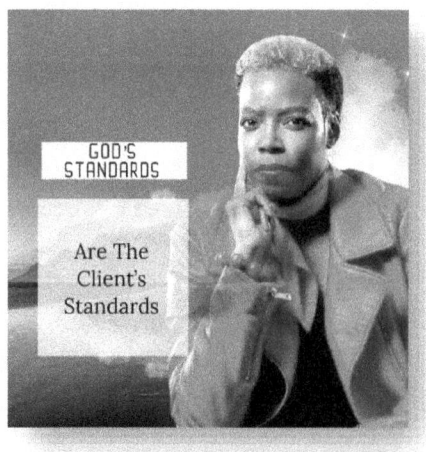

GOD'S STANDARDS

Are The Client's Standards

Chapter 17

MAINTAINING BIBLICAL STANDARDS

Most are willing to set goals for fulfilling various goals and objectives concerning our natural life. Goals are great for achieving temporal success. Destiny, however, is not a goal to be conquered, put the plaque on the wall, and mark it off your to-do list. Destiny is not a one-hit wonder. A person should never plateau in destiny. Once there is an achievement, there should always be an acceleration by increasing, growing, constantly filling and fulfilling, conquering, and protecting, all that has been accomplished. Faith based counseling strategies must always be built at the destiny level. Simply getting a client to find relief by setting goals is not the purpose of faith-based counseling. This is the dividing line between many secular theories and the vision of counseling through biblical standards.

Genesis 1:28 And God blessed them, and God said unto them, Be fruitful, and multiply, and replenish the earth, and subdue it: and have dominion over the fish of the sea, and over the fowl of the air, and over every living thing that moveth upon the earth

Destiny is a continually evolving lifestyle. It is an intentional standard of living that God has designed.

 **Destiny is a continually evolving lifestyle.**

Philippians 3:12-14 Not as though I had already attained, either were already perfect: but I follow after, if that I may apprehend that for which also, I am apprehended of Christ Jesus. Brethren, I count not myself to have apprehended: but this one thing I do, forgetting those things which are behind, and reaching forth unto those things which are before. I press toward the mark for the prize of the high calling of God in Christ Jesus.

Verse 12-20 I'm not saying that I have this all together, that I have it made. But I am well on my way, reaching out for Christ, who has so wondrously reached out for me. Friends, don't get me wrong: By no means do I count myself an expert in all of this, but I've got my eye on the goal, where God is beckoning us onward—to Jesus. I'm off and running, and I'm not turning back. So, let's keep focused on that goal, those of us who want everything God has for us. If any of you have something else in mind, something less than total commitment, God will clear your blurred vision—you'll see it yet! Now that we're on the right track, let's stay on it.

Stick with me, friends. Keep track of those you see running this same course, headed for this same goal. There are many out there taking other paths, choosing other goals, and trying to get you to go along with them. I've warned you of them many times; sadly, I'm having to do it again. All they want is easy street. They hate Christ's Cross. But easy street is a dead-end street. Those who live there make their bellies their gods; belches are their praise; all they can think of is their appetites. But there's far more to life for us. We're citizens of high heaven! We're waiting the arrival of the Savior, the Master, Jesus Christ, who will transform our earthy bodies into glorious bodies like his own. He'll make us beautiful and whole with the same powerful skill by which he is putting everything as it should be, under and around him. (MSG)

Apprehend in Greek is *katalambanō* and means:
1. to take eagerly, i.e. seize, possess, etc. (literally or figuratively)
2. apprehend, attain, come upon, comprehend, find, obtain, perceive, (over) take
3. to lay hold of, to lay hold of so as to make one's own, to obtain, attain to, to make one's own
4. to take into one's self, appropriate, seize upon, take possession of

God does not want us to have goals about our relationship with him. He wants us to live a life that demonstrates our belief and faith in him. He wants it to be our system, our standard, our lifestyle.

Isaiah 59:19 *So shall they fear the name of the Lord from the west, and his glory from the rising of the sun. When the enemy shall come in like a flood, the Spirit of the Lord shall lift up a standard against him.*

Standard is *nus* in Hebrew and means:
1. to flit (to move lightly and swiftly, fly, change one's address)
2. vanish away (subside, escape; causatively, chase, impel, deliver)
3. disappear quickly, make invisible, disappear by ceasing to exist; come to an end
4. abate (annul, extinguish, suppress), away, be displayed, (make to) flee (away)
5. put to flight, hide, lift up a standard
6. to drive hastily, to cause to disappear, hide

When we know God's standard and we STAND in it, our standard becomes the weapon to abate, send fleeing, drive away, vanish, and put an end to the challenging or fiery trials in our life. Even though the Apostle Peter tells us to not think it is strange when fiery trials come (*1 Peter 4:12*), he lets us know that the purpose is to glorify God and increase our joy. He actually calls it exceeding joy which speaks to the fulfillment of divine promise.

A standard is an approved model, and in this case one approved by God, and that aligns with his word and will for a person's life.

Dictionary.com defines *standard* as:
1. something considered by an authority or by general consent as a basis of comparison
2. an approved model
3. a rule or principle that is used as a basis for judgment
4. an average or normal requirement, quality, quantity, level, grade, etc.
5. standards, those morals, ethics, habits, etc., established by authority, custom, or an individual as acceptable

A flood is a great overflowing or outpouring of water that covers, fills, submerges, overwhelms, overtakes, damages, destroys, and drowns land, people, and material objects.

When the enemy comes in like a flood, he seeks to:

- Make himself comparable or above God,

- Become governor and rule of a thing by covering and overtaking it,

- Flood a person's life with people, things, conditions, and situations, that are not God,

- Overwhelm people so they become weary, pressured, weighty, while giving into drowning by that which has consumed them,

- Damage the identity and purpose of a person or thing,

- Destroy the identity and purpose of a person or thing,

- Cause settling and compromise that leads to death.

Let's consider what happens when we settle and compromise our standards. As you examine this fact, think about your own life or even of a potential client.

Most structures cannot withstand a flood because the influx of water has intensively destructive power. When flood waters settle on land, it causes erosion to occur in the soil. This can destroy the foundation of buildings, whether the structure collapses immediately or permanent damage results in the need for demolition. As extended flooding occurs, erosion wears on the land which compromises the ground's productivity. This eventually compromises the natural state of the land by change the natural composition and proposition of whatever it flooded (changes the identity and purpose of a thing).

> *"Floods can cause even more damage when their waters recede. The water and landscape can be contaminated with hazardous materials, such as sharp debris, pesticides, fuel, and untreated sewage. Potentially dangerous mold can quickly overwhelm water-soaked structures. As flood water spreads, it carries disease. Flood victims can be left for weeks without clean water for drinking or hygiene. This can lead to outbreaks of deadly diseases."*[40]

Essentially, the flood acts as a thief, while God's standard gives life and that more abundantly. **John 10:10** says, *"The thief cometh not, but for to steal, and to kill, and to destroy: I am come that they might have life, and that they might have it more abundantly."*

Standards prevent:

- the enemy from stealing, killing, and destroying, the identity of a person or thing,
- the person from settling and compromising beneath God's identity for their life,
- the person from cycling into old behavioral patterns,
- the person from failing and aborting their success and progress,
- the person from developing new sin issues, unhealthy behaviors, and experiencing trials and challenges that God did not intend,
- health hazards and disease from emotionally, spiritually, and naturally, infecting a person,

---

[40]Encyclopedic Entry. (n.d.) Flood. Retrieved from National Geographic website at https://www.nationalgeographic.org/encyclopedia/flood/

- The person from becoming consumed and transformed by the identity of the enemy, while being transformed into something God did not intend for them to be.

Levees are used to keep waters within their respective habitats and borders. Standards provides clear boundaries that serve as a levee from the floodwaters of the enemy. When we live by the standards the Lord has established, the spirit of the Lord can raise these standards up against the enemy's floodwater. If we have no standards, minimal standards, compromised standards, contaminated standards, or confused standards, our levee can easily be overtaken by the flood of the enemy. It is important to know who we are and what God's standards are, so we live a fortified lifestyle that supports our progress.

Counselor, help clients define their godly standards so they can sustain in destiny with God.

Isaiah 59:19 So [as the result of the Messiah's intervention] they shall [reverently] fear the name of the Lord from the west, and His glory from the rising of the sun. When the enemy shall come in like a flood, the Spirit of the Lord will lift up a standard against him and put him to flight [for He will come like a rushing stream which the breath of the Lord drives]. (AMP)

In the west they'll fear the name of GOD, in the east they'll fear the glory of GOD, For he'll arrive like a river in flood stage, whipped to a torrent by the wind of GOD. (MSG)

Identify Client Standards In The Following Areas:

- **Life** - As a woman or man and for one's life in general
- **Identity** - Character, nature, integrity, morals, reputation
- **Judgments** - Judge self and others, respect the freewill of others, while maintaining one's own judgments
- **Presentation** - Clothing, attire, what the person desire to speak to people through their attitude and demeanor
- **Purity** - Chastity, virginity, abstinence, righteousness, holiness, virtue, sexual image
- **Acquaintances and Stranger Interactions** - Politeness, respect, resolving of conflicts, favor, treatment from others, and vice versa
- **Friendships** - Love, belonging, communication, maintain healthy relationships and boundaries, avoid drama, accept constructive criticisms and truth, resolve conflicts
- **Singleness** - Fulfillment in singleness, ability to handle loneliness, consider and prepare for marriage if that is God's will
- **Dating Relationships** – Perception of dating, what dating entails, whose date worthy, curfews, boundaries, casual dating, dating for marriage
- **Marriage** – Personal and godly desires and needs regarding marriage, engagement standards, premarital counseling, wedding planning, conduct while handling stressors of wedding planning
- **Submission** – Biblical and personal perceptions of submission in marriage, God's requirement regarding marriage and submission and honor, one's ability to accept criticism, grow in relationship and submission
- **Home** – Biblical and personal perspective regarding the home life of a family; what will be allowed or will not be tolerated in the home, e.g. guests, music, tv, media standards, respect, honor, atmosphere
- **Parenting Style** – Biblical and personal standards for raising children; expectations, bring correction, instill healthy and godly standards
- **Immediate & Extended Family Relationships & Interactions** – A person does not choose family can choose how family engage in our lives and what loyalties align with one's standards. This determines what strongholds, curses, bondages and blessings are passed down from generation to generation. Loyalty, false loyalty, obligations, culture, customs, traditions and the effects on what God requires of a person
- **Social Interaction** - Conduct on the internet, social media, public interaction
- **Physical Body** – wellness regarding care for one's body; body treatment, preservation, lifespan, exercise regimen
- **Disposition** - emotional stability, state of mind, emotional outlook on life and situations, mood, inclinations

- **Health** - Breaking generational and culture curses related to health, eating habits, doctor visits, faith in God to heal
- **Finances** - Debt perspective, prosperity and wealth goals and standards, future security
- **Education** - Peer interaction, teacher interactions, procedures for handling conflict and challenges, sports goals, extracurricular activities, grades, scholarships, educational level desired, degree pursuit desired, purpose of educational level and degree; its relations to destiny and calling
- **Job** - Type of occupation desired, goals for advancing in a career
- **Workplace Setting** - Interactions in the workplace with coworkers; compromises as it relates to the laws of the world, the policies and procedures the workplace
- **Entrepreneur** – Self-employment, business plan, vision, purpose of goals for sustained success
- **Church** – Religious and spiritual views; church and leadership desires and needs, personal, leadership, church, perception
- **Church Fellowship** - Commitment to fellowship, the building spiritual relationships, and church community; expectations of other believers, evangelizing, soul winning, deliverance, healing, spiritual wellness
- **Giftings** – Knowing and governing one's talents, gifts, abilities; understanding God's will for gifts, intent in utilizing and growing in these areas, e.g., trainings, certifications, workshops, licenses
- **Calling** – Knowing and maturing in one's purpose in life, creating, seasonally examining, and maintaining goals, focuses, and plans for learning and sustaining in a destiny lifestyle
- **Spiritual Walk** - Desire for one's relationship with God, willingness to put him first and allow his spirit to guide destiny; goals for a productive prayer life, study habits, fasting lifestyle, accountability
- **Future** – Identifying, mentoring, and establishing successors; creating, working, building, and leaving a written and working destiny plan to help successors sustain; setting standards for making sure what is built, imparted, invested in, broken off the bloodline, instilled in the bloodline, sustain throughout the generations

Standard Exploration Assignment For Clients:

Provide this as a homework assignment. Have the client add a scripture to each standard.

1. What is the purpose of the flood of the enemy?
2. What is settling?
3. What is compromise?
4. How do the client know when they are settling beneath God's standard for their life?
5. What are some areas in life that could cause the levee to break should the enemy send a flood into the client's life?
6. What are some behaviors and cycles a client need to have cleansed and broken in their life?
7. What are some positive attributes and behaviors the client possess but need to strengthen to increase their standard for who they are and how God desires their life to be?
8. What is the client willing to do in order to receive deliverance in areas that compromise their levee?
9. How can the client take steps to receive that deliverance and healing?
10. Will the client commit to practicing their standard until it becomes a normal part of their everyday life? If they are, encourage the client to keep a journal of their progress and to have at least two accountability partners that can assist them with maintaining their standards.
11. What steps can the client take for accountability in improving their standards?

Chapter 18

TEACHING CLIENTS ABOUT SELF-WORTH

After a client has determined their standards, they must determine:

- What is their personal worth?
- How valuable are their standards as a lifestyle?

This is essential because many will state they believe certain things or will state they have a moral conscious about particular matters, but do not possess the self-worth or moral godly value level needed to hold to their standards. When there is no sense of self-worth or moral godly value, clients tend to sway in their standards even though their belief system does not change.

Self-worth and godly values confirm how important something is to a client.

- How valuable do they believe they are? What do they believe their worth is?
- How important is it to live within the standard God has set for their lives?

Because living for God is a choice, a client must have revelation in this area if they are going to live their standards no matter what unfolds in their life.

Self-worth is a client's self-respect or self-esteem. It is:

- A favorable or realistic perception of oneself.
- A feeling or perception that they are a good person who deserves to be treated with respect and should have the best regarding life in any given situation.
- The belief that they are worth God's best. They are worth God's standard for their lives.

Sometimes clients will not possess healthy self-respect and self-esteem, because of inadequacies, insecurities, and negative opinions of themselves.

Inadequacy is defined as, *"having a feeling of deficiency, incompleteness, or insufficiency, regarding life or for a position, task or duty."*

Insecurity is defined as, *"a lack of confidence, self-assurance; self-doubt, instability, inferiority, low self-esteem, fear of what others will think, timidity, shyness, embarrassment, self-consciousness, or uncertainty about one's self and life endeavors."*

Low self-esteem is defined as *"having a general negative opinion of oneself; judging or evaluating oneself negatively and placing a negative value on oneself as a person."*

A client may have challenges of inadequacy, insecurity and low self-esteem, because they did not have an adequate empowering of confidence and self-worth growing up that made them feel at peace with themselves, or that empowered them to value who they are. There are also those clients where confidence has not been sufficiently developed in their identity, thus they struggle in these areas. In addition, a client could have been stripped of feeling confident through experiences of criticism, belittling, abuse, control, bullying, intimidation, and even subtle remarks or jokes, which sifted their character and worth, while causing a deficiency or brokenness of their identity.

Inadequacy, insecurity, and low self-esteem can be intertwined in the personality and identity. Deliverance ministry will most likely need to be part of the counseling process to aid the client in being delivered from the underlying roots. This will provide a greater chance for wholeness to develop. It will be important to build up the client's identity in the areas of self-confidence and self-worth, so they can mature in their identity and not need the accolades, attention, and approval, of others to make them feel adequate and valuable. Aligning a client with who God says they are is key to building and solidifying their confidence. The more the client is doing and becoming what God says, the greater their life success will be. God becomes the source for feeling whole and complete, as his likeness and nature instills a peace for the client to be comfortable with their unique identity.

Self-Worth Assignment for Client:

1. Examine and journal the underlying reasons for feeling inadequate, insecure, having low self-esteem. Examples - past childhood experiences, not being praised, supported, provided complements or accolades growing; been in abusive and neglectful relationships; lack development in these areas.

2. Spend time in prayer asking God to heal past issues and experiences where you were devalued, abused, neglected, teased, and so on. Forgive and release the person to God. Ask God to heal the wounds and pains of these situations.

3. Explore and journal the behaviors you engage in to fulfill the need for attention and affirmation of your value. Search with God how to get these needs and desires met in a healthy way without giving into negative or unhealthy attention seeking behaviors.

4. Search out with God your purpose and life's destiny. Do what he says to align with what he is speaking. Connect with a mentor and like-minded individuals that can encourage you, provide wise counsel, and hold you accountable to your destiny walk.

5. At least once a week, spend time verbally proclaiming what God has said about you. Put little reminders in various places in your home (bathroom mirror, closet door) that can encourage you. The more you speak and connect to God's truths, the more you become what he says, want to be what he says, become accountable to what he says, and manifest what he says.

6. Every other week, study at least three scriptures that build your confidence and acquire three confidence attributes that you need to be built up in. Spend time weekly praying them into your life by verbally speaking them over yourself and using them as weekly standards.

7. Confidence means to have complete and full trust in self, others, or a situation. The word full lets us know that there is a pouring that must be done before confidence is

completely solidified within us. Continually use these practical guides to pour into your identity such that your confidence becomes full. Refer to them at different seasons in your life when you need a confidence boost. ***Philippians 1:6*** *Being confident of this very thing, that he which hath begun a good work in you will perform it until the day of Jesus*

Decreeing deliverance and healing to your identity as inadequacy, insecurity, and low self-esteem is dismantled, uncoiled, and dislodged from your life.

SHIFT!

Chapter 19

OVERCOMING INFERIORITY

Inferiority is when a client feels or thinks lower or less of themselves in relations to the rank, position, stature, or perception of others. The client has a perception that they do not measure up to others or to the standard needed for the task or position at hand. They continuously underrate and underestimate there:

- Identity (who they are),
- Worth (value and purpose in life),
- Potential (opportunities, capabilities, and abilities).

The inferior client lives from a posture of fear, helplessness, hopelessness, and unworthiness, while constantly sacrificing their needs, desires, and worth at the expense of others.

Inferiority tends to be rooted in unresolved experiences of abuse, bullying, intimidation, control, unsuccessful feats, or can stem from inadequacy, low self-esteem, and low self-worth. When people bully others or strive to strip them of their confidence and identity, it can cause an inferiority complex. When a person's confidence and identity has been compromised and demeaned, they will have false loyalties and false obligations to those who have intimidated or abused them, or to those who they feel are higher in rank, stature, position, or perception, than they are. False loyalties, humilities, and obligations will have the person committing and engaging in behaviors for approval and people pleasing, to avoid further abuse and degradation. Some tend to:

- Overcompensate where they behave in opposition to their identity character and nature,
- Overachieve in effort to prove worth or feel valuable or successful,
- Underachieve where the person will not try for fear of failing or further feeling bad about ones' self,

- Become indifferent where they are socially withdrawn or engage in behaviors to ensure they will not be accepted (psychology calls this asocial behavior).

When a client who struggles with inferiority engages in overcompensation, overachieving, underachieving, or indifference, they yield to pride because they SHIFT into operating from a place of high or inordinate opinion about themselves. Their feelings and actions become rebellious, unconstrained, uncontrolled, disorderly, and unreasonable, as they are not in a place to receive truth because of the false perception of self has become the truth to which they live by. This is an extremely dangerous place as *Proverbs 16:18* tells us that "*Pride goeth before destruction, and a haughty spirit before a fall.*" When the inferior person enters this place, they often end up sabotaging their own life and progress. Even with being justified in that they may have been abused, controlled, bullied, belittled, etc., they have now become their own offender in killing their identity and worth.

Inferiority Assignment for Client:

1. Explore and journal areas in your life where you have been abused, bullied, controlled, intimidated, belittled, or challenged, in your identity and worth?

2. Explore and journal areas in your life where you have been constantly compared to others, ostracized, or outcast by peers, popular or esteemed groups, sabotaged in opportunities by people or circumstances, given mix message about your identity, abilities, or capabilities. Spend time forgiving and letting God heal you in these areas.

3. Repent and cleanse from behaviors of pride stemming from overcompensation, overachieving, underachieving, and indifference.

4. Consistently build your self-esteem in the following areas:
   A. Who you are in God and what he says about you.

   B. Who God is in and to you.

   C. God's promises in the scripture concerning being there for you and trusting him.

   D. Learn and acknowledge your gifts and calling; seek to grow and operate in what God has placed in you and who you are called to be.

   E. Surround yourself with people who empower and celebrate you rather than competing and degrading you.

   F. Build others up as you build yourself up.

   G. Build yourself up in knowing you are unique and no one can be you and you cannot be anyone else. Then there is no reason to be jealous or to compare yourself.

   H. Celebrate the successes of others and empower them to be even greater in what they already are and have accomplished.

   I. Celebrate your successes and be okay with rejoicing in your victories.

Scriptures to Combat Inferiority

Song of Solomon 6:3 *I am my beloved's and my beloved is mine: he feedeth among the lilies.*

I am my beloved's [garden] and my beloved is mine! He feeds among the lilies [which grow there]. (AMP)

Songs of Solomon 7:10 *I belong to my beloved, and his desire is for me.*

Romans 8:28 *And we know that all things work together for good to them that love God, to them who are the called according to his purpose.*

Job 22:6 *Delight in the Almighty and lift up your face to God.*

Psalm 37:4 *Delight thyself also in the LORD; and he shall give thee the desires of thine heart.*

Matthew 7:7 *Ask and it will be given to you; seek and you will find; knock and the door will be opened to you.*

Psalm 149:9 *For the LORD takes pleasure in His people; He will beautify the afflicted ones with salvation.*

Psalm 145:19 *He fulfills the desires of those who fear him; he hears their cry and saves them.*

Psalm 79:7 *But God is the judge: he putteth down one, and setteth up another.*

Psalm 118:6 *The LORD is on my side; I will not fear: what can man do unto me?*

Hebrews 13:5-6 *Let your conversation be without covetousness; and be content with such things as ye have: for he hath said, I will never leave thee, nor forsake thee. So that we may boldly say, The Lord is my helper, and I will not fear what man shall do unto me.*

Proverbs 29:5 *The fear of man bringeth a snare: but whoso putteth his trust in the LORD shall be safe.*

Philippians 2:3 *Let nothing be done through strife or vainglory; but in lowliness of mind let each esteem other better than themselves*

2 Corinthians 10:12 For we dare not make ourselves of the number, or compare ourselves with some that commend themselves: but they measuring themselves by themselves, and comparing themselves among themselves, are not wise.

2 Corinthians 2:14-16 Now thanks be unto God, which always causeth us to triumph in Christ, and maketh manifest the savour of his knowledge by us in every place. For we are unto God a sweet savour of Christ, in them that are saved, and in them that perish: To the one we are the savour of death unto death; and to the other the savour of life unto life. And who is sufficient for these things?

<u>*Sufficient* in Greek is *hikanos* and means:</u>
1. competent (as if coming in season)
2. content, worthy, able, good, great, enough
3. ample in amount or fit in character
4. secure, suffice to in ability

2 Corinthians 3:4-5 And such trust have we through Christ to God-ward: Not that we are sufficient of ourselves to think any thing as of ourselves; but our sufficiency is of God.

John 15:4-5 Abide in me, and I in you. As the branch cannot bear fruit of itself, except it abide in the vine; no more can ye, except ye abide in me. I am the vine, ye are the branches: He that abideth in me, and I in him, the same bringeth forth much fruit: for without me ye can do nothing.

Philippians 2:13 For it is God which worketh in you both to will and to do of his good pleasure.

[Not in your own strength] for it is God Who is all the while effectually at work in you [energizing and creating in you the power and desire], both to will and to work for His good pleasure and satisfaction and delight. (AMP)

Philippians 4:13 I can do all things through Christ which strengtheneth me.

I can do all things [which He has called me to do] through Him who strengthens and empowers me [to fulfill His purpose—I am self-sufficient in Christ's sufficiency; I am ready for anything and equal to anything through Him who infuses me with inner strength and confident peace.] (AMP)

Kingdom Wellness Counseling and Mentoring Center

Faith Based Counseling

Manual I

Part 6: Chapters (20 –21)

Learning Objectives:

- To provide biblical understanding of destiny and how to journey in destiny as a lifestyle.
- To provide strategic wisdom on godly fulfillment and how to sustain in the fullness of salvation with God.
- To provide counseling guidance for clients who have a distorted perception of God, hate God, or blame God for their issues.

Chapter 20

DESTINY AS A LIFESTYLE

Let us take a moment to dispel misconceptions, misperceptions, impure motives, and myths, that may hinder a client from receiving revelation of their destiny, and truly committing to walking in a lifestyle of destiny with God.

- *Misconception* is a mistaken notion.
- *Misperception* is to understand incorrectly.
- *Impure Motives* are motives that are unclean, mixed, contaminated, or covetous. The motive is birthed out of lust or focus on self without considering what is best or appropriate for self or for others.
- *Myths* are something lived or perceived as true but is more of a fairy tale, fantasy, or lie.

Destiny Misconceptions and Misperceptions:

- Destiny is not necessarily a destination or a goal a client is trying to reach as those points of success are just destiny moments. Destiny, however, is a lifestyle of living in the purpose and plan God ordained for the client at birth. Destiny is not just a moment with God but a journey in and with God.

- A destiny moment is temporary success. A destiny lifestyle is lifetime success with constant destiny moments.

- Destiny is not always easy. It requires strategic efficient work to maintain and sustain in destiny. Even people who were handed a destiny moment have to work that moment to maintain a lifestyle of destiny. This is the reason a client should keep working once they have attained or succeeded in a particular area, or to a particular level. They are striving to maintain and sustain in what they have achieved.

Ephesians 2:10 *For we are God's [own] handiwork (His workmanship), recreated in Christ Jesus, [born anew] that we may do those good works which God predestined (planned beforehand) for us [taking paths which He prepared ahead of time], that we should walk in them [living the good life which He prearranged and made ready for us to live]. (AMP)*

Psalm 139:16 *Your eyes saw my unformed substance, and in Your book all the days [of my life] were written before ever they took shape, when as yet there was none of them. (AMP)*

From creation, God had already committed to walking in destiny with us. He made it part of our DNA, our very substance, and instilled it into the plans for our lives.

Many clients may achieve destiny things (e.g. money, fame, material goods, temporary happiness, rewards, successes) without God, as he put these talents and gifts in them at birth. Yet despite achievements, many clients will be unhappy, longing, and constantly searching, while filling themselves up with things in effort to acquire fulfillment. This is because true destiny fulfillment can only come through and with God.

Destiny is not necessarily about what a client can do or attain as this is a biproduct of destiny. This is the result of destiny.

SHIFT!

Destiny is about:
- Who the client uniquely is in God (Identity).
- What clients are to do through the identify of God (Purpose).
- The reason clients are God chosen (His Plan).

Jeremiah 1:5 Before I formed thee in the belly I knew thee; and before thou camest forth out of the womb I sanctified thee, and I ordained thee a prophet unto the nations.

Isaiah 49:1 Listen, O isles, unto me; and hearken, ye people, from afar; The Lord hath called me from the womb; from the bowels of my mother hath he made mention of my name.

Sometimes clients are committed to the idea of destiny or the part of destiny that benefits them, but not destiny itself. Their drive to pursue destiny may be intact. However, they tend to be focused on what they are to do and achieving those goals, rather than the reason they are to do what they do, and allowing that to be the drive for attaining their life's desires and goals.

Being driven by what they do rather than the purpose God chose them to do what they do can cause a client's motives to be distorted, mixed, contaminated, and misalignment with the committed purposes and plans God instilled in them at creation.

Proverbs 20:24 Man's goings are of the Lord; how can a man then understand his own way?

Interestingly that word *goings* means *"companionship or steps which insinuates walking with God."*

Jeremiah 10:23 LORD, O Lord, I know that the way of man is not in himself: it is not in man that walketh to direct his steps.

Steps means *goings* and *a course of life*. Jeremiah was saying that man was not designed to walk without God. Man was not designed to do his own thing aside from God.

Psalm 37:23 The steps of a good man are ordered by the Lord: and he delighteth in his way.

God is invested in the steps – the goings and course of a man. God takes delight – pleasure - in journeying with his people. He takes pleasure in helping us accomplish what he has instilled in us and enjoys watching us become what he has created us to be.

Being able to help a client focus on the reason God chose them rather than what they are to attain has to do with the position and state of their heart.

Proverbs 16:9 *A man's heart deviseth his way: but the Lord directeth his steps.*

Proverbs 19:21 *Many are the plans in a person's heart, but it is the LORD's purpose that prevails.*

Proverbs 16:2-3 *All the ways of a man are clean in his own eyes; but the Lord weigheth the spirits. Commit thy works unto the Lord, and thy thoughts shall be established.*

The scriptures caution us to resist being redirected by our hearts. *Proverbs 4:23* states: *Keep thy heart with all diligence; for out of it are the issues of life."* The Amplified Bible says, *"Out of it flows the springs of life."*

Matthew 15:18 *But the things that come out (issue forth) of a person's mouth come from the heart, and these defile them. For out of the heart proceed evil thoughts, murders, adulteries, fornications, thefts, false witness, blasphemies: These are the things which defile a man: but to eat with unwashen hands defileth not a man.*

Some clients will feel uncomfortable with a commitment to counseling. Letting them know that we all have issues and are working on something may help them rest in the counseling process. Even as we live through salvation with God, we are rarely without a challenge – an issue - that requires conquering. This is because we are constantly SHIFTING from level to level and glory to glory with God.

2 Corinthians 3:18 *But we all, with unveiled face, beholding as in a mirror the glory of the Lord, are being transformed into the same image from glory to glory, just as by the Spirit of the Lord.*

Issues derive from unhealed, wounded, hurt, frustrated, sinful, unchallenged, or unfulfilled areas within our soul. These areas affect our emotions and thoughts by distorting the truth of who we are, who God is, and how our lives are to be in him.

Such distortions make our heart unreliable as it causes us to make decisions that are:

- Not the notion of God (misconception),

- Not the perception of God (misperception),

- Not the motive or intent of God (impure motives),

- Not the will of God for our lives (myths and fantasy lifestyles).

When a client makes decisions with their heart, they veer from a committed destiny walk with God. The client resorts to doing their own thing and consult God more out of convenience than through a committed lifestyle relationship with him. The client may equate any good, success, and achievements that come from their life to God, even though it is their gifts flourishing in them simply because that is what they have been placed in them to do. Yet, a client may not recognize that since they are not committed to God, he is not getting any glory out of their lives, nor is his hand upon them or their flourishing giftings. It is like having the essence of God working in them, but the presence of God is not there.

A client can have the gifts of God working in them, but the presence of God is not authenticating them. God is not there.

Proverbs 16:3 *Commit thy works unto the Lord, and thy thoughts shall be established.*

Commit in Hebrew is gâlal means:
1. to roll (literally or figuratively)
2. remove, roll (away, down, together)
3. run down, seek occasion, trust, wallow

Dictionary.com defines *roll* as:
1. to move along a surface by revolving or turning over and over
2. to move as in a cycle
3. to revolve or turn over once or repeatedly

Dictionary.com defines *wallow* as:
1. to roll about or lie in something
2. to live self-indulgently; luxuriate; revel
3. to flounder about; move along or proceed clumsily or with difficulty

These definitions further confirm how God's commitment to destiny is intertwined in us, and how God rolled his purposes and plans into us, where true fulfillment comes from wallowing in life with him. Living a destiny lifestyle in him. Counselors, equip your clients to wallow in God.

Verse 2-3 *All the ways of a man are pure in his own eyes, but the Lord weighs the spirits (the thoughts and intents of the heart). Roll your works upon the Lord [commit and trust them wholly to Him; He will cause your thoughts to become agreeable to His will, and] so shall your plans be established and succeed. (AMP)*

Thoughts in Hebrew is *machashebeth* and means:
1. a contrivance (plan or force), i.e. (concretely) a texture, machine
2. (abstractly) intention, plan (whether bad, a plot; or good, advice)
3. cunning (work), curious work, device, imagination, invented, means, purpose, thought

Some of the successes, rewards, and plans, that a client is experiencing in the world, are not the destiny of God. God is not committed to them, and they are not the establishment and successes of God. What they are experiencing are their own ways, ways of man, or the ways of the devil. They are rolled into what man or the devil deems as purposeful intentions, inventions, devices, workings, or achievements. Because it possesses a form of God's grace and blessings, but not his essence, many clients assume their workings are of God, and that these ways and lifestyles are the representation of destiny. They are baffled when they lack joy and fulfillment which is their reason for entering counseling. The counselor must be able to help them decipher that a form of godliness does not produce the joy and fulfillment of God.

2 Timothy 3:5 Having a form of godliness, but denying the power thereof: from such turn away.

That word *form* means *an appearance or likeness,* but it also means *semblance. Semblance* means *to have an affinity or attraction to something.* This means a client can be drawn into their own way of destiny, yet in their pursuit, they are left empty or incomplete, because without God, there is no true destiny.

Without God, there is no true destiny!

We see many people walking in a form of destiny with lots of power. However, God's power,

- Possesses his spirit and his fruit - his nature and his character (*Matthew 7:15-23, 1Samuel 24:13, Luke 6:43-44, Psalm 1:5-6*).
- Draws people to him (*John 12:32*).
- Transforms lives for the good and betterment of his kingdom and the world as a whole (**seven mental areas of warfare**).

One key truth we must help clients understand about how God created us is, whatever gifts and abilities he put in them, they will manifest whether they live for him or not.

Romans 11:29 For the gifts and calling of God are without repentance.

God does not recall or annul his gifts simply because we do not use them for his glory. Whether we use them for him or the devil, they will manifest. Even though God does not repeal his gifts, he does not accept whatever we do with them. God is clear about serving him or the devil. And though we think we may not be rejecting God, when we use our gifts for the devil or without consulting him, he does reject us.

Revelations 3:15-16 *I know thy works, that thou art neither cold nor hot: I would thou wert cold or hot. So then because thou art lukewarm, and neither cold nor hot, I will spew thee out of my mouth.*

"*Spew*" means to "*vomit up.*" When we vomit, our bodies are essentially rejecting whatever it is we took in. Whatever we consumed did not agree with our body system so it regurgitated it. *Lukewarm* means "*indifferent or unconcerned.*" Lukewarm means having no concern about what pleases God as it relates to one's destiny. Many clients will be lukewarm because they live in survive mode. They are more focused on paying bills and getting their immediate needs and desires met, as opposed to exploring whether what they are doing in life is the purpose and plan of God. God says because a person is lukewarm in their works – their destiny - he vomits them out of his mouth. He rejects them. Silence, lack of conviction, or lack of public judgment, do not mean he approves. He has *spewed* your client out of his mouth. Unless they want to repent, be delivered from lukewarmness, and be transformed through God identity, there is no need for dialog. This is because a vomiting mouth does not speak with words, it speaks with sounds of disgusts and with a disapproved rejected substance.

A vomiting mouth does not speak, it gags!

The challenge most of us have with destiny is it is not really discussed in our households until we are in high school and are seeking to find a path in life. Even then, the concern is more about us going to college or getting a job so we can take care of ourselves. There is minimal focus on identifying our God ordained purpose and calling. It is God's plan however, that we are cultivated in destiny from the womb; that we are grounded from birth in his word and purpose concerning who we are to be.

Proverbs 22:6 *Train up a child in the way he should go: and when he is old, he will not depart from it.*

Train up in Hebrew "*hanak*" and means:
1. figuratively to initiate or discipline
2. dedicate, inaugurate (induct into office with a formal ceremony or install)
3. to train, train up

In our youth, many of us are placed in sports, dance classes, singing and music lessons. We are cultivated in our talents. There is minimal discussion of destiny. Even if we do well in these areas, the focus is more on fame and fortune, rather than the purpose for the fame and fortune, and how God can acquire glory out of our lives. Counselor, this needs to change in society, especially since much fame and fortune yields to secular and worldly means, which is rooted in the devil and not God. Even if a person has a Godly upbringing because they lack revelation regarding the purpose of their calling, they succumb to the devil's demise. They end up using their gifts to bring the devil glory or to bring themselves glory, while calling it God.

This is the reason God says he desires that we were either hot or cold, and not lukewarm. When we are lukewarm, we strive to serve two masters, God and the devil, and call it God. Since we are desensitized to truth, we equate our success to God and think we are pleasing and serving him. But whether we discern truth or not, God will not share his glory with the devil. In God's perspective, it is the devil's glory whether we acknowledge that or not. God is spewing us out of his mouth.

Matthew 6:24 *No man can serve two masters: for either he will hate the one, and love the other; or else he will hold to the one, and despise the other. Ye cannot serve God and mammon.*

Counselor, you must share the following truth with your clients:

As they enter the counseling process, and God begins to deal with them about destiny, it is important for them to adhere to what he is speaking. He is striving to SHIFT their life in alignment with him. God knows their destiny pathway and their potential. He desires to align them so they will not miss destiny. They must be willing to relinquish their plan for the plan of God. They must reject striving to fit God into their plan and surrender to his plan. As they surrender to God's will and desires, he will identify what is of him and what is not of him regarding their plans, so true destiny can be revealed.

Isaiah 14:24 The Lord of hosts has sworn saying, Surely as I have thought, so shall it come to pass; and as I have purposed, so shall it stand:

Regardless to whether we live out God's plans, his plans remain. The Lord's plan do not change. What changes is whether we achieve them or not, and whether we live a life of true fulfillment and experiencing real lasting joy in what we do and who we have become.

Psalm 16:11 Thou wilt shew me the path of life: in thy presence is fulness of joy; at thy right hand there are pleasures for evermore.

Dispelling Destiny Myths

Counselor, you will have to dispels myths that are more fantasy and fairy tales of destiny but are not necessarily the truth about destiny regarding your client. **SHIFT!**

Though destiny can entail the following, destiny is not necessarily about:

1. Being rich, famous, being well known, having large platforms, an abundance of followers, or likes on social media. A client can still have fulfilled destiny and never have any of these things.

2. Being perfect. The client needs to understand that they will make mistakes in their destiny walk. If they were perfect, we would not need God.

    Psalm 37:23-24 The steps of a good man are ordered by the Lord: and he delighteth in his way. Though he fall, he shall not be utterly cast down: for the Lord upholdeth him with his hand.

    The key is remaining rooted and grounded in God so he can pull the client back into the standards they need to continue their destiny journey.

    The Lord directs the steps of the godly. He delights in every detail of their lives. Though they stumble, they will never fall, for the Lord holds them by the hand. (NLT)

    The steps of a [good] man are directed and established by the Lord when He delights in his way [and He busies Himself with his every step]. Though he falls, he shall not be utterly cast down, for the Lord grasps his hand in support and upholds him. (AMP)

    Stalwart walks in step with God; his path blazed by God, he's happy. If he stumbles, he's not down for long; God has a grip on his hand. (MSG)

3. Pleasing people or being approved by people. Some of the loneliest and most unfulfilled people are the most famous, rich, and popular people pleasers.

    John 12:43 For they loved the praise of men more than the praise of God.

    Luke 16:15 And he said unto them, Ye are they which justify yourselves before men; but God knoweth your hearts: for that which is highly esteemed among men is abomination in the sight of God.

1 Samuel 16:7 But the LORD said to Samuel, "Do not consider his appearance or his height, for I have rejected him. The LORD does not look at the things people look at. People look at the outward appearance, but the LORD looks at the heart."

1 Thessalonians 2:4 But as we were allowed of God to be put in trust with the gospel, even so we speak; not as pleasing men, but God, which trieth our hearts.

Colossians 3:22 Servants, obey in all things your masters according to the flesh; not with eyeservice, as menpleasers; but in singleness of heart, fearing God: And whatsoever ye do, do it heartily, as to the Lord, and not unto men

4. Avoiding hardship or trials or having the easy road in life. Be honest with your clients and let them know that there will be trials and tribulations.

2 Timothy 2:3-4 Thou therefore endure hardness, as a good soldier of Jesus Christ. No man that warreth entangleth himself with the affairs of this life; that he may please him who hath chosen him to be a soldier.

John 16:33 These things I have spoken unto you, that in me ye might have peace. In the world ye shall have tribulation: but be of good cheer; I have overcome the world.

Psalm 34:19 Many are the afflictions of the righteous: but the LORD delivereth him out of them all.

Diagram 20.0 Destiny Requirements

Commitment	Sacrifice	Impacting people & the world	Living on purpose
Obedience	Responsibility	Glorifying God	Achieving success
Hard work	Accountability	Being one's authentic self	Building a generational legacy

Source: Baker 2019

Destiny Wisdom Keys to Instill in Your Client

- Destiny is not necessarily about having a lot of ideas or huge plans. The most effective people who sustain in destiny have one or a few ideas. They work that those ideas into something bigger, impacting, and long lasting. Once they are sustained in a few ideas, they expand into other areas of their destiny.

Matthew 25:23 His lord said unto him, Well done, good and faithful servant; thou hast been faithful over a few things, I will make thee ruler over many things: enter thou into the joy of thy lord.

- Even though God's plans for a person's destiny may not have been part of their life plans or what they considered their destiny would be, if they align with God, they will never resent destiny. He will unveil what he has instilled in them to achieve destiny, and they will enjoy being what he has destined for their lives.

- Destiny is like an unfolding prophecy. Destiny will pull a person towards a truth that does not exist in their present world. The person will continuously evolve in who they are personally, in their relationship with God, and what they know about him.

2 Corinthians 3:8 But we all, with open face beholding as in a glass the glory of the Lord, are changed into the same image from glory to glory, even as by the Spirit of the Lord.

Isaiah 46:10-11 Declaring the end from the beginning, and from ancient times the things that are not yet done, saying, My counsel shall stand, and I will do all my pleasure: Calling a ravenous bird from the east, the man that executeth my counsel from a far country: yea, I have spoken it, I will also bring it to pass; I have purposed it, I will also do it.

Isaiah 14:24 The LORD of hosts hath sworn, saying, Surely as I have thought, so shall it come to pass; and as I have purposed, so shall it stand:

- Walking in destiny has a sense of fulfillment to it that does not always make sense to the person or onlookers. This will initially cause the person and other people to speak against certain destiny requirements, as the natural mind cannot comprehend what is unfolding from the spirit. The person must trust the Holy Spirit within them more than what others think. They must trust the vision God is giving and trust him to provide clarity and understanding as they journey in destiny with him.

Psalm 138:8 The LORD will perfect that which concerneth me: thy mercy, O LORD, endureth for ever: forsake not the works of thine own hands.

John 13:5-7 After that he poureth water into a bason, and began to wash the disciples' feet, and to wipe them with the towel wherewith he was girded. Then cometh he to Simon Peter: and Peter saith unto him, Lord, dost thou wash my feet? Jesus answered and said unto him, What I do thou knowest not now; but thou shalt know hereafter.

Jeremiah 4:22 For my people are foolish, they have not known me; they are stupid children, and they have no understanding: they are wise to do evil, but how to do good they have no knowledge.

- Destiny births God's unique blueprint through a person. Even if there are similarities of someone or something else, there will always be something unique about a person's identity and what they are producing that is different from others. This is because each of us hold a unique representation of God, therefore destiny in and of itself, has no competitor. Destiny is often attached to an initiative that is new to the world but not new to God. It was always part of God's plan. The timing of a person's birth and the development of who they are allowed, "Thy will be done in the earth as it is in the heaven . . . ." With destiny, the history of the world was waiting on the person to be in place.

2 Corinthians 5:17 Therefore if anyone is in Christ, he is a new creature; the old things passed away; behold, new things have come.

Isaiah 43:18-19 Remember ye not the former things, neither consider the things of old. Behold, I will do a new thing; now it shall spring forth; shall ye not know it? I will even make a way in the wilderness, and rivers in the desert.

Client Destiny Exploration Worksheet

- What are the misconceptions, misperceptions, and myths, you have regarding destiny? (Spend time repenting and cleansing yourself of these negative attributes)

- What are your motives as you pursue destiny?

- Are you more focused on surviving, attaining, or achieving, the purpose to which you were called to attain in life? (Examine yourself and explore this before God).

- What are some of your heart issues that may affect your decisions as you journey in destiny? (Constantly check yourself in these areas and seek God for deliverance and healing).

- Is your way of pursuing destiny clean and pure to you but not necessarily to God?

- Does your pursuit of destiny line up with the word, standard, and nature of God? (Anything that is of God should be in line with his word and character).

- Have you asked God how he feels about how you are living your life and whether it is pure in his eyes, or whether it aligns with his purposed destiny for your life? If not ask him. Journal what he says. Make changes as he leads.

- Do you trust God to lead you in your destiny journey? How so? How not?

- In what ways do you need to be healed in the areas of trust to walk with God? Ask God to teach you how to trust him. Practice what he says until it becomes a lifestyle.

- In what ways do you need to surrender your will to submit in a destiny lifestyle with God?

- How can your counselor help you to assess and attain true destiny with God?

Chapter 21

CONNECTING CLIENTS TO GOD

Some clients may have a difficult time entering the faith-based counseling process because they are mad at God, blame God, hate God, do not believe in God. For those clients who desire a productive faith-based experience, this will have to be confronted so that they can fully connect to and receive from the counseling theory. Addressing these challenges will enable them to SHIFT into God identity and a destiny lifestyle of wholeness with him.

Some clients cannot fathom how God could stand by and watch them experience the traumas they have endured. As a counselor, you will have to help them understand that God cares, hurts when they hurt, yet there is the concept of freewill; God does not violate a person's freewill. Let us SHIFT on a journey to process this truth.

God's Principle Of Freewill

Freewill is defined as a person's voluntary right to choose as he or she pleases. Though God sent Jesus to save the entire world, he does not demand people chose him as God or enter into covenant relationship with him.

> **John 3:16** *For God so loved the world, that he gave his only begotten Son, that whosoever believeth in him should not perish, but have everlasting life.*

This word *believeth* actually means to commit to or to entrust. Belief is not just a matter of perception but an act of living what a person says they believe. Many claim they believe in God and his works on the cross, but their lifestyle reveals otherwise. They make choices that are contrary to God and his principles with no understanding that when they say they believe, they are committing to a relationship with God, and to live through his identity and standards.

God Cares

The entire reason God sent Jesus to be sacrificed for our sins is because he cared about our sufferings and wanted us to have a chance at eternal life.

> **2 Corinthians 5:21** *For he hath made him to be sin for us, who knew no sin; that we might be made the righteousness of God in him.*

God Sympathizes

God is moved physically and emotionally by what hurts us.

> **Hebrews 4:15** *For we have not an high priest which cannot be touched with the feeling of our infirmities; but was in all points tempted like as we are, yet without sin.*

Feelings is *sympatheō* in Greek and means:
1. to feel "sympathy" with, i.e. (by implication) to commiserate
2. have compassion, be touched with a feeling of.
   to be affected with the same feeling as another
3. to sympathize with, to feel for, have compassion on

Infirmities is *astheneia* in Greek and means:
1. feebleness (of mind or body); by implication, malady, morally, frailty
2. disease, infirmity, sickness, weakness
3. want of strength, weakness, infirmity
   - A. of the body
     - a. its native weakness and frailty
     - b. feebleness of health or sickness
   - B. of the soul
     - a. want of strength and capacity requisite
     - b. to understand a thing, to do things great and glorious
     - c. to restrain corrupt desires, to bear trials and troubles

God has compassion for what we endure in life and is affected in the same way we are as he sympathizes with our experiences. God bears our trials and troubles with us and is just as heartbroken and pained by what happens to us as we are.

Everyone Has Free Will

Even those who have committed to God still have a right to choose God on a daily basis. The more we commit and SHIFT into God likeness, the easier it is to choose God's will and principles over our own, other people, or the devil. However, the choice is still ours and we have to want to be guided into God's truth via the Holy Spirit, and to live in godly truth as a lifestyle.

John 14:17 Even the Spirit of truth; whom the world cannot receive, because it seeth him not, neither knoweth him: but ye know him; for he dwelleth with you, and shall be in you.

John 16:13-14 Howbeit when he, the Spirit of truth, is come, he will guide you into all truth: for he shall not speak of himself; but whatsoever he shall hear, that shall he speak: and he will shew you things to come. He shall glorify me: for he shall receive of mine, and shall shew it unto you.

The Holy Spirit resides in a believer when they commit to God, but they still have to act upon the guidance that the Holy Spirit provides them. They must choose the ways of their Spirit over their flesh, the world, and demon forces.

Romans 7:21-25 So I've discovered this truth: Evil is present with me even when I want to do what God's standards say is good. I take pleasure in God's standards in my inner being. However, I see a different standard at work throughout my body. It is at war with the standards my mind sets and tries to take me captive to sin's standards which still exist throughout my body. What a miserable person I am! Who will rescue me from my dying body? I thank God that our Lord Jesus Christ rescues me! So I am obedient to God's standards with my mind, but I am obedient to sin's standards with my corrupt nature. (GW)

1 Corinthians 10:13 There hath no temptation taken you but such as is common to man: but God [is] faithful, who will not suffer you to be tempted above that ye are able; but will with the temptation also make a way to escape, that ye may be able to bear [it].

The Amplified Translation provides expounding clear insight regarding this scripture.

For no temptation (no trial regarded as enticing to sin), [no matter how it comes or where it leads] has overtaken you and laid hold on you that is not common to man [that is, no temptation or trial has come to you that is beyond human resistance and that is not adjusted and adapted and belonging to human experience, and such as man can bear]. But God is faithful [to His Word and to His compassionate nature], and He [can be trusted] not to let you be tempted and tried and assayed beyond your ability and strength of resistance and power to endure, but with the temptation He will [always] also provide the way out (the means of escape toa landing place), that you may be capable and strong and powerful to bear up under it patiently.

God wants **ALL** people to want to live for him, not have to live for him. He wants people to want to be in relationship with him, not have to be in relationship with him. He wants people to choose to be his child, not have to be his child. Whether a believer or nonbeliever, God will never change his nature on this fact.

Revelation 3:20 Behold, I stand at the door, and knock: if any man hear my voice, and open the door, I will come in to him, and will sup with him, and he with me.

God is waiting to enter covenant but will not force covenant.

- No matter how much he longs for people to choose him.
- No matter how much he longs to be their God.
- No matter how much evil a person does.
- No matter how much he longs for a person to choose good over evil.

God is waiting, but people have freewill.

Freewill has always been in the earth. Even with the fall of man, God continued to allow freewill. It is an eternal principle that will never perish.

Genesis 2:16-17 And the LORD God commanded the man, saying, Of every tree of the garden thou mayest freely eat: But of the tree of the knowledge of good and evil, thou shalt not eat of it: for in the day that thou eatest thereof thou shalt surely die.

The Contrivance Of Evil

Everything a person plans or does may not necessarily be God. God operates through divine order and direction that is in alignment with the course of life he has ordained for a person at birth. A person can alter those plans through their own devises. Freewill enables a person to be directed by what they devise versus what God is directing.

> ***Proverbs 16:9*** *A man's heart deviseth his way: but the LORD directeth his steps.*

The Choice Of Evil

God does not tempt with evil. People choose to be evil. Demon forces can also sway people to do evil.

> ***James 1:12-14*** *Blessed is the man that endureth temptation: for when he is tried, he shall receive the crown of life, which the Lord hath promised to them that love him. Let no man say when he is tempted, I am tempted of God: for God cannot be tempted with evil, neither tempteth he any man: But every man is tempted, when he is drawn away of his own lust, and enticed. Then when lust hath conceived, it bringeth forth sin: and sin, when it is finished, bringeth forth death.*

> ***Galatians 5:13-23*** *For, brethren, ye have been called unto liberty; only use not liberty for an occasion to the flesh, but by love serve one another. For all the law is fulfilled in one word, even in this; Thou shalt love thy neighbour as thyself. But if ye bite and devour one another, take heed that ye be not consumed one of another. This I say then, Walk in the Spirit, and ye shall not fulfil the lust of the flesh. For the flesh lusteth against the Spirit, and the Spirit against the flesh: and these are contrary the one to the other: so that ye cannot do the things that ye would. But if ye be led of the Spirit, ye are not under the law.*

> *Now the works of the flesh are manifest, which are these; Adultery, fornication, uncleanness, lasciviousness, Idolatry, witchcraft, hatred, variance, emulations, wrath, strife, seditions, heresies, Envyings, murders, drunkenness, revellings, and such like: of the which I tell you before, as I have also told you in time past, that they which do such things shall not inherit the kingdom of God. But the fruit of the Spirit is love, joy, peace, longsuffering, gentleness, goodness, faith, Meekness, temperance: against such there is no law.*

John 10:10 The thief comes only to steal and kill and destroy; I have come that they may have life, and have it to the full.

James 4:7 Submit yourselves therefore to God. Resist the devil, and he will flee from you.

The Consequences Of Evil

Evil breeds harm, trauma, pain, wickedness, viciousness, hardship, tragedy, destruction, turmoil, bewilderment, and death. The more people engage in evil, the viler they became. These evil people devour others as they have no regard for life, for people, and how their actions impact people or the earth.

Proverbs 6:12-15 A naughty person, a wicked man, walketh with a froward mouth. He winketh with his eyes, he speaketh with his feet, he teacheth with his fingers; Frowardness is in his heart, he deviseth mischief continually; he soweth discord. Therefore shall his calamity come suddenly; suddenly shall he be broken without remedy.

Job 15:35 They conceive mischief, and bring forth vanity, and their belly prepareth deceit.

Jeremiah 12:6 Your relatives, members of your own family— even they have betrayed you; they have raised a loud cry against you. Do not trust them, though they speak well of you.

Micah 2:1 Woe to those who plan iniquity, to those who plot evil on their beds! At morning's light they carry it out because it is in their power to do it.

Matthew 12:34 You brood of vipers, how can you who are evil say anything good? For the mouth speaks what the heart is full of.

2 Timothy 3:2 People will be lovers of themselves, lovers of money, boastful, proud, abusive, disobedient to their parents, ungrateful, unholy.

Isaiah 32:6 For fools speak folly, their hearts are bent on evil: They practice ungodliness and spread error concerning the LORD; the hungry they leave empty and from the thirsty they withhold water.

The Devil's Children

Some people are children of the devil and therefore choose evil. They are oppressed and possessed by demon forces and will choose his ways. They are not lovers of God and have no regard for how their actions impact others. These people can engage in some horrendous unthinkable acts that traumatize others. There is no explaining away their actions or making excuses for their behavior. It can indeed be evil and wicked. However, God is not allowing it for he is not their god. Their god is the devil. The devil is controlling them and is the influencer of their evil.

> *John 8:44 Ye are of your father the devil, and the lusts of your father ye will do. He was a murderer from the beginning, and abode not in the truth, because there is no truth in him. When he speaketh a lie, he speaketh of his own: for he is a liar, and the father of it.*

> *1 John 3:7-10 Dear children, don't let anyone deceive you. Whoever does what God approves of has God's approval as Christ has God's approval. The person who lives a sinful life belongs to the devil, because the devil has been committing sin since the beginning. The reason that the Son of God appeared was to destroy what the devil does. Those who have been born from God don't live sinful lives. What God has said lives in them, and they can't live sinful lives. They have been born from God. This is the way God's children are distinguished from the devil's children. Everyone who doesn't do what is right or love other believers isn't God's child. (GW)*

People Reap What They Sow

A person can make choices contrary to the Lord. When such a choice yields negative consequences, the person may become angry at God rather than accepting responsibility for their actions. These choices can bring them to counseling. They must accept responsibility in order to be delivered, healed, and guided into making better choices.

> *Proverbs 19:3 The foolishness of man perverteth his way: and his heart fretteth against the LORD.*

> *Galatians 6:7 Make no mistake about this: You can never make a fool out of God. Whatever you plant is what you'll harvest.*

Generational Impact Of Sin

A person's choices can have generational consequences. This is the reason some clients come to counseling. They are battling the sins and consequences of their forefathers. As a counselor, you will have to help them break free while teaching them to choose God and life over Satan and death, so the generational line can SHIFT under the blessings of God.

> *Deuteronomy 30:19-20 I call heaven and earth to record this day against you, that I have set before you life and death, blessing and cursing: therefore choose life, that both thou and thy seed may live: That thou mayest love the LORD thy God, and that thou mayest obey his voice, and that thou mayest cleave unto him: for he is thy life, and the length of thy days: that thou mayest dwell in the land which the LORD sware unto thy fathers, to Abraham, to Isaac, and to Jacob, to give them.*

Experiencing Challenges Due To One's Calling

Some life experiences can be due to a person's calling or destiny. Believers will call these types of experiences warfare, accusation, persecution, betrayal. These acts can be done by demonic forces, people being used by the devil, witches, warlocks, and wicked people who are against God and his people, demonic, worldly, and manmade systems, and people who make poor choices due to their own ignorance, immaturity, or unresolved hurts.

> *Psalm 34:19 Many are the afflictions of the righteous, But the LORD delivers him out of them all.*

> *Jeremiah 18:18 They said, "Come, let's make plans against Jeremiah; for the teaching of the law by the priest will not cease, nor will counsel from the wise, nor the word from the prophets. So come, let's attack him with our tongues and pay no attention to anything he says."*

> *Matthew 5:10 Blessed [are] they which are persecuted for righteousness' sake: for theirs is the kingdom of heaven.*

> *Matthew 5:44 But I say unto you, Love your enemies, bless them that curse you, do good to them that hate you, and pray for them which despitefully use you, and persecute you.*

> *Matthew 11:12 And from the days of John the Baptist until now the kingdom of heaven suffereth (allows) violence, and the violent take it by force.*

Mathew 26:49 The chief priests and the whole Sanhedrin were looking for false evidence against Jesus so that they could put him to death.

Luke 6:22 Blessed are ye, when men shall hate you, and when they shall separate you [from their company], and shall reproach [you], and cast out your name as evil, for the Son of man's sake.

John 15:18 If the world hate you, ye know that it hated me before [it hated] you.

Acts 6:11 Then they secretly persuaded some men to say, "We have heard Stephen speak blasphemous words against Moses and against God."

2 Timothy 3:12 Yea, and all that will live godly in Christ Jesus shall suffer persecution.

1 Peter 3:16 Having a good conscience; that, whereas they speak evil of you, as of evildoers, they may be ashamed that falsely accuse your good conversation in Christ.

The Sovereignty of God

There is a sovereignty regarding God's character. He is the supreme authority. He is above all things and before all things. He rules over everything and is in control of all things. How much authority he actually asserts is by his own volition. Clients must be taught this as there are some things they will endure and that they will not understand. And they will not comprehend if it is God's perfect will, God's permissive will, or God's design. In these instances, they need to be counseled on how to maintain honor and regard for God. They will have to relinquish their choice to blame God, be angry at God, hate God, curse God, and reject God's existence for the truth that God cares, sympathizes, loves, wants covenant relationship, and is working everything in their life for a greater good.

2 Samuel 16:12 It may be that the LORD will look upon my misery and restore to me his covenant blessing instead of his curse today.

Romans 8:28 And we know that all things work together for good to them that love God, to them who are the called according to his purpose.

Romans 8:30 And those He predestined, He also called; those He called, He also justified; those He justified, He also glorified.

An example of God's sovereignty would be God hardening Pharaoh's heart to demonstrate greater signs through Moses, or God allowing Satan to inflict demonic plans on Job for a greater purpose of glory.

Joshua 11:20 For it was of the LORD to harden their hearts to engage Israel in battle, so that they would be set apart for destruction and would receive no mercy, being annihilated as the LORD had commanded Moses.

Romans 9:14-21 What then shall we say? Is God unjust? Not at all! For he says to Moses, "I will have mercy on whom I have mercy, and I will have compassion on whom I have compassion." It does not, therefore, depend on human desire or effort, but on God's mercy. For Scripture says to Pharaoh: "I raised you up for this very purpose, that I might display my power in you and that my name might be proclaimed in all the earth. Therefore God has mercy on whom he wants to have mercy, and he hardens whom he wants to harden.

One of you will say to me: "Then why does God still blame us? For who is able to resist his will?" But who are you, a human being, to talk back to God? "Shall what is formed say to the one who formed it, 'Why did you make me like this?' Does not the potter have the right to make out of the same lump of clay some pottery for special purposes and some for common use? (NIV)

Verse 21 Has the potter no right over the clay, to make out of the same mass (lump) one vessel for beauty and distinction and honorable use, and another for menial or ignoble and dishonorable use? (AMP)

Verse 21-23 Isn't it obvious that a potter has a perfect right to shape one lump of clay into a vase for holding flowers and another into a pot for cooking beans? If God needs one style of pottery especially designed to show his angry displeasure and another style carefully crafted to show his glorious goodness, isn't that all right? (MSG)

Job 1:8-12 And the LORD said unto Satan, Hast thou considered my servant Job, that there is none like him in the earth, a perfect and an upright man, one that feareth God, and escheweth evil?" Then Satan answered the Lord, and said, Doth Job fear God for nought? Hast not thou made an hedge about him, and about his house, and about all that he hath on every side? thou hast blessed the work of his hands, and his substance is increased in the land. But put forth thine hand now, and touch all that he hath, and he will curse thee to thy face. And the Lord said unto Satan, Behold, all that he hath is in thy power; only upon himself put not forth thine hand. So Satan went forth from the presence of the Lord.

Job 42:10 And the LORD turned the captivity of Job, when he prayed for his friends: also the LORD gave Job twice as much as he had before.

Paul suffered great hardships due to his calling and due to the sovereignty of God. Some of his experiences appeared to be God's perfect will and others appeared to be God's permissive will. Paul described his journey with God as one dying a daily death so that eternal life could live in him.

2Corinthians 4:8-12 We are hard pressed on every side, but not crushed; perplexed, but not in despair; persecuted, but not abandoned; struck down, but not destroyed. We always carry around in our body the death of Jesus, so that the life of Jesus may also be revealed in our body. For we who are alive are always being given over to death for Jesus' sake, so that his life may also be revealed in our mortal body. So then, death is at work in us, but life is at work in you.

Paul experienced a buffeting from Satan permitted by God so that he would not become prideful due to the abundance of revelations he received from God. He sought God three times for deliverance and God expressed that the sufficiency of his grace strengthened him to endure the buffeting.

2Corinthians 12:7-11 And lest I should be exalted above measure through the abundance of the revelations, there was given to me a thorn in the flesh, the messenger of Satan to buffet me, lest I should be exalted above measure. For this thing I besought the Lord thrice, that it might depart from me. And he said unto me, My grace is sufficient for thee: for my strength is made perfect in weakness. Most gladly therefore will I rather glory in my infirmities, that the power of Christ may rest upon me. Therefore I take pleasure in infirmities, in reproaches, in necessities, in persecutions, in distresses for Christ's sake: for when I am weak, then am I strong.

Sufficient is *arkeo* in Greek and means *"to ward off, to defend, to suffice, to be content, to be enough to be satisfied."* Paul had to live with the buffeting, while resting in the sovereign truth that even though he felt and appeared weak, he was actually strong. Had Paul resisted the sovereignty of God, he most likely would have been angry with God, resisting to live for him, and dreading the call upon his life. Counselors, some clients will have to be processed to accept the sovereign truths regarding their lives and how to live through the sufficiency of the grace of God.

We Forgive - God Avenges

Many people want their persecutors to experience swift judgement.

- Sometimes an offender is never caught or exposed.

- Sometimes the statute of limitations has passed regarding the ability to prosecute an offender.

- Sometimes the law can fail a victim where there is little to no consequences for an offender's actions.

- Sometimes the situation is not criminal but very traumatic, and the offender refuses to apologize or accept responsibility for their actions.

- Sometimes an offender will justify their hurtful actions with no regard for how it impacted the victim.

The idea of vengeance feels like a moment of catharsis that will translate the offended person into a victor, but there are scientific studies that find the opposite to be true. There are two intriguing theories about vengeance and likely, most offended people identify with the first which is called comparative suffering, ". . . the idea that simply seeing an offender suffer restores an emotional balance to the universe."[41] The idea of "payback" is drive out of a base human emotion to not only get even but to feel that the offended person has a right to rebalance their world by seeing the other person suffer. Trusting God to rebalance an offense also gives God the power to do it according to his plan and in his timing.

Though justice may not occur via the law or regarding one accepting responsibility for their actions, that does not mean God will not avenge a matter on our behalf. Whether in this life or the next, sinners will have their day of judgment before the Lord. God is all authority. He determines when and how he will avenge. He has postured us to forgive, while he avenges our adversaries as he deems suitable. This truth can be difficult for some clients to accept because God is making the decision based on his judgement. It will be important for a person to work through their thoughts and feelings concerning God and the situation. I encourage clients to

---

[41] Eric Jaffe, (2011, October 4). The complicated psychology of revenge. Retrieved from Association for Psychological Science website at https://www.psychologicalscience.org/observer/the-complicated-psychology-of-revenge

express their true thoughts and feelings to God, even regarding how they feel about him and his decisions. This can be done in a respectful and honorable way and is needful so they can release the barriers these emotions hold in their hearts, mind, and soul. Then they can hear God more effectively and work through resolving the matter with God. I do not believe God requires us to like everything he chooses to do. Faith is about trusting God even when we do not understand or enjoy his pathway. We are trusting God to know what is best for us, and we have faith that his way will keep us in right alignment with him, his principles, and his purpose for our lives. Clients can be honest with God and enter a dialog with him where he can SHIFT them to a place of peace about whatever decisions he is making.

- There have been times in my life where I thought I wanted justice for a matter, and when God showed me what he was going to do to the person, I was so scared for them, I asked God to have mercy and not ensue the judgement.

- There have been times where I felt God's judgment was not swift enough and I was angry with him. After being honest with him, he revealed areas where I needed to mature in my ability to forgive and let go of hurts and pains. I would not have recognized this if he had brought swift judgement. I would have misperceived him releasing judgment as me being rectified and healed of the experience. His way drew me into a conversation that enabled me to be delivered and healed from my pains, and not have my wholeness be dependent what he chose to do concerning the matter.

- There have been times where God brought swift judgement and I felt a greater punishment was warranted. God revealed to me that the person had repented. He also revealed how my heart was hardened and susceptible to evil. Sometimes we think we want God's job, but if we truly think about it, we would not properly carry the rod of avenging. We may do well with avenging some situations properly, then there are other situations where we would fail miserably. Even with all the laws and court procedures, the justice system fails at times, especially because the laws are based on what man believe is right, rather than seeking or living through God's justice and

Biblical laws. Justice was never meant to in man's hands. This is only a position for God.

Deuteronomy 32:4 *[He is] the Rock, his work [is] perfect: for all his ways [are] judgment: a God of truth and without iniquity, just and right [is] he.*

Psalm 75:7 *But God is the judge: he putteth down one, and setteth up another.*

Isaiah 33:22 *For the LORD is our judge, the LORD is our lawgiver, the LORD is our king; he will save us.*

Ecclesiastes 12:4 *For the LORD is our judge, the LORD is our lawgiver, the LORD is our king; he will save us.*

Luke 6:37 *Do not judge, and you will not be judged. Do not condemn, and you will not be condemned. Forgive, and you will be forgiven.*

James 4:12 *There is only one Lawgiver and Judge, the one who is able to save and destroy. But you—who are you to judge your neighbor?*

Romans 1:1-3 *You, therefore, have no excuse, you who pass judgment on someone else, for at whatever point you judge another, you are condemning yourself, because you who pass judgment do the same things. Now we know that God's judgment against those who do such things is based on truth. So when you, a mere human being, pass judgment on them and yet do the same things, do you think you will escape God's judgment?*

Romans 13:1 *Let every soul be subject unto the higher powers. For there is no power but of God: the powers that be are ordained of God.*

Romans 14:12 *So then every one of us shall give account of himself to God.*

1 Corinthians 4:3-4 *I care very little if I am judged by you or by any human court; indeed, I do not even judge myself. My conscience is clear, but that does not make me innocent. It is the Lord who judges me.*

We often wonder the reason God requires us to forgive while he accepts the role of the avenger. As I consider my experiences, there are some situations where no amount of avenging would make me feel better about my offender or what I endured. If I had my way, the greatest gift anyone could give me was to turn back the hands of time where that situation never occurred in my life. God knows that ultimately avenging may provide some temporary satisfaction. But avenging in and of itself will not make us well. There is also the truth that whether intentionally or unintentionally, we are all subject to hurting someone at some point. The mercy that we probably should have given a person, we may need at some time in our lives. In addition, I learned that God's judgment is incomparable to anything I could bestow upon a person. It is one matter for a person to deal with me. It is a whole other matter to have to stand before God regarding wrongdoings. It may be essential to have clients study the scriptures concerning God avenging and forgiveness so they can grasp God's principle in this area.

Deuteronomy 32:35 *It is mine to avenge; I will repay. In due time their foot will slip; their day of disaster is near and their doom rushes upon them.*

Hebrews 10:30 *For we know him that hath said, Vengeance [belongeth] unto me, I will recompense, saith the Lord. And again, The Lord shall judge his people.*

Proverbs 20:22 *Do not say, "I'll pay you back for this wrong!" Wait for the LORD, and he will avenge you.*

Romans 12:19 *Do not take revenge, my dear friends, but leave room for God's wrath, for it is written: "It is mine to avenge; I will repay," says the Lord.*

Psalm 94:1-2 *The LORD is a God who avenges. O God who avenges, shine forth. Rise up, Judge of the earth; pay back to the proud what they deserve.*

Matthew 18:15-17 *If your brother sins against you, go and tell him his fault, between you and him alone. If he listens to you, you have gained your brother. But if he does not listen, take one or two others along with you, that every charge may be established by the evidence of two or three witnesses. If he refuses to listen to them, tell it to the church. And if he refuses to listen even to the church, let him be to you as a Gentile and a tax collector. (EST)*

Matthew 18:21-22 *Then came Peter to him, and said, Lord, how oft shall my brother sin against me, and I forgive him? till seven times? Jesus saith unto him, I say not unto thee, Until seven times: but, Until seventy times seven.*

1 Thessalonians 5:15 *Make sure that nobody pays back wrong for wrong, but always strive to do what is good for each other and for everyone else.*

Forgiveness is an internal heart transformation. A person can actually feel divine liberation when they have forgiven someone. There will be a liberation in the person's heart and soul in knowing they are no longer bound by that person or situation. There is an exchange of God's freedom for our pains and bondages that takes place when we forgive. If such a freedom does not exist, then the person has not experience true forgiveness.

> *Mark 11:25-26 And when ye stand praying, forgive, if ye have ought against any: that your Father also which is in heaven may forgive you your trespasses. But if ye do not forgive, neither will your Father which is in heaven forgive your trespasses.*

Forgive is *aphiēmi* in the Greek and means:
1. cry, forgive, forsake, lay aside, leave, let (alone, be, go, have)
2. omit, put (send) away, remit, suffer, yield
3. let alone, to send away, to bid going away or depart
4. to expire, to let go, let be, to disregard, to leave, not to discuss now

Trespass is *paraptōma* and means:
1. a side-slip (lapse or deviation)
2. i.e. (unintentional) error or (willful) transgression
3. fall, fault, offence, sin, trespass
4. to fall beside or near something
5. a lapse or deviation from truth and uprightness a sin, misdeed

When harboring unforgiveness, a person can deviate from handling matters in a righteous manner. They may be yield to willful sin because of offense and choose to remain bound to the offense. The situation can be so traumatizing that it appears impossible to forgive. It is not that a person cannot forgive, trauma has become so consuming or exalting that it blocks the truth and pathway to forgiveness. God views this as sin because nothing should consume or exalt itself above him. The trauma has become a stronghold and idol such that is starts to dictate our thoughts, feelings, and actions. Even though the person may have a right to be upset, the transgression of unforgiveness as become god in the person's life.

When considering *Mark 11:25-26*, a person must process through and release their hurts so God can forgive them for unforgiveness. In order to really forgive: A person has to relinquish the need for vindication to God and trust him to handle the matter however he chooses.

Psalm 51:17 The sacrifices of God are a broken spirit; a broken and contrite heart, O God, you will not despise.

already broken and contrite. You feel crushed, destroyed, ripped apart, mentally and physically distraught. However, those feelings must be sacrificed.

A sacrifice is the killing or offering of something.

Sacrifice in *Zebah* in Hebrew and means:
1. Sacrifices of righteousness
2. Sacrifices of strife
3. Sacrifices to dead things
4. The covenant sacrifice (for the sake of covenant with God or sacrifice an ungodly covenant for God's covenant
5. The Passover
6. Annual sacrifice
7. Thanks offerings

Counselors, you will have to help clients to sacrifice the justifications, trauma, anguish, and need for revenge.

For true forgiveness to occur, unforgiveness has to be killed.

Matthew 11:28-30 "... Come to me, all who labor and are heavy laden, and I will give you rest. Take my yoke upon you, and learn from me, for I am gentle and lowly in heart, and you will find rest for your souls. For my yoke is easy, and my burden is light."

Unforgiveness can way on a person like labor - causing one to be heavy ladened.

Labor is kopiaō in Greek and means:
1. to feel fatigue; by implication, to work hard
2. (bestow) labour, toil, be wearied, bestow labour, to grow weary, tired

3. exhausted (with toil or burdens or grief)to labour with wearisome effort, to toil

Heavy laden is *phortizō* and means:
1. to load up (properly, as a vessel or animal)
2. i.e. (figuratively) to overburden with ceremony (or spiritual anxiety)
3. lade, by heavy laden, to place a burden upon, to load
4. metaph. to load one with a burden (of rites and unwarranted precepts)

Releasing the load requires honesty, while exchanging hurts for healing. Forgiveness can be instant and sometimes it requires a process. God is willing to journey in the forgiveness process with a client. He is aware of their tears and wants to wipe every last one of the away.

> **Psalm 56:8** *Thou tellest my wanderings: put thou my tears into thy bottle: are they not in thy book?*

> *You know how troubled I am; you have kept a record of my tears. (GNT)*

> **Revelations 21:4** *And God shall wipe away all tears from their eyes; and there shall be no more death, neither sorrow, nor crying, neither shall there be any more pain: for the former things are passed away.*

Religion Versus Relationship

Some clients will be rooted in religion but not relationship with God. They will have all the religious answers and be able to quote the Bible. They may initially have a difficult time resting in the counseling as their religious beliefs will make them think they know how to heal themselves. They will be controlling due to their religious rhetoric and wanting to prove they know what is best for them and understand God. They will want to interject quick fixes, rather than surrender to a process of wholeness. They may challenge your wisdom and the counseling process, and be resistant to implementing what is being required to receive breakthrough. These religious barriers will have to be exposed and confronted. They will have to be taught how to engage God in relationship and not religious works or religious cliches. Patience is essential with this type of client. It will also be important to regard their process and not take their actions personal.

There might even be a spirit of religion at work. Jesus encountered religious spirits. Some he confronted and let them know they were religious and others he drew them into spiritual and self-examination. Many of them were too busy trying to correct his actions to recognize he was savior. When he confronted them, they were even more resistant to him as savior and were more focused on quoting their traditions than exploring whether he was the Messiah. People dread hearing they have a spirit of religion. Often times, it is best only to tell a person they have a religious spirit if God is leading you as counselor to reveal that information. If he is not leading you to expose it to the client, confront and break down its workings through the counseling process itself, then identify other areas where deliverance is needed. When the client agrees to deliverance ministry, the spirit of religion can be cast out at the time as it is sure to rear its ugly head in the deliverance session. However, within the deliverance session, it will not be able to enmesh within the person's personality or use biblical reasoning to hide as if it is maturity or wisdom. Due to the deliverance environment, it will be obvious that it is a demon and need to be cast out. You can inform the deliverance minister ahead of time that it is there, and they can be led by God on when to confront it and break its power over the person's life.

Becoming God Focused

It is important to help clients understand that they cannot adequately experience kingdom wellness if,

- They are problem focused, pain focused, and not solution focused.
- They are so busy being God instead of surrendering to God.
- They are focused on blaming others and God, rather than processing through their pain so they can forgive and let go.

Even these areas of breakthrough are about choice – freewill. Their ability to experience the truth concerning their situation, to recognize God's compassion for their infirmities, to breakthrough to freedom and wellness, resides in this very choice. At some point a client must want their wholeness more than they want an accuser, revenge, or justice. There will be experiences where letting go of their right for justice is easy. Other times, it will be the choosing of freewill in and of itself, that will help them relinquish their right to have justice.

With some experiences, the greatest justice the client can give themselves, will be refusing to allow the pain, bondage, and unforgiveness of those situations to control them. The justice system may not work for them, they may not believe God is working fast enough for them, but they have freewill to SHIFT in justice by riding their lives of everything that tried to destroy them through that experience.

Counselor, teach clients the freewill they possess to be delivered, healed, and whole.

Counselor's Freewill Homework Activation:

1. How would you counsel a client who was a sex trafficking victim, who received no justice, is angry, unforgiving, blames God, understand freewill? How would you help the client see God's compassion for them?

2. How would you counsel a client who made poor choices that caused grave consequences to their destiny, yet they blamed God for how their life has unfolded?

3. Study the story of Tamar in *2 Samuel 13*. How would you assist Tamar with forgiving herself, forgiving her offender, forgiving God, not succumbing to the cultural customs regarding rape victims? How would you assist her with SHIFTING out of a lifestyle of shame and isolation into destiny?

4. How would you counsel a religious client who was dealing with a relationship problem regarding their leader? The client continued to share scriptures to justify their actions, and spiritual insights regarding what they believed God was saying, but was not accepting responsibility for their actions, and what they were sharing was not in alignment with what God was speaking to you as their counselor.

5. Study the story of Job. How would you help a client that had a story like Job understand the sovereignty of God?

6. Study the story of Moses. In what ways would you counsel Moses regarding governing his calling and destiny more efficiently?

Kingdom Wellness Counseling and Mentoring Center

Faith Based Counseling

Manual I

Part 7: Chapters (22 –24)

Learning Objectives:

- To provide insight on proper counseling session etiquette,
- To provide biblical understanding of healthy boundaries and balance when engaging clients and maintaining proper self-care.
- To charge counselors and other social service workers to partner together to establish kingdom wellness centers that save, deliver, heal, and make people whole.

Chapter 22

_____

COUNSELING SESSION ETIQUETTE

Start each session with prayer and end with prayer. If the client is not a believer, ask them if you can pray. Sometimes they are open to it even if they do not believe. If they are not open to this, be mindful to pray before they come for their appointment and after they leave. Prayer should entail setting the atmosphere for the session, for the client to be open to processing, and for divine wisdom concern the issues at hand. Ending in prayer should entail a measure of deliverance and healing of whatever was discussed and bringing peace to your client's heart, mind, and soul, so they will not leave your office vulnerable and exposed. Be sure to start closing a session about ten to fifteen minutes before it actually ends so you can process a client to a place where they are not left in the middle of a serious issue, and so you can spend time praying for them. It is also beneficial to start and end a counseling session with positive affirmations and spiritual revelations that empower the client if prayer in not an option.

Start sessions by asking about the client's day or any situations that are going on in their lives that may hinder them from effectively engaging in the counseling process. Address these issues first, while considering ways to connect them into the main counseling issue.

Be observant of a client's nonverbal cues from the time they arrive for their session until they leave. Gauge their eye contact, facial responses, body language, speech, voice tone, emotions, behaviors, and ask open ended questions that provoke processing what they are displaying.

Find opportunities to accolade a client and celebrate their progress and growth, even minimal growth. The more clients feel empowered, the more they will share in counseling.

Though it is faith-based counseling, be sensitive in discerning where the client is in life and with God. Do not force God or the Bible on clients. God is inside of you. His word and presence will speak through you and guide you. Trust him and allow him to lead you in what to say, how to say it, when to use scripture, how to use scripture, and what approach works best with your client.

Some of your clients may not be believers or believe in God but will want you to counsel them. Though I may not quote scripture chapters and verses or use biblical jargon, I inform such clients that my approach is still biblically grounded. My focus is to assist them as best as I can under the stipulations that are presented to me, but to be a light so that they are drawn to salvation, where I can truly SHIFT them into a process of destiny. Some clients have not wanted to work with me because I am a faith-based counselor; they believe my views will infringe upon their beliefs. I respect their choice and encourage them to find a counselor they will feel comfortable processing with. I have been successful in counseling non-believers, while remaining grounded in my counseling theory. Usually it is with people who have been recommended to me, so they trust the reputation regarding my counseling services. I am very respectful of their views, while providing the same opportunities for prayer, biblical exploration, spiritual assignments, inner healing, and deliverance ministry, that I do any other client. I allow them to decide what they desire to participate in and inform them of the benefits and consequences of their choices. Clients have freewill so they control what measure of breakthrough they receive. I respect a client's decision in whether they receive a measure of deliverance and healing, or wholeness.

Let clients know the more in-depth they share, the more effective their counseling process is. Ensure them the counseling environment is safe, nonjudgmental, and whatever they share is confidential, as long as they are not a threat to themselves or others. Be mindful to encourage them to go deeper and take them deeper when necessary.

Confrontation is important to the counseling process. I tell clients during the first session that I am a confronter. I do not mind asking the hard questions nor am I afraid of conflict. I express that confrontation will be essential to examining and breaking through certain issues. I also allow them to confront me regarding anything I say in our sessions as long as they are respectful. I encourage clients to be honest if they are challenged by something I say or do, as it gives us an opportunity to build an authentic counseling relationship and to resolve matters in a healthy productive manner. This also teaches clients communication and conflict resolution skills.

Use open-ended questions with clients. These are questions that cannot be answered with a simple 'yes' or 'no,' and require the client to elaborate on their points. Open-ended questions allow you to listen to the client's perspective, identify information that they are not speaking or that is hidden within what they are sharing, observe body language for unconscious thoughts, feelings, behaviors, and triggers, while listening to the Holy Spirit for revelation and insight on how to help them process what they are sharing.

Open-ended questions begin with:
- What (reveals facts, information, and considerations)
- When (reveals timing, seasons, proceedings, follow up information, patterns, and cycles)
- Where (reveals location, environment, and situations)
- How (provokes thoughts, feelings, consideration, exploration and processing)
- Could (allows processing of alternative perceptions, thoughts, feelings, and behaviors)
- Who (reveals people, targets, and options)
- Provides opportunities for expounding on information that is shared:
  - Explain that a bit more
  - Share more about that
  - Elaborate on that

Closed-ended questions are phrased in the form of ratings, scaling, and multiple-choice. They can also be 'yes' or 'no' questions, blanket statements that overgeneralize a matter where the client feels grouped into a perspective that does not necessarily fit their experience, or is too straightforward where it does not offer consideration of how the client has been impacted by their experience.

Closed-ended questions begin with:

- Is
- Are
- Do
- Can
- Should
- Why (can cause defensiveness and feeling the need to justify actions so limit use)

Closed-ended questions provoke limited responses that may cause a client to become defensive, negative, and pessimistic, while sharing minimal information from a posture of protecting and justifying their perspective, versus exploring and processing comfortably and progressively. I recommend using closed-ended questions as little as possible.

Whether open-ended or closed-ended, do not bombard a client with back-to -back questions. Should you use closed questions, and the client becomes defensive, trust the counseling process. Give them an opportunity to answer and elaborate. Encourage them to examine themselves beyond their walls and offenses. Do not be afraid of silence. Trust God with your client and with you as their counselor. Resting in the silence allows clients to hear God. I also leave opportunities for them to share freely what they are thinking or what God is speaking to them, and enable you to decipher what roots they need deliverance from.

Counseling sessions will not always run smoothly. There can be awkward moments and intensity. Some counselors are uncomfortable with this. There are instances where a level of shaking and SHIFTING is necessary for clients to confront themselves and their issues, and pursue the courage needed to tackle them head on. I am a KINGDOM SHIFTER. My very presence is going to stir some things in a client. Because I know this, I am comfortable with it and expect it to occur. As a counselor, parts of your character and identity will be prevalent to your counseling approach. This is called your "niche." Knowing your niche is vital to understanding the impact you will have on your clients. Clients know they will SHIFT when they encounter me. They know I am not a downer, that I am seeking that SHIFT that will draw them into deliverance and healing, and that I am destiny focused. What can clients expect when they encounter you?

What is your niche that will SHIFT a client?

Always provide homework assignments. There is no way to deal with everything in counseling. Also, you are teaching the client to be accountable for their progress, how to seek God for deliverance and healing, and teaching them how to pursue applicable tools and skills to further sustain in their wholeness.

- ❑ If a client cannot answer a question in counseling, I may give that question as a homework assignment. This allows them to think about the question in-depth and explore the matter at hand with God. It also allows us to explore other questions that they can answer, and limits them from shutting down or becoming defensive, due to not having an immediate response regarding a topic.
- ❑ At times, I complete the homework assignment as I am taking noting throughout the counseling session. Other times, I text or email them after I have explored what assignments would be beneficial for a client.
- ❑ Kingdom Wellness has a host of materials that are beneficial to clients at kingdomshiftingbooks.com.
- ❑ Counselors should build their own collection of materials that can be readily available for clients on various topics. In addition to my books, God inspired articles and documents, I have built email and cloud folders on different topics that I have gathered from various resource, which has proved beneficial to my clients over the years.

- Sometimes, I have clients Google topics and gather their own information and insights. Google is full of free information that can be a blessing to clients. This also teaches clients how to research information for themselves and decipher what is God and what is not of him, and what is and is not beneficial to them.

- Exploring topics and unresolved issues in prayer is always in order and is the best assignment to give a client. You are teaching them how to hear God, spend time with him, and build a relationship with him.

- Scriptural studies are great assignments because they help clients build a solid foundation in God, ground them in his word, and mature them in their walk with the Lord. They also teach clients how to apply the Bible to their daily life and situations, and how to journey with God and his word in a destiny lifestyle.

- Providing skills building assignments is necessary for equipping the client in how to sustain in their wholeness. Clients need to learn applicable tools so they can utilize them in their everyday life. This helps to transform how they view their experiences, and how they engage and handle future experiences. Without applicable tools, clients risk returning to old patterns or being exposed to new hurtful issues.

I take notes as I am counseling a client. Depending on the client, I may voice record the session. If I deem it beneficial, I will give a copy to the client so they can listen to it again; especially if it has wisdom keys they need. Sometimes I will only tape the prayer at the end or have the client tape it on their cell phone. This enables them to partake of it later; it also gives them guidance on how to pray for themselves. Some counselors take notes after the session or at the end of the day. You will have to do what is best for you. I recommend making sure you choose a method that is effective but does not have you swamped with paperwork. I use bullet form notation and only record the important details of a session. I keep all my notes for seven years on a secure cloud folder that is HIPPA compliant. No one can access my files but me.

After my last session of the day, I pray for myself. I cleanse myself of stress, grief, sadness, frustrations, concerns, etc. and I release all my clients to God. I cleanse myself of anything that would try to become a burden or would transfer from my clients to me. One day a week, I spend time praying for all my clients. I pray for breakthrough and explore God for revelation on how to help them. Unless the Lord leads, I do not spend time praying for a client more than this. This helps maintain balance, while trusting God with my clients. God is always speaking as he wants my clients whole. He is constantly giving me revelation and insight for every client. Often, I know within the first few sessions how to process a client to wholeness and even the measure to which they will achieve in counseling. This is because I am not being God in their lives. I am staying in my place and allowing God to guide me. This enables me to hear God effectively and to be at peace with the impact I will have on my clients.

I may have instrumental music on low or no music playing at all when working with a client. I keep scriptures and music playing in my office constantly when I am not working with a client and when I am not at work, as this cultivates a glory environment that incites a heavenly atmosphere. I constantly pray over my office and our building. I invite the Holy Spirit, strong glory, and the angels to reside there. Clients are able to be refreshed, feel safe exploring issues, and hear God for themselves, because the atmosphere is conducive to him and his healing power.

Every year I take seasons where I do not have sessions with clients for two months. For me this is December and January. Usually people are focused on the holidays, so it is easy to take this time for myself. I focus on resting, renewing, and refreshing. I do not waver in taking this time for self-care. I refer clients who cannot wait until I return to another counselor. This has helped me sustain in my career and avoid burnout.

I only counsel between certain hours of the day. I do not counsel clients past 7pm. I do not respond to phone calls, texts, online messengers, or emails, past this time. Clients and people in my personal life are aware of this boundary. This ensures that I am not drawn into providing counseling past my allotted hours and that I am maintaining proper self-care. This ensures that I am not going to sleep with peoples' issues weighing on my heart. If a person becomes upset, then that is someone who does not care about my personal health and does not need to be a client or part of my personal life. I do not apologize for my self-care and for making sure I do not become god to people. I recommend you create a system that works for you and stick to it. There will always be issues. People will always view their issue as an emergency. Counseling is not a 911 service. That is what crisis hotlines are for. Provide this option for clients who may need someone to talk to after your scheduled hours. Once you start allowing people to treat you like a 911 service, they will start to take advantage of you.

When I do respond, my questions are, "Did you pray about it?" "What did God say?" Since counseling is not advice but guiding people into hearing God's counsel, I respond in a way to help people hear God for their situation. This usually entails questions they can explore with him or providing materials that draw them into a seek of him and his answers. I usually only provide insight after a client or loved one has sought God for themselves.

I do not counsel people in private messengers online. When people ask me questions about their issues, about my services, or about something I post, I provide minimal insight that does not draw me into rescue counseling. I refer people to one of my books or such materials that would be beneficial to them. I also let them know I can email them the paperwork for counseling services, or that they can refer to my website and schedule a paid consultation or inner healing session. This keeps me healthy, balanced, and focused on clients who are truly invested in their healing process. I highly recommend this as when people realize you are a counselor, they will want to confer with you about their issues. But many people just want to rehash issues but not heal from them. Such people will drain the life out of you. Referring people for services can be the best way to separate the drainers from those who genuinely want help. People invest in what is important to them.

True counseling ministry entails a process. It is not a 911 intervention.

Though I do have sliding scales for less fortunate clients, I do not cut my prices or offer free services unless God leads me too. Clients need to make the necessary sacrifices to invest in their services. They can cut back on eating out, getting their hair and nails done, buying clothing, etc., to invest in their counseling services. When clients start making money excuses, I remind them of these options. Their sacrifices are temporary. but the healing that they will receive is forever. I do not allow people to guilt me into cutting my prices or counseling them for free. These same people will be posting pictures eating at expensive restaurants and of their new outfits, while you struggle to make ends meet. These same clients usually will quit counseling before they are fully processed to wholeness, because they are hustlers who are seeking a quick fix to their pain. Save yourself some time by creating standards for pricing that entail your self-worth, your educational and spiritual pursuits, your expertise, years of experience, and the time and attention you invest in making sure your clients are made whole. Your remnant of clients will draw to you. They will find you and want to invest in their wellness and what you offer to their lives.

SHIFT!

Sample Form

Here is a list of recommended forms for the counselor to use with each client. Whether you are counseling individuals, families, or couples, each person requires a set of paperwork. Always be aware of confidentiality, particularly if you are operating from a home office. It is recommended that you use the following checklist as a cover sheet for the client file. Include the date of the form completion and the signature of the assigned counselor.

Date	Counselor Signature	Form
		Intake / Application Form
		Personal Data Form
		Confidentiality Agreement
		# of Sessions Agreement
		Financial Responsibility Agreement
		Insurance Submission Agreement (if applicable)
		Counseling Fee Agreement
		Deliverance Ministry Agreement (if applicable)
		Follow-Up Agreement

For consistency of reporting, set a file system with the exact order of forms on the righthand side of the file and exact order of forms on the left-hand side of the file. Please contact me at kingdomwellnesscenter@gmail.com if you need to order a sample packet.

Chapter 23

BALANCE: RESPITE FOR LEADERS

It is imperative for counselors to have balance. It is not optional. Without balance, burnout and crossing boundaries with clients is inevitable. Self-care is essential. A counselor cannot be a role model or impart healthiness and wholeness if they are not healthy and whole.

Matthew 10:8 *Heal the sick, cleanse the lepers, raise the dead, cast out devils: freely ye have received, freely give.*

Received is *lambano* in Greek and means:
1. to take (get a hold of, have offered to one, violently - to seize or remove)
2. attain, be amazed, assay, attain, when God calls, to hold, catch

God gives a counselor power to heal, cleanse, raise, and cast out. The counselor can also lay hold of these transformation mechanisms for themselves. As the counselor freely receives from God, they are able to impart these salvation wells into others.

Psalm 42:7 *Deep calleth unto deep at the noise of thy waterspouts: all thy waves and thy billows are gone over me.*

A counselor cannot take a person in deep deliverance and healing if they:
- Have not received deep deliverance and healing for themselves.
- Do not consistently go deep in God's presence for answers and strategies for their clients.
- Are not constantly refreshed and replenished in God's presence.
- Do not seek seasons of healing, refreshing, respite, counseling, and consecration, for themselves, where they are taken deep, purged of sins, soul challenges, war wounds, burdens, and challenges of helpings others.

Freely receiving from God provides respite and rejuvenation that enables a counselor to give what they have received and have become. A counselor must pursue deliverance and healing for themselves, so they can be a representative of wellness and, can give from a fruitful and replenished well.

Many counselors have trouble taking time to refresh. We tend to have a mindset that if we take time away, or we get caught up in work inertia (marathon work habits):

- Things will not get done.
- Clients and duties will become stagnant or even regress.
- Clients and duties cannot survive and grow without us.
- We are failing or neglecting clients or duties.
- We are failing God and our calling.
- We are failing the vision of our business, organization, or ministry.
- We are not equipped, as if we were, we would not need respite.
- We are weak, as resting means we cannot handle what has been granted to our hands.

"One of the perceptions is that you make yourself indispensable (by working more)," says ACA member Julia Porter, an associate professor of counselor education at Mississippi State University-Meridian. But the increased pressure to perform and contribute often creates unrealistic expectations, Porter says. "That puts a tremendous demand on people to do more than they're really physically or mentally capable of sustaining over a long period of time."[42]

Most of our mindsets regarding resting is rooted in pride. The focus is more about us and how our identity and self-worth, is rooted in what we do, rather than who God is, and what he does through us. Such a disposition is error, and lends the impression that we constantly need to do and help in order to have a sense of value or self-importance. This is idolatry, because much of what we are doing is about building up our own kingdom, where we are glorified, rather than establishing God's kingdom

---

[42] Lynn Shallcross, (2009, June 15). Regaining life balance. Retrieved from *Counseling Today*.

where he is glorified. There is also a fear that someone will take our clients and what we have built. This is pride at work as the focus is self. There is a false sense of security, and obligation in and to God, when really the counselor's trust and commitment is rooted in self, and in his or her accomplishments. This is a dangerous place to be in because we as counselors, are operating as if God is with us, when really, he is no longer governing us. We are governing ourselves and are now positioned for a great fall.

Proverbs 16:18 *Pride goeth before destruction, and an haughty spirit before a fall.*

As counselors, we are not called to micromanage our clients. If a client can only sustain in their deliverance and healing when we are excessively pouring into them and managing them, then error and imbalance has occurred. We have either become the fixer, the rescuer, or God in their lives. We are playing roles that makes them dependent on us, rather than independent and accountable to God and their deliverance and healing process.

Jesus did not achieve identity as savior from people. He made stepping away from people a regular part of his ministry. Jesus did not micromanage people. Jesus knew that some would fall. And though he equipped and prayed for them, he recognized that some would yield to sin, error, backsliding, and go to hell, no matter how much they knew him as savior. We see examples of this with Judas and Peter.

Judas was an apostle that was taught and equipped by Jesus. However, that did not stop him for betraying Jesus for money.

Matthew 26:21-25 *And as they did eat, he said, Verily I say unto you, that one of you shall betray me. And they were exceeding sorrowful, and began every one of them to say unto him, Lord, is it I? And he answered and said, He that dippeth his hand with me in the dish, the same shall betray me. -- The Son of man goeth as it is written of him: but woe unto that man by whom the Son of man is betrayed! it had been good for that man if he had not been born. Then Judas, which betrayed him, answered and said, Master, is it I? He said unto him, Thou hast said.*

Peter was one of the first initial disciples of Jesus. He was also one of the first initial apostles. Jesus not only counseled and mentored him, but Peter was also in Jesus' inner circle, and was chosen to be a fisherman of men by Jesus.

Mathew 26:31-35 Then saith Jesus unto them, All ye shall be offended because of me this night: for it is written, I will smite the shepherd, and the sheep of the flock shall be scattered abroad. But after I am risen again, I will go before you into Galilee. Peter answered and said unto him, Though all men shall be offended because of thee, yet will I never be offended. Jesus said unto him, Verily I say unto thee, That this night, before the cock crow, thou shalt deny me thrice. Peter said unto him, Though I should die with thee, yet will I not deny thee. Likewise also said all the disciples.

- Jesus did not try to counsel or rescue them from what would occur.
- Jesus did not stop his purpose or go out of his way to make sure they did not abort all he had poured into him.
- In *Matthew 26:36*, Jesus took time to pray and refresh with the Lord in the garden of Gethsemane. His focus was not on Judas or Peter, but on being further empowered in his purpose.

Jesus saved, delivered, and healed people, but it was their responsibility to maintain their breakthrough. Even as Jesus was on the cross and it appeared as if he was defeated, he was accomplished. This is the reason he could pray for forgiveness of his persecutors and declare in *John 19:30*, "*it is finished.*" He did his part, and now it was left in our hands to accept the gift of redemption he provided and live our lives through it.

It is important for counselors to have a balanced lifestyle of resting and replenishing with the Lord, and to enter seasons of rest with the Lord.

One of the Greek words for *rest* is *anapausis* and means:
1. intermission; by implication, recreation:— rest
2. cessation of any motion, business or labour

Rest is a literal putting to death of our works. The only way to enter true rest is to cease all works, and not be drawn into battles that are not God ordained. This is the reason I shared strict boundary etiquettes in the previous chapter. My boundaries allow me to put to death my works as a counselor, while SHIFTING into the refreshing rest of God.

Matthew 11:28-30 Come unto me, all ye that labour and are heavy laden, and I will give you rest. Take my yoke upon you, and learn of me; for I am meek and lowly in heart: and ye shall find rest unto your souls. For my yoke is easy, and my burden is light.

There is a changing of guards in the place of rest. The counselor exchanges their strength, and their workings for God's easy yoke and burden. God promises refuge and lightheartedness when there is a true positioning of rest. At times we are not able to discern God's refuge because resting usually manifests what is already unrested/disquieted within us. If we are anxious, agitated, murmuring, complaining, sick, tired of warring, overworked, overburdened, it is usually an indication of the weariness that has already settled in us. This is the reason God requires a time of rest. He wants to arrest the unrest in us and SHIFT us into restored peace and rejuvenation.

Rest is a fixed and stable place or position. In this place, the counselor is submitted to being seated in God, while trusting him to consume them with what is needed to transform the lives of clients.

Psalm 91:1-2 HE WHO dwells in the secret place of the Most High shall remain stable and fixed under the shadow of the Almighty [Whose power no foe can withstand]. I will say of the Lord, He is my Refuge and my Fortress, my God; on Him I lean and rely, and in Him I [confidently] trust! (AMP)

You who sit down in the High God's presence, spend the night in Shaddai's shadow, Say this: "God, you're my refuge. I trust in you and I'm safe!" (MSG)

Hebrews 4:11 Let us labour therefore to enter into that rest, lest any man fall after the same example of unbelief.

Let us therefore be zealous and exert ourselves and strive diligently to enter that rest [of God, to know and experience it for ourselves], that no one may fall or perish by the same kind of unbelief and disobedience [into which those in the wilderness fell]. (AMP)

As we further consider *Mathew 11:28*,

Labour is *spoudazo* in the Greek and means:
1. seed (used in sowing): to use speed, to do
2. i.e. to make effort, be prompt or earnest
3. (give) diligence, be diligent (forward), endeavor, labour
4. due diligence, be diligent, give diligence, be forward, study
5. to hasten, make haste, to exert one's self

The Greek word for labor denotes that when the counselor is diligent to enter a place of rest in God, it is seed used for sowing. The counselor is sowing into being diligent to rest. God rewards the counselor by renewing them so they can effectively accomplish all the counseling duties that has been granted to their hands.

Jesus often took moments of respite. It enabled him to balance his ministry, his calling, and live a lifestyle of personal wellness.

Luke 5:16 And he withdrew himself into the wilderness, and prayed.

Matthew 14:23 And when he had sent the multitudes away, he went up into a mountain apart to pray: and when the evening was come, he was there alone.

Luke 6:12 And it came to pass in those days, that he went out into a mountain to pray, and continued all night in prayer to God.

Luke 9:28 And it came to pass about eight days after these sayings, he took Peter and John and James, and went up into a mountain to pray.

To my Counselor colleagues,

YOU MUST OPERATE IN THE TRUE SPIRIT OF COUNSELING WITH BALANCE!

YOU MUST GOVERN YOUR GIFT OF COUNSELING BALANCE AND EXCELLENCE!

YOU ARE NOT A 911 SERVICE!

DO NOT STEAL A CLIENT'S GIFT OF PROCESSING TO WHOLNESS WITH GOD!

WHEN YOU NEED REST, YOU MUST TAKE IT!

YOU MUST SCHEDULE REST IN YOUR WEEK AND SCHEDULE SEASONS OF RESPITE!

YOU MUST DIE TO SELF - DIE IN REST - SO RENEWAL CAN BE RESTORED IN YOU!

YOU MUST RESPECT YOUR OWN BOUNDARIES SO THAT OTHERS WILL RESPECT THEM!

YOU MUST PRACTICE SELF-CARE SO YOU CAN IMPART IT INTO YOUR CLIENTS!

YOU ARE WORTH REST AND A BALANCED LIFE!

I DECREE YOU WILL PURSUE REST LIKE YOU PURSUE WHOLENESS FOR YOUR CLIENT!

Chapter 24

COUNSELING CENTER CHARGE

I want to CHARGE spiritual counselors, psychiatrist, psychologists, behavioral specialists, life coaches, exercise coaches, massage therapists, social workers, human service workers, mentors, pastors, ministers, deliverance workers, faith healers, to partner together and establish faith based counseling centers in their communities. These centers can be within the ministry structure or in a separate building within the community.

It is time for us to SHIFT out of the world's system and take our rightful place as God's healers in the earth. Together we can establish successful kingdom wellness centers that truly save, deliver, heal, instill wholeness into people and communities, while SHIFTING forth generational deliverance. We do not have to be subjected to the world's policies and procedures. We can operate through kingdom standards that release God's healing power.

The Kingdom Wellness team and I would love to assist you in this endeavor. The four Kingdom Wellness Counseling Manuals can be used to equip, train, and certify, all those who wish to work in your center. My team has already established a center which includes our:

- Kingdom Shifters Empowerment Center (apostolic ministry hub)
- Kingdom Wellness Counseling and Mentor Program
- Life Coaching Services
- Exercise To Life Program
- Manifold Grace Dance Classes
- Euodoo Enterprises Business Services
- Kingdom Shifters Destiny Equipping Network Services
- Be Made Whole Mentoring Fellowship
- Kingdom Shifters Bookstore
- Shift Culture Kingdom Apparel

As we grow, we hope to add psychiatric services, massage services, healing rooms, hospice programs, shelters, and much more.

Ask God for a vision of a Kingdom Wellness Center that would bless your community. Partner with those among you who have a heart to work in this field, while experiencing the kingdom of God through what they do. Seek God for a name, vision, and take the necessary steps to establish an LLC wellness center in your midst. For step by step information on how to seek God for a vision plan and establish a legalized business, obtain my "Sustaining The Vision Workbook," on Amazon or Kingdomshiftingbooks.com.

Decreeing kingdom vision invades you with divine boldness to establish Kingdom Wellness Centers that awaken revival and kingdom culture in your sphere!

SHIFT!

KSM BOOKSHELF

Available at kingdomshifters.com or Amazon

Healing The Wounded Leader

Dismantling Homosexuality Handbook

Releasing The Vision

Apostolic Mantle

God's Shifting Power

The Great Awakening: Igniting Regional Revival

Feasting In His Presence

Let There Be Sight

Apostolic Governing Of Destiny

Annihilating The Powers Of Church Hurt

Atmosphere Changers (Weaponry)

Kingdom Decrees For Releasing The Vision

Sustaining The Vision

There Is An App For That

Kingdom Shifters Decree That Thang

Kingdom Watchman Builder on the Wall

Kingdom Watchman

Embodiment Of A Kingdom Watchman<u>COUNSELING MANUALS</u>

Kingdom Wellness Counseling & Mentoring Center

Manual I (Winter 2020)

Manual II (Spring 2021)

Manual III (Summer 2021)

Manual IV (Fall 2021)

<u>BOOKS FOR DANCE MINISTERS</u>

Dancers! Dancers! Decree That Thang

Dance & The Fivefold

Spirits That Attack Dance Ministers & Ministries

Dance from Heaven to Earth

REFERENCES

Ayodele, B. (2007, September 5). "The significance of spiritual wells." Retrieved from Sermon Central website at https://www.sermoncentral.com/sermons/the-significance-of-spiritual-wells-bode-ayodele-sermon-on-holy-spirit-in-believers-111359.

Boa, K. (n.d.) "The gifts of the Spirit." Retrieved from *The Bible* website at https://bible.org/article/gifts-spirit.

"Carditive therapy: A distinctly Christian Model of Psychotherapy and Counseling." (n.d.) Retrieved from the Christian Psychology website at http://www.christianpsych.org/wp_scp/

Coutu, C. & Kaufmann, D. (2009, January). "What can coaches do for you?" Retrieved from *The Harvard Business Review* website at https://hbr.org/2009/01/what-can-coaches-do-for-you.

Davey, G. C. L. (2014, December 31). 'Spirit possession' and mental health. Retrieved from Psychology Today website at https://www.psychologytoday.com/us/blog/why-we-worry/201412/spirit-possession-and-mental-health

Duvall, J.S. & Hays, J.D. (2012). *Grasping God's Word*, 3rd ed. Grand Rapids, MI: Zondervan.

Encyclopedic Entry. (n.d.) Flood. Retrieved from National Geographic website at https://www.nationalgeographic.org/encyclopedia/flood/

Etymology of purpose. (n.d.). Retrieved from *The Blue Letter Bible* website at https://www.blueletterbible.org/lang/lexicon/lexicon.cfm?Strongs=G4286&t=KJV.

Fain, K.M. & Alexander, G.C. (2015, April 1). "Mind the gap: Understanding the effects of pharmaceutical Direct-to-Consumer advertising." Retrieved from U.S. National Library of Medicine website at https://www.ncbi.nlm.nih.gov/pmc/articles/PMC4031617/

"Fast facts about American religion." (n.d.) Retrieved from the *Hartford Institute for Religious Research* at http://hirr.hartsem.edu/research/fastfacts/fast_facts.html.

Forey, J. (2016, August 26). "Growing in discernment." Retrieved from Biblical Counseling website at https://biblicalcounselingcoalition.org/2016/08/26/growing-in-discernment-part-1/

Gillen, A.L. (2007, June 10). "Biblical leprosy: Casting light on the disease that shuns." Retrieved from *Answers in Genesis* website at https://answersingenesis.org/biology/disease/biblical-leprosy-shedding-light-on-the-disease-that-shuns/

Gonzalez, V.M., Goeppinger, J., and Lorig, K. (1990). Four psychosocial theories and their application to patient education and clinical practice. Retrieved from Wiley online library at https://onlinelibrary.wiley.com/doi/pdf/10.1002/art.1790030305

Hackman, R. (2017, April 19). "When therapists also need therapists: 'Suffering is not unique to one group." Retrieved from *The Guardian* website at https://www.theguardian.com/society/2017/apr/19/therapists-go-to-therapy-prince-harry-mental-health

"History of wellness." (n.d.) Retrieved from the *Global Wellness Institute* website at https://globalwellnessinstitute.org/industry-research/history-of-wellness/

Instinct. (n.d.) Retrieved from American Psychological Association website at https://dictionary.apa.org/instinct

Jaffe, E., (2011, October 4). The complicated psychology of revenge. Retrieved from *Association for Psychological Science* website at https://www.psychologicalscience.org/observer/the-complicated-psychology-of-revenge

Kuhn, T. S. (2012). *The Structure of Scientific Revolutions.* Chicago, IL: The University of Chicago Press.

Marcia, J. (1966). Development and validation of ego-identity status. *Journal of Personality and Social Psychology*, 3(5), 551.

Miller, S.G. (2016, December 13). "1 in 6 Americans take a psychiatric drug." Retrieved from *Scientific American* website at https://www.scientificamerican.com/article/1-in-6-americans-takes-a-psychiatric-drug.

Moody, G. (n.d.). *Deliverance Manual 1.1.* Retrieved from Deliverance Ministries website at www.gbmoody.com

Nickels, T. (2011). "The role of religion and spirituality in counseling." Retrieved from California Polytech State University website at https://digitalcommons.calpoly.edu/cgi/viewcontent.cgi?referer=https://search.yahoo.com/&httpsredir=1&article=1024&context=psycdsp

Nordqvist, C. (2017, August 24). "What is mental health?" Retrieved from *Medical News Today* website at https://www.medicalnewstoday.com/articles/154543.php.

Rosenberg, R.S. (2013, April 12). "Abnormal is the new normal." Retrieved from *Health and Science* website at http://www.slate.com/articles/health_and_science/medical_examiner/2013/04/diagnostic_and_statistical_manual_fifth_edition_why_will_half_the_u_s_population.html

Ross, M. (1987). *The Fountain & the Furnace: The Way of Tears and Fire.* New York, NY: Paulist Press.

Saad, G. (2014, October 31). "New age gurus: Dispensers of nonsense." Retrieved from *Psychology Today* website at https://www.psychologytoday.com/us/blog/homo-consumericus/201410/new-age-gurus-dispensers-nonsense.

Shallcross. L. (2009, June 15). "Regaining life balance." Retrieved from *Counseling Today* website at https://ct.counseling.org/2009/06/regaining-life-balance.

Snodgrass, J.L. (n.d.) "Why pastoral counseling?" Retrieved from *American Association of Pastoral Counselors* website at https://www.aapc.org/page/WhyPastoral.

State-secular vs. Christian counseling. (n.d.). Retrieved from the *Pastoral Counseling Center* website at http://www.pastoral-counseling-center.org/Christian-Counseling-vs-Secular-Counseling.htm

Stitzinger, J.F. (1995, Fall). "Pastoral ministry in history." Retrieved from *The Master's Seminary* website at https://www.tms.edu/m/tmsj6f.pdf.

Thagard, P. (2017, October 24). "What is a psychological theory?" Retrieved from *Psychology Today* website at www.psychologytoday.com.

Tollboll, M. (n.d.) "The devastating New Age turn within psychotherapy." Retrieved from Morton Tollboll's website at https://mortentolboll.weebly.com/the-devastating-new-age-turn-within-psychotherapy.html.

Whitler, K.A. (2014, July 17). Why word of mouth advertising is the most important social media advertising. Retrieved from *Forbes* website at https://www.forbes.com/sites/kimberlywhitler/2014/07/17/why-word-of-mouth-marketing-is-the-most-important-social-media/#35f3530f54a8

Winnail, D.S. (2009, May-June). "Biblical principles of health." Retrieved from *Tomorrow's World* website at https://www.tomorrowsworld.org/magazines/2009/may-june/bible-principles-of-health.

Witherington, B. (2011). *Work: A Kingdom Perspective on Labor*. Grand Rapids, MI: William B. Eerdmans Publishing Company

www.ingramcontent.com/pod-product-compliance
Lightning Source LLC
Chambersburg PA
CBHW080233270326
41926CB00020B/4221